Enjoying Research in Counselling

CW00821786

"This book supports the development of our next ɡ   n
clear and understandable language, with engaging c   ɟf
counselling methodologies, from specific qualitative aᵖᵖᵣᵤₐᵤₙₑₛ ᵗᵤ quantitative and mixed methods,
ending with a recent example of a randomised control trial. It is current, drawing on research in areas
of interest to counsellors today and fills the current gap for a textbook providing a comprehensive
approach to successfully completing counselling and psychotherapy research. Covering the principles
of research, as well as some of the details required for those wishing to consider research at a higher
level, it provides an excellent resource for students studying research at all levels of counselling and
psychotherapy. I will be recommending it to my MSc and PhD students."

— Dr Jeannette Roddy, *Senior Lecturer in Counselling and Psychotherapy,*
University of Salford, UK

"I congratulate the editors and authors of this important book. It is filled with insights into the breadth
and depth of research frameworks and methodologies. The book can contribute to the promotion and
shaping of high quality practitioner-friendly research. Well done."

— Michael Helge Rønnestad, *Professor Emeritus, Department of Psychology,*
University of Oslo, Norway

"This timely new book beautifully and critically reflects knowledge and insights on a range of research
frameworks and methodologies. The editors and authors are to be congratulated on offering and
summing up multiple perspectives that empower therapists, research teachers and researchers alike. It
offers essential tools to engage in research and developing or sharpening key research skills. 'Enjoying
Research in Counselling and Psychotherapy' will take its place as a key text for many years to come,
particularly as the psychotherapy and counselling professions are increasingly valuing both evidence-
based practice and practice-based evidence."

— Professor Divine Charura, *UKCP Research Group, Director of the Counselling*
Psychology Doctorate, York St John University, UK

"'Enjoying Research in Counselling and Psychotherapy' lives up to its title and is a pleasure to read! The
book is aimed at counsellors and psychotherapists, and it clearly speaks to this audience informing
about different methodologies and encouraging in equal measure. It is very clearly written, and yet it
succeeds in communicating complexity and richness of psychotherapy research methods. I would
recommend it as essential reading to all research students and novice researchers."

—Dr Biljana van Rijn, *Psychotherapist and a Faculty Head of Research*
and Doctoral programmes, Metanoia Institute, UK

Sofie Bager-Charleson • Alistair McBeath
Editors

Enjoying Research in Counselling and Psychotherapy

Qualitative, Quantitative and Mixed Methods Research

Editors
Sofie Bager-Charleson
Metanoia Institute
London, UK

Alistair McBeath
Metanoia Institute
London, UK

ISBN 978-3-030-55126-1   ISBN 978-3-030-55127-8   (eBook)
https://doi.org/10.1007/978-3-030-55127-8

Cover Illustration: Bernhard Fritz/gettyimages

This Palgrave Macmillan imprint is published by the registered company Springer Nature Switzerland AG
The registered company address is: Gewerbestrasse 11, 6330 Cham, Switzerland

Acknowledgements

We want to thank our colleagues and Metanoia students for their invaluable input: your research is an ongoing source of inspiration and enrichment. We would also like to thank our families and friends.

Contents

About the Editors

Sofie Bager-Charleson

is a British Association for Counselling and Psychotherapy (BACP)- and United Kingdom Council for Psychotherapy (UKCP)-registered psychotherapist and supervisor, who works as Director of Studies on the MPhil/PhD in Psychotherapy at the Metanoia Institute. Sofie specialises in psychotherapy research, reflexivity and reflective practice. She chairs the Metanoia research group 'Therapists as Research Practitioners' aimed to support psychotherapists and counselling psychologists to become confident researchers. She is the co-founder of the annual Metanoia Research Academy for practitioners, and has published widely in the field of research methodology and reflexivity, including the text-book *Practice-based Research in Therapy: A Reflexive Approach* (2014). She has guest edited the *Counselling and Psychotherapy Research* journal issues on 'Therapists and Knowledge' and 'Mixed methods research in therapy' together with her Metanoia colleagues Alistair McBeath and Simon du Plock. She also guest edited the *Psychotherapist* journal issue on 'Therapists' Creative Use of Self in Research'. She holds a PhD from Lund University in Sweden in attachment issues within families and reflective practice amongst teachers.

Alistair McBeath

is a Chartered Psychologist and BACP- and UKCP-registered psychotherapist. Trained at Regents College and Guys Hospital, he is a doctoral Research Supervisor at the Metanoia Institute and the New School of Counselling and Psychotherapy. He also works for an Edinburgh-based therapeutic consultancy. Alistair considers himself to be a researcher-practitioner and is keen to promote this identity within the psychotherapy profession. Alistair is a strong advocate of mixed methods research and has recently used this approach to explore topics such as the motivations of psychotherapists and psychotherapists' attitudes to academic writing. Alistair favours a collaborative approach to research and has published research-led papers with Sofie Bager-Charleson and has been a co-editor with her (and Simon du Plock) for a special edition of the journal *Counselling and Psychotherapy Research* entitled 'Therapists and Knowledge'. Alistair is a senior practitioner member on the BPS Register of Psychologists Specialising in Psychotherapy and a member of the Editorial Board of the *European Journal for Qualitative Research in Psychotherapy*.

Deborah Bailey-Rodriguez

is a lecturer in Psychology within the Psychology Department at Middlesex University in London, UK. Deborah's PhD used a pluralistic case study approach to explore the dynamics and changes in attachment behaviours in a couple relationship as they transitioned to second-time parenthood. She is an Executive Committee member of the International Attachment Network as well as a member of the Network for Pluralistic Qualitative Researchers and of the Centre for Abuse and Trauma Studies (at Middlesex University). Amongst other subjects, Deborah teaches research methods and is also programme director of the MSc in Psychological Therapies and Interventions at Middlesex University.

John Barton

is a counselling psychologist and psychotherapist and writer. In his private practice in his hometown of London, he often works with clients who are experiencing or avoiding transitions in their lives; or who are having difficulties in their relationships with others and with themselves; or who otherwise struggle to live and love. He also works with psychotherapy trainees. During his training, he spent time at the Samaritans, the West London Centre for Counselling, Ealing Abbey, Mind and the NHS, both primary and secondary care. His doctoral research was an exploration into the lived experience of progressive disability. Before training to be a therapist in midlife, he lived in America for a decade and travelled the world in his previous career as a magazine writer and editor. He believes that living well can be a choice, and that death is not the end.

Emma Broglia

is a senior researcher and policy lead working across the British Association for Counselling and Psychotherapy (BACP) and the University of Sheffield. Emma has 12 years' research experience working in settings ranging from hospitals to schools and counselling services. This includes holding a PhD supervised by Professor Michael Barkham and Dr. Abigail Millings, partially funded by BACP, to explore the effectiveness of university counselling services. It was through her PhD that she met Louise Knowles and had the privilege of working with the counselling service and alongside Louise and Michael to embed research into the service for the first time. Emma later worked as a postdoctoral researcher with the policy department and continues to make research, practice and policy links in her work. She believes that these three components are necessary to build an evidence base born from counselling and psychotherapy practice.

Charlie Duncan

is Senior Research Fellow at the British Association for Counselling and Psychotherapy (BACP) and primarily leads on their Children, Young People and Families research. She is also pursuing a part-time PhD at the University of Roehampton on the goals that young people set for school-based humanistic counselling. Charlie's research interests are varied, but she particularly enjoys practice-based research in counselling and psychotherapy and analysing large datasets of routinely collected outcome measures.

Kim Etherington

is Emeritus Professor at the University of Bristol, Fellow of BACP, BACP senior accredited counsellor and supervisor, and accredited EMDR practitioner in private practice. She has presented workshops and seminars in New Zealand, Malta, South Africa, Crete and the USA. Invited keynote speeches and conference presentations have taken her to Canada, Ireland, the USA and across the UK. She is a leading writer in the field of reflexivity and narrative inquiry. Her books and peer-reviewed journal papers reflect her passion for linking practice with research, and her intention to write with an emancipatory purpose, using a style of writing that is accessible by academics, practitioners and clients, as well as the public in general. Kim lives in Leicestershire and offers freelance support to doctoral and master's candidates who are interested in creative, reflexive, collaborative research such as Narrative Inquiry and Autoethnography and other arts-based approaches. Details at: ▶ http://kim.etherington.com

Linda Finlay

is an existentially orientated relational integrative psychotherapist and supervisor (UKCP registered) in private practice in York, UK. Previously she was an occupational therapist (not presently registered) working in the mental health field. She teaches psychology, counselling and research methodology at the Open University (UK), and she also teaches and mentors doctoral students across various European institutions. She has published widely. Her most recently published books are *Practical ethics in counselling and psychotherapy: A relational approach* (2019) and *Relational integrative psychotherapy: Engaging process and theory in practice* (2019). Among her books relevant to research are *Phenomenology for therapists: Researching the lived world; Relational-centred research for Psychotherapists* (written with Ken Evans) and *Qualitative research for health professionals: Challenging choices* (edited with Claire Ballinger). Her particular research interests include exploring relational dynamics and applying relational-reflexive approaches to investigate the lived experience of disability and trauma.

She is Editor of the *European Journal for Qualitative Research in Psychotherapy* (EJQRP.org). Website: ▶ http://lindafinlay.co.uk/

Nollaig Frost

is Adjunct Professor at the School of Applied Psychology, University College Cork, Ireland. After many years as a psychodynamic counsellor in psychiatric and community settings she pursued a PhD at Birkbeck, University of London, to research women's transitions to second-time motherhood within a psychosocial framework. Her interest in pluralistic research was piqued, and on completion of her PhD she began to work with a team of researchers to explore the benefits and tensions of combining methods. This project led to one of the first books about pluralistic research: Frost, N. (ed) (2011), *Qualitative Methods in Psychology: Combining Core Approaches.* She is working on a second edition. Nollaig established the Network for Pluralism in Qualitative Research (▶ www.npqr.wordpress.com) and the Ireland Network for Pluralism in Qualitative Research (▶ www.ucc.ie/en/inpqr/inpqr) to provide resources, support and training to researchers and practitioners interested in pluralistic research.

Rupert King

is a UKCP registered existential-phenomenological psychotherapist and supervisor in private practice. He studied at Regents University and is a graduate of the ADEP programme. Over the years he has taught phenomenology and existential philosophy on a number of postgraduate diploma courses. He is a module leader and an academic advisor on the DPsych at Metanoia Institute. His research interests include hermeneutic phenomenology, the later works of Martin Heidegger and the use of images in research. He is a keen gardener with a particular interest in Japanese gardens. His West London garden has featured in a number of magazines and on television.

Louise Knowles

is a UKCP registered psychotherapist who describes her professional journey as a non-traditional one. Louise left school at 16 with few qualifications and started her working life as a youth worker, working in some of the most deprived areas of Sheffield and Manchester. She decided to return to education and graduated with an MA in Gestalt Psychotherapy. For the last 8 years Louise has been the University of Sheffield's Head of Counselling and Psychological Wellbeing. Louise's commitment to ensuring the highest clinical quality in service provision is highlighted by the fact that she oversaw a considerable expansion in provision and the achievement of the University of Sheffield becoming the first UK university to be accredited by the Accreditation Programme for Psychological Therapies. Louise believes that quality has to be backed up by sound evidence and that the relationship between research and practice is critical to the ongoing development of psychotherapy.

Elvis Langley

is a counselling psychologist and psychotherapist with a background in management and consultancy in the UK voluntary sector. He works full-time in his private practice in London as a UKCP (UK Council for Psychotherapy) and BPS (British Psychological Society) practitioner. Elvis brings substantial experience from working in mental health. He has a special research interest in hearing voices (as the topic of his doctoral research) and has extensive experience of working with people with severe mental health diagnoses and trauma, outside of NHS settings.

Barry McInnes

is an independent therapist, service consultant, writer and blogger, and co-creator of Therapy Meets Numbers. He started in the therapy field more than 35 years ago as a volunteer youth counsellor. Other roles have included Head of Service for the Royal College of Nursing Counselling Service and Director of Training for CORE Information Management Systems. Barry is passionate about the role of research, evaluation and feedback in creating the best therapy experience for every client.

Alan Priest

is a UKCP registered integrative psychotherapist, with over 20 years' experience working at the NHS in Yorkshire and Greater Manchester. He is Director of Studies (Programme Management) on the Doctorate in Counselling Psychology & Psychotherapy programme at Metanoia and continues to maintain a small private practice. His research focuses on conceptions of self, with special interest in the way that clients relate to self in the language they use in therapy and the impact of this on process and outcome. Alan has mixed qualitative and quantitative methods in research, combining in-depth interviews with computerised text analysis and the use of CORE outcome measures to research this area. He has also utilised a similar approach to understand the developing reflective and reflexive capacities of psychotherapy trainees. His projects include a mixed methods study of doctoral candidates' experiences of academic supervision.

Megan R. Stafford

is a UKCP (United Kingdom Council for Psychotherapy) registered psychotherapist in private practice, a lecturer at the University of Roehampton and an academic tutor at Metanoia Institute, where she teaches on integrative, relational counselling and psychotherapy training programmes. She has worked for many years as a researcher, including work in mental health and wellbeing, developing guidelines for the National Institute for Health and Care Excellence at the National Collaborating Centre for Mental Health, and most recently evaluating humanistic therapy for young people at the University of Roehampton. Megan integrates a developmental, relational and transpersonal approach in her practice to consider working therapeutically with her clients' developmental traumas, current relational difficulties and future aspirations. She lives in West London, where she works in private practice and enjoys yoga, cooking and painting furniture.

Contributors

Sofie Bager-Charleson
Metanoia Institute, London, UK
sofie.bager-charleson@metanoia.ac.uk

Deborah Bailey-Rodriguez
Middlesex University, London, UK
D.Bailey-Rodriguez@mdx.ac.uk

John Barton
Metanoia Institute, London, UK
help@johnbartontherapy.com

Emma Broglia
(BACP) The British Association for Counselling and Psychotherapy, Lutterworth, UK
emma.broglia@bacp.co.uk

Charlie Duncan
(BACP) The British Association for Counselling and Psychotherapy, Lutterworth, Leicestershire, UK
charlie.duncan@bacp.co.uk

Kim Etherington
University of Bristol, UK, London, UK
kim@etherington.com

Linda Finlay
Open University, London, UK
linda@lindafinlay.co.uk

Nollaig Frost
University College Cork, Cork, Ireland
nollaig.frost@ucc.ie

Rupert King
Metanoia Institute, London, UK
rupert.king@metanoia.ac.uk

Louise Knowles
University of Sheffield, Sheffield, UK

Elvis Langley
Metanoia Institute, London, UK

Alistair McBeath
Metanoia Institute, London, UK
Alistair.mcbeath@metanoia.ac.uk

Barry McInnes
(BACP) The British Association for Counselling and Psychotherapy, Lutterworth, Leicestershire, UK

Alan Priest
Metanoia Institute, London, UK
alan.priest@metanoia.ac.uk

Megan R. Stafford
Metanoia Institute, London, UK
megan.stafford@metanoia.ac.uk

Introduction: Considering Qualitative, Quantitative and Mixed Methods Research

Alistair McBeath and Sofie Bager-Charleson

Contents

© The Author(s) 2020
S. Bager-Charleson, A. McBeath (eds.),
Enjoying Research in Counselling and Psychotherapy,
https://doi.org/10.1007/978-3-030-55127-8_1

Learning Goals

After reading this chapter, you should be able to:

- Distinguish between qualitative, quantitative and mixed methods research;
- Gain familiarity with the meaning of ontology and epistemology;
- Consider the difference between positivist and interpretivist research;
- Consider idiographic versus nomothetic research interests;
- Consider the difference between inductive and deductive perspectives;
- Start to consider yourself in the field of research.

Grappling with Quantitative and Qualitative Approaches to Research

Mental health and emotional wellbeing have not enjoyed the priority awarded to physical health. They are usually deprived of funds and qualified staff, and despite one in four of us estimated to experience mental health problems, mental health research has 'lagged behind many other areas in terms of priority, funding, and therefore discoveries' (Departmen of Health and Social Care 2017, p. 2). This book approaches research with mental health *practitioner*s in mind. We are particularly aiming at counsellors, psychotherapists and counselling psychologists who–over the last 30 years–we have witnessed often feel marginalised and 'homeless' as researchers. Therapists are natural investigators, exploring, tracing and considering underlying meanings–it is what we do. Most of our research students enter their research training with this enthusiasm for finding out. In our studies into therapists' relationship to research (Bager-Charleson et al. 2018) one therapist said, for instance, that 'reading and writing–finding out–it's like breathing for me', whilst another summed up her sense of enjoyment as follows:

» 'Every day I talk about research [I am] really passionate about the process, the exciting process about not knowing anything and then finding out, experiment with ideas and then finding new knowledge…'

However, regrettably we also notice obstacles for therapists wanting to take their research further. One therapist explained, 'when I ask my manager in the NHS about doing more research training – I'd love to do a PhD – she just says "Nevine, you're already overqualified for what you do, you're a counsellor…"'

A reoccurring theme is a sense of 'gap' between an emotional, embodied and intuitive practice on the one side and research often construed as detached and rational on the other. In the same study (Bager-Charleson et al. 2019) a psychoanalytic therapist working within the NHS says:

» When I think of research I associate it with feeling lonely, the largest upset is to not find research which reflects what I work with. Being a psychotherapist can feel like being a second-class citizen in the NHS. Cognitive, neuro, biological, outcome measures – there's a whole bunch of people I can contact and speak to. But I'm not working within those approaches … I struggle with the idea that emotions are measurable, and that I need a scientific practice. We can't work with the mind without

1

thinking about what we mean by the mind … I mean, in the 80s I worked in - well what best would described as asylums, which were quite sickly, immoral and abusive really. Those things, the bigger picture is massively important to me.

Therapists are often caught between two contrasting schools of thought, with an evidence-based approach emphasising the importance of certainties contrasted by social constructionist-inspired approaches emphasising differences with socio-cultural, linguistic and gender-related interests. Both argue for transparency and accountability, but from conflicting angles. For more therapists to enjoy and take part in research, we believe it is important to become familiar with both, whilst enjoying freedom and confidence in building on questions, problems and approaches which best suit the therapists and clinical practice. We regard the divide between the two approaches to mental health and emotional wellbeing as important to acknowledge and explore, and will refer to concepts such as ontology, epistemology and methodology to highlight a longstanding dispute about 'reality' and relevant knowledge. Ellis and Tucker (2015) assert, for instance, that the 'scientisation of psychology as a discipline has to some extent repressed its emotional history' (p. 180), and in the following chapter, we will look more closely at emotions and embodied awareness as sources of knowledge. Whilst largely adopting a pragmatic approach to research ourselves, we do believe that an emotionally repressed research runs the risk of repressing clinical practice if it shuns, rejects and detaches itself from the messiness and ambivalence of life.

On the other hand, our studies (McBeath et al. 2019; Bager-Charleson et al. 2019) also highlight the risk for therapists of being marginalised in research contexts through lack of knowledge. Whilst counselling psychologists often bring basic knowledge in quantitative research from their first degree, counsellors and psychotherapists tend to be unprepared for this kind of research. As one of our participants said, 'I don't agree with measuring, at least I think I don't. I don't really know anything about it. I've assumed that that kind of research doesn't work for me but to be honest I don't understand it and haven't even tried it. I'd actually like to learn more'.

This book is written for our research students as well as for various research participants to support them in making informed decisions. It advocates an overarching pluralist framework on research, with approaches chosen from qualitative, quantitative, mixed methods and pluralistic research. We have invited researchers to share key features of their methodology and approaches to therapy-related matters. This means that the chapters will differ in tone, emphasis and focus. We hope by this to encourage you to connect with *your* research problem, interest and approach to issues directly or indirectly related to your clinical practice to further our knowledge in the field of mental health and emotional wellbeing in general.

Reflection

We have interspersed the text with Reflection and Activity sections to encourage you as a reader to reflect on theories discussed and apply them to your own work and experiences.

Considering Research Approach

Today's research discourse is often punctuated by concepts such as evidence, efficacy and effectiveness. We will return to these concepts. In this introduction consideration will be given to some of the differences and similarities between quantitative and qualitative research, which we believe is a significant distinction to become 'at ease' with, to dispel some of the perceived mysteries within research. We aim to briefly introduce some of the advantages and disadvantages of both approaches. There will also be an introduction to some of the philosophical assumptions that underpin quantitative and qualitative research methods, with specific mention made of ontological and epistemological considerations. These two terms broadly relate to assumptions about the nature of existence (*ontology*) and how we might gain knowledge about the nature of existence (*epistemology*).

Your Methodology

In counselling and psychotherapy most research activity is commonly associated with either qualitative or quantitative research methods, although there is a growing trend in so-called mixed methods approaches wherein a blend of quantitative and qualitative techniques is utilised.

The importance of ontology and epistemology considerations within a research context will have a significant bearing on the choice of research methodologies and the perceived relationship of researchers to their research. Although not often made explicit, the choice between quantitative and qualitative methods reflects contrasting ontological and epistemological positions. In choosing quantitative or qualitative methods (or both) the researcher is tacitly revealing a choice of preferred research philosophies. Scotland (2012) makes a key point which all researchers should keep in mind when he states that 'It is impossible to engage in any form of research without committing (often implicitly) to ontological and epistemological positions' (p 10).

Ontological and Epistemological Considerations

There are different ontological positions. Two commonly used positions are *realism* and *relativism*. Briefly, the differences between realism and relativism reflect significantly differing assumptions about the nature of reality and existence. A realist view assumes that there is an objective reality out there that exists independently of our cognitions, perceptions or theories. In contrast, a relativist view proposes that reality, as we know it, is constructed inter-subjectively through the social creation of meaning and understanding; there is no objective reality within a relativist view. The American poet Muriel Rukeyser (1968) succinctly captured the essential heart of relativism with these few words:

>> The universe is made of stories, not of atoms. (p 486)

From a research perspective these two contrasting ontological positions raise some profound questions which we believe are relevant when formulating research in areas such as mental and emotional wellbeing: What is reality and what kind of knowledge is helpful, relevant and regarded as 'true' or valid–and why?

An important starting point is how we position ourselves in our research. Does the researcher believe they are independent of the reality of their research or do they believe that they somehow participate in the construction of the reality of their research? These are two very basic and different research philosophies and they signal very different relationships between the researcher and their research.

From an epistemological perspective there are competing philosophies. An often-used distinction is between *positivism* and *interpretivism* (or constructionism, or social constructionism) that follow from and complement the ontological positions of realism and relativism. A positivist stance assumes that reality is objective and that casual factors between events can be discovered by scientific observation. An interpretivist stance assumes that reality is subjective and that reality can only be observed as approximations or estimates. Finally, positivism assumes that social phenomena and their meanings are fixed, whilst interpretivism assumes that social phenomena and their meanings are constantly being revised through social interaction and language.

The difference between positivism and interpretivism is really quite striking. Crotty (1998) has eloquently captured the difference with reference to trees. Here is his account of positivism:

» That tree in the forest is a tree, regardless of whether anyone is aware of its existence or not. As an object of that kind, it carries the intrinsic meaning of treeness. When human beings recognize it as a tree, they are simply discovering a meaning that has been lying in wait for them all along. (p 8)

And here is Crotty's account of interpretivism:

» We need to remind ourselves here that it is human beings who have constructed it as a tree, given it the name, and attributed to it the associations we make with trees. (p 43)

As Scotland (2012) has commented, 'a tree is not a tree without someone to call it a tree'.

The differing epistemological positions of positivism and interpretivism have significant implications for research activity. Quantitative methodologies are grounded in positivism where the researcher is a scientist, an empiricist interested in facts, testing hypotheses and confirming causality. In contrast, qualitative methodologies are based on interpretivism and constructionism wherein there are no realities that pre-exist independently of our perceptions and thoughts. The qualitative researcher adopts a subjective stance and is intimately involved in the co-creation of knowledge through the exploration and discovery of meaning. In one sense the quantitative researcher sees individuals as numbers whereas the qualitative researcher sees individuals as people.

It is important at this point to briefly mention the philosophy of *critical realism*, which, in part, grew from a reaction against positivism. Originally formulated by Bhaskar (1975, 1998), critical realism is an alternative philosophical position to the classic positivist and interpretivist paradigms and, to some extent, offers a unifying view of reality and the acquisition of knowledge. Critical realism can be viewed as being positioned somewhere between positivism and interpretivism. Critical realism accepts the principle of an objective reality independent of our knowledge. It also accepts that our knowledge of the world is relative to who we are and that, ultimately, our knowledge is embedded in a non-static social and cultural context.

Critical realism has several key–sometimes complex–concepts. One proposition is the notion that reality is layered into different domains, that is, the empirical, the actual and the real. This 'stratified ontology' allows both quantitative and qualitative research approaches to co-exist and to have more relevance in certain domains than in others. Critical realism also acknowledges the complexity of the world and recognises 'the fallibility of knowledge', which refers to the probability that our knowledge of the world may be misleading or incomplete. From a research perspective a key element of critical realism has been neatly captured by Danermark et al. (2002) with these words:

» there exists both an external world independently of human consciousness, and at the same time a dimension which includes our socially determined knowledge about reality. (pp. 16–17)

Critical realism has been regarded as a philosophical position which would promote both quantitative and qualitative approaches as being important and relevant within research (e.g. McEvoy and Richards 2006).

Quantitative and Qualitative Research: Comparisons

Given the significantly differing ontological and epistemological assumptions that underpin quantitative and qualitative research methods it is not surprising that they differ in a number of important ways. Perhaps most obvious is the scale of research and, ultimately, the numbers of participants involved in research activity. Because quantitative and qualitative research methods are focused on different outcomes or potential knowledge claims they require quite differing numbers of participants.

The objective, scientific basis of quantitative research which is focused on hypothesis testing needs large numbers of participants to offer statistical confidence in research findings and also in the power to generalise from those findings. Surveys are a classic example of a large-scale quantitative approach where several hundred participants could be involved (e.g. McBeath 2019). In contrast, the exploratory and interpretative nature of qualitative research methods, where the focus is to reveal the social reality and lived experience of individuals, requires only a few research participants and often fewer than ten (Smith and Osborn 2008).

The sharp contrast in the numbers of research participants associated with quantitative and qualitative methods is sometimes described using the terms *nomothetic research* and *idiographic research* respectively. Nomothetic research is about the pursuit of 'objective' knowledge through scientific methods, which tends to involve collecting large amounts of quantitative data from large numbers of peo-

1

ple. The objective of nomothetic research is to establish rules and classifications that can be generalised to wider groups of people. In contrast, idiographic research focuses on the individual who is considered to be unique, and thus there can be no meaningful search for rules and generalisations.

As we will explore further in later chapters, one of the key characteristics of qualitative research is its emphasis on the individual and the meanings that individuals ascribe to experiences and various social phenomena. This focus on the exploration of *experience* through meaning, at an individual level, is in sharp contrast to quantitative approaches where the views and characteristics of individuals are aggregated together in large numbers and manipulated using a variety of statistical procedures. A shorthand way to characterise the differences between the two approaches is to say that qualitative research seeks to explore experience and meaning whereas quantitative research seeks to confirm meaning.

One important difference between quantitative and qualitative methods concerns the basis of their reasoning or logic. Quantitative research methods are associated with *deductive reasoning* or a top-down approach where data are tested to confirm an existing theory or hypothesis. Qualitative research methods are associated with *inductive reasoning* or a bottom-up approach. Hence, in this case data and observations are examined with the potential to suggest the emergence of theory. An example of a specific qualitative approach that captures the inductive approach is *grounded theory*, described by Glaser and Strauss (1967) as 'the discovery of theory from data systematically obtained from social research'. This will be explored more in Chap. 6 by Elvis Langley on grounded theory in regard to his study on 'hearing voices'.

Quantitative and qualitative research differs in several other respects. For example, qualitative research is really quite process orientated whereas quantitative research tends to be results orientated. By the nature of their enquiry quantitative research findings tend to be generalisable whereas qualitative research findings are not. The output of qualitative research is usually narrative whilst that of quantitative research is often statistical. Finally, sample size is usually important in quantitative research and aspires to follow a random sampling method, whereas sample size in qualitative research is seldom a critical issue and sampling usually follows a purposive method.

In seeking to differentiate the two research methodologies it is sometimes suggested that qualitative research is essentially 'non-numeric' whilst quantitative research is wholly numeric. In reality the situation is not so clear-cut, and Sandelowski (2001) has challenged the identification of qualitative research as non-numeric, calling it the 'anti-number myth'. In fact within qualitative research there are established methods for transforming qualitative data into a quantitative representation to aid pattern recognition and interpretation. The basic Likert scale is a good example of ascribing quantitative values to qualitative data. Here subjectively judged qualitative statements such as 'strongly agree' and 'strongly disagree' are assigned numerical values to aid analysis.

As noted earlier, one crucial difference between quantitative and qualitative research is the role of the researcher. In quantitative approaches the researcher is essentially a detached figure who is considered to be independent and separate from the object of study. From this position it follows that the values and opinions of the quantitative researcher are considered to have no real influence on the research process. Denscombe (1998) has described quantitative research as a 'researcher detachment' approach.

In contrast, the qualitative researcher is inherently immersed within the research process and is the research instrument trying to capture the lived experience of individuals. There is an interactive relationship in qualitative research between the researcher and research participants where, ultimately, there is a co-creation of meaning. In qualitative research the researcher's own biography and values are recognised as a contributing factor in the research process and the interpretation of meaning. Evered and Louis (1981) have neatly captured the differing vantage points of the researcher in quantitative and qualitative research by respectively characterising the two research approaches as 'inquiry from the outside' and 'inquiry from the inside'.

Good Questions

It is important to emphasise that there is no sensible question to be asked about whether quantitative or qualitative research approaches are better than one other. Quantitative and qualitative research methods have their value in the context in which they are applied; they both allow different sorts of questions to be asked and they offer different perspectives on exploring research topics.

Consider the notion of compassion fatigue amongst counsellors and psychotherapists and how this might be researched. From a quantitative perspective an online survey could be delivered to large numbers of practitioners, which might well provide useful information such as the perceived incidence of the phenomenon and how practitioners might respond to it (e.g. supervision, reduction of workload). However, as useful as such information might be, what would be missing is detail around such key questions as: *What does compassion fatigue feel like? How does one recognise compassion fatigue? Do different people have different definitions of compassion fatigue?* Questions such as these are much more appropriately addressed using *qualitative research* methods such as Interpretative Phenomenological Analysis where meaning is distilled from the experience of individuals.

One way to think of the difference between quantitative and qualitative research is to consider what types of information they may provide. Quantitative methods with a key emphasis on measurement are good at describing phenomena and confirming facts. In contrast, qualitative research methods are good at exploring phenomena and illuminating their meaning. Malterud (2001) described the aim of qualitative research: 'to investigate the meaning of social phenomena as experienced by the people themselves'.

1

Combining Questions

Of course there doesn't need to be an either or choice; the two approaches can be combined to create a potent and flexible research method. So, for example, in researching the phenomenon of compassion fatigue it might well seem sensible to conduct some initial qualitative research, which could give some understanding of what might be meant by the term. This could be a first stage of a research effort, which subsequently informs the content of a later second-stage quantitative survey. Thus, in this case the differing approaches would be complementary, with each offering a different set of research advantages. What is being proposed here, in the example of researching compassion fatigue, is a mixed methods research approach.

The potential advantages of mixed methods approaches has been eloquently articulated by Landrum and Garza (2015):

>> We argue that together, quantitative and qualitative approaches are stronger and provide more knowledge and insights about a research topic than either approach alone. While both approaches shed unique light on a particular research topic, we suggest that methodologically pluralistic researchers would be able to approach their interests in such a way as to reveal new insights that neither method nor approach could reveal alone (p 207).

Historically, views on the appropriateness of quantitative and qualitative research methods have become polarised and captured by the notion of a 'paradigm war' (Ukpabi et al. 2014). In a mixed methods approach there is no inherent conflict, with quantitative and qualitative research methods able to make their own distinctive contribution. The growing popularity of mixed methods approaches to research seems to make perfect sense. For example, whilst a large survey with all its quantitative processes may provide compelling evidence of the incidence of a condition such as social anxiety, it is unlikely to be able to offer an explanation as to why individuals suffer from this condition and, most importantly, what it might feel like. And that is precisely why a complementary qualitative element of research is warranted.

This Book

As editors of this book, we both feel very much aligned with the mixed methods approach to research and have used it in several different contexts. These include subject areas such as the motivations of psychotherapists (McBeath 2019), the relationship between psychotherapy practice and research (Bager-Charleson et al. 2019) and psychotherapists' views around academic writing (McBeath et al. 2019). The wealth and richness of data that research in these areas has produced has confirmed the power and unifying principles of mixed methods research. However, there is an undoubted challenge and that is to do with the acquisition and competent use of both quantitative and qualitative research methodologies. It takes time and commitment to become competent in both areas but the rewards can be compelling.

In a considered review of the historical notion that qualitative and quantitative research methods are somehow competing or incompatible approaches, Landrum and Garza (2015) have championed what they term 'methodological multiculturalism'. In using this term there is an underlying recognition that both qualitative and quantitative approaches have specific strengths and limitations and these need to be respectfully acknowledged. It is also recognised that neither approach is 'privileged' and that 'methodological plurality' actually allows researchers to more fully encounter and describe the phenomena under study.

Summary

This introductory section has from the outset emphasised the issue of considering the philosophical assumptions which inevitably underpin and influence research activities. The chapter refers to the importance of reflecting upon our own ontological and epistemological positioning, which as researchers we cannot escape but only choose. We have also aimed to reject some of the historical and false dichotomies that have been popular over time in association with research activity and approaches to research. This introduction suggests the need to consider ways to approach research, both philosophically and in methodology, which are inclusive rather than exclusive. In this regard specific mention has been made of the benefits of the mixed methods approach. Throughout this book, the issue of research-supported practice will remain an underlying theme. Research-based practice will be considered based on multiple routes into research. We hope this book encourages you to familiarise yourself with approaches ranging from phenomenological experiences to more nomothetic, generalising and comparing foci such as outcome measuring and RCTs, which in turn, is best understood with a basic knowledge of statistics. Our book revolves around a broad range of research, including approaches where inductive—deductive combinations–as in grounded theory together with pluralistic and mixed methods approaches–provide multi-layered understandings to develop rich and realistic support in the field of mental health and emotional wellbeing. Primarily, we hope that the chapter will encourage you to start considering your own research. Enjoy!

References

Bager-Charleson, S., McBeath, A. G., & du Plock, S. (2019). The relationship between psychotherapy practice and research: A mixed-methods exploration of practitioners' views. *Counselling and Psychotherapy Research, 19*(3), 195–205. https://doi.org/10.1002/capr.12196.

Bager-Charleson, S. du Plock, S and McBeath, A.G. (2018) Therapists Have a lot to Add to the Field of Research, but Many Don't Make it There: A Narrative Thematic Inquiry into Counsellors' and Psychotherapists' Embodied Engagement with Research. Psychoanalysis and Language, 7 (1), 4–22.

Bhaskar, R. (1975). *A realist theory of science.* Hassocks, England: Harvester Press.

Bhaskar, R. (1998). *The possibility of naturalism.* London: Routledge.

Crotty, M. (1998). *The foundations of social research.* London: Sage Publications.

Danermark, B., Ekstrom, M., Jakobsen, L., & Karlsson, J. C. (2002). *Explaining society: Critical realism in the social sciences.* New York: Routledge.

Denscombe, M. (1998). *The good research for small –Scale social research project*. Philadelphia: Open University Press.

Department of Health and Social Care (2017). A Framework for mental health research.

Ellis, D., & Tucker, I. (2015). Social psychology of emotions. London, United Kingdom: Sage.

Evered, R., & Louis, R. (1981). Alternative Perspectives in the Organizational Sciences: 'Inquiry from the Inside' and 'Inquiry from the Outside. *Academy of Management Review, 6*(3), 385–395.

Glaser, B. G., & Strauss, A. L. (1967). *The discovery of grounded theory: Strategies for qualitative research*. New York: Aldine de Gruyter.

Landrum, B., & Garza, G. (2015). Mending fences: Defining the domains and approaches of quantitative and qualitative research. *Qualitative Psychology, 2*(2), 199–209. https://doi.org/10.1037/qup0000030.

Malterud, K. (2001). The art and science of clinical knowledge: Evidence beyond measures and numbers. *The Lancet., 358*, 397–400. https://doi.org/10.1016/S0140-6736(01)05548-9.

McBeath, A. G. (2019). The motivations of psychotherapists: An in-depth survey. *Counselling and Psychotherapy Research, 19*(4), 377–387. https://doi.org/10.1002/capr.12225.

McBeath, A. G., Bager-Charleson, S., & Abarbanel, A. (2019). Therapists and Academic Writing: 'Once upon a time psychotherapy practitioners and researchers were the same people. *European Journal for Qualitative Research in Psychotherapy, 19*, 103–116.

McEvoy, P., & Richards, D. (2006). A critical realist rationale for using a combination of quantitative and qualitative methods. *Journal of Research in Nursing, 11*, 66–78. https://doi.org/10.1177/1744987106060192.

Rukeyser, M. (1968). *The speed of darkness*. New York: Random House.

Sandelowski, M. (2001). Real qualitative researchers do not count: The use of numbers in qualitative research. *Research in Nursing and Health, 24*(3), 230–240. https://doi.org/10.1002/nur.1025.

Scotland, J. (2012). Exploring the philosophical underpinnings of research: Relating ontology and epistemology to the methodology and methods of the scientific, interpretive and critical research paradigms. *English Language Teaching, 5*(9), 9–16. https://doi.org/10.5539/elt.v5n9p9.

Smith, J. A., & Osborn, S. (2008). *Interpretative phenomenological analysis*. In J. A. Smith (Ed.), *Qualitative psychology* (pp. 53–80). London: Sage.

Ukpabi, D. C., Enyindah, C. W., & Dapper, E. M. (2014). Who is winning the paradigm war? The futility of paradigm inflexibility in Administrative Sciences Research. *IOSR Journal of Business and Management, 16*(7), 13–17.

Doing Qualitative Research

Sofie Bager-Charleson

Contents

© The Author(s) 2020
S. Bager-Charleson, A. McBeath (eds.),
Enjoying Research in Counselling and Psychotherapy,
https://doi.org/10.1007/978-3-030-55127-8_2

🖱 Learning Goals

After reading this chapter, you should be able to:

- Consider research in terms of different activity domains and research interests;
- Recognise where and how qualitative research can be useful and on what basis decisions about methodology can be taken;
- Be aware of what constitutes reliability and validity in qualitative research, for instance 'specificity' and 'reflexivity';
- Consider different types of reflexivity, for instance introspective, intersubjective and social critique.

Research Interests and Activity Domains

Mental health and emotional wellbeing are neglected and notoriously difficult areas to research. Under the umbrella of a research group called Therapists as Research Practitioners, we have explored obstacles and opportunities to do research from the perspectives of counsellors, psychotherapists and counselling psychologists (Bager-Charleson, du Plock and McBeath 2018, ii. Bager-Charleson, McBeath and du Plock 2019, iii. McBeath, Bager-Charleson and Abarbarnel 2019). We introduced some of our findings in the previous chapter. Our literature review highlighted first how studies often describe therapists' research activity as 'limited' and the research knowledge as 'unstructured' or 'patchy' (Prochaska and Norcross, 1983; Morrow-Bradley and Elliott 1986; Beutler, Williams, and Wakefield, 1995; Boisvert and Faust 2005; Morrow-Bradley and Elliott; Castonguay et al. 2010; Darlington and Scott, 2002; Tasca 2015). This literature review suggested, for instance, that:

- Therapists, historically, have rarely initiated research.
- Therapists rely more on discussions with colleagues than on research.
- Therapists' knowledge around research tends to be 'patchy' and in-depth knowledge is associated with topics of personal interest.
- Therapists are, for instance, more informed by clinical experience, supervision, personal therapy and literature than by research findings.
- Therapists' research also often stems from an unstructured integration of knowledge gained from workshops, books and theoretical articles.
- Therapists do read research, but not as often as other researchers do.
- Therapists tend to be critical of the clinical relevance of much research and also about the clarity of presentation.
- Therapists and researchers are developing disconnected bodies of knowledge.

Our own research, and subsequently this book, developed in response to this critique. A number of questions have guided our interest: How do therapists describe their relationship to research? How might they position themselves epistemologically when doing research compared to in clinical practice? And how do therapists access others and disseminate own research, for instance in academic journals?

Regrettably, lack of opportunities, fear and lack of confidence appeared several times (McBeath, Bager-Charleson and Abarbanel 2019) in the replies, for instance:

- Lack of support to do research at work;

2

— Fear of seeming self-important and emotionally detached by focusing on research as a counsellor;
— Fear of not being able to write to the required standard;
— Fear of negative evaluation;
— Fear of criticism or doing harm or being found to be a 'rubbish' therapist and others are better than me;
— Fear of being rejected;
— Fear of failure and peer judgement.

Where to Start – And Why?

Research interests and focuses vary enormously, but an obvious starting point is usually something in our clinical practice which doesn't quite work. This can relate directly or indirectly to your practice. Some typical 'activity domains' (Barkham et al. 2010) for therapy related-research are:

— *Efficacy research*, which is rated highly in the NICE guidelines favouring specific, measurable aspects of therapy to produce clinically measurable effects under 'ideal' conditions; this means testing hypotheses under conditions that are as similar as possible.
— *Effectiveness research*. Effectiveness refers to what extent therapy achieves the intended results under as 'normal' or usual circumstances as possible, often by exploring efficacy in a wider context (Barkham et al. 2010: 23).
— *Practice research,* which reflects a broad 'research domain' and will remain in focus throughout this book. Barkham et al. (2010) assert that 'rather than controlling variables as in an RCT [as in Efficacy studies], practice research aims to capture data from routine practice … to reflect everyday clinical practice' (p.39). In this chapter we will expand on the concept of 'practice research' with a special focus on practice-based *qualitative* research.

We will explore all domains in this book. Depending on activity domain and research question, your methodology will vary; we hope that each chapter will give you a full flavour of different potentials with each approach.

> **Activity**
> What do you wonder about, and perhaps regard as a problem or a burning interest?
> List three issues which you can return to and choose from later on.

How to Do It?

The most common distinction is whether to use a 'qualitative' or 'quantitative' approach, which we have already introduced but will expand on slightly here.

Object   Experience/Representation

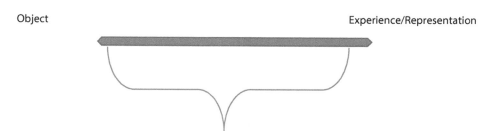

■ **Fig. 2.1**   Qualitative research for the gap between object and experience

Quantitative research, as mentioned, suits studies where generalisations and causal lines of enquiry are considered relevant. It is helpful for exploring change and considering questions about how many and how much. Questionnaires and statistical records are examples of quantitative methods which can transform many responses into numbers for statistical analysis. *Qualitative research* will, as mentioned, be at the forefront in this chapter. It is a broad church ultimately revolving around the complex area of *experiences*. It positions itself in the gap between objects and their representations (Ritchie, Lewis, McNaughton Nicholls, Ormston 2014), with an interest in human existence in terms of how we experience it (■ Fig. 2.1).

On a simple level, for instance if we wanted to research traffic behaviour at a traffic light, a quantitative research will be helpful to measure traffic behaviour. A survey can help to measure *how many times* and *how often* the driver slows down, accelerates and stops at the changing lights. Qualitative research can help to understand how different drivers *experience* the traffic light; what meaning might the changing lights have for them? Such meanings will be assumed to differ and involve ambivalent and ever-changing meanings.

Interviewing drivers might help to understand more about what changing lights represent to different drivers in terms of their personal, socio-cultural, gender and life stage-related contexts. Such an understanding is, in turn, from the perspective of qualitative research meaningful in relating to the conundrum of living in general but will also be useful for understanding more about the motivations behind traffic light behaviours. Qualitative research strives in this sense for a "three-dimensional" (Saldana 2012) understanding of people, focusing on depth of being and on what each of us might believe, think and feel, and why, as illustrated in ■ Fig. 2.2.

Seeking to Connect with the Experience of Doing Research

Our own first study (Bager-Charleson, du Plock and McBeath 2018) into how therapists experienced research was a qualitative study. We focused on therapists' spoken and written accounts in dissertations, research journals and interviews. This included exploring doctoral dissertations ($n = 50$), interviews ($n = 7$) and research

2

Object ⟵━━━━━━━━━━━━━━━⟶ Experience/Representation

Gap of interest for qualitative research

◪ **Fig. 2.2**   Object and representation

journals ($n = 20$) across 19 cohorts and years from one professional doctoral pro-gramme. Our 'narrative-thematic' study (Bager-Charleson, du Plock, McBeath 2019) aimed to capture the richness and complexity involved in peoples' ways of making meaning.

Several therapists described becoming unwell during their data analysis work, with unexplained pain, hypertension, palpitations, chest pains, panic attacks and difficulty sleeping being some of the self-disclosed symptoms recorded. Therapists described especially the process of data analysis as an intense and deeply challeng-ing one, referring to visceral, embodied upsets from an 'excessive immersion' with the data. One therapist said, 'I've agonised so much, feeling like a fraud, so stupid … all the time thinking that I am doing this right with themes and codes and tables'. Another therapist referred to the intense workload, to 'the sheer amount of data … I really did eat, sleep and breathe the research'. Some therapists commented on feeling 'heady'; one said, 'I became stuck at the structural level of data analysis. I had played in the words so much I lost sight of the body'. And 'my immersion in their stories [made it] difficult to 'let go'. Engaging with transcripts was often over-whelming from an emotional point of view; whilst used to reflect and seek support to process emotions in clinical practice, they referred to difficulties in knowing where to turn for their responses in research. One therapists said, 'I was over-whelmed by mixed emotions. I found myself laughing at some and crying at others

... Where do you take theses feeling in research?' Many therapists expressed feeling unprepared for the lack of self-care in research, one addressing how 'the literature on qualitative research emphasises the importance of protecting the research participants. There is not much on protecting the researcher'.

Storying Our Findings

For us, trying to communicate and 'story' our own findings was difficult. We shared the participants' despair: How could we choose and do the accounts justice? We kept some full stories to communicate the often both intense and reflective rhythm and tone of the participants. Group or pair analysis was helpful; when analysing we shared a sense of the narratives following certain trajectories, or plot lines. One particularly common 'trajectory' was one beginning in good intentions, reflecting therapists' enthusiasm for 'finding out', followed by feeling overwhelmed and lost, but usually moving on to communicating a 'happy ending'. The example below is an account from a therapist who is 45 years old and works as a lead therapist in the NHS. His expansion on his experiences of what to use came across as a rich example of transformative learning. It communicates the level of agony which can be associated with letting go of something as part of new learning. We will call him 'Peter'.

What Transformative Learning *Feels* Like

'I am writing this and sending it immediately without any editing because I think that will help me tell it as it is ...', writes Peter, who has volunteered to share his experience from doing his doctoral research 5 years ago in the field of therapy for clients from the LGBT community.

» ... [Starting the study] I struggled to find a good, simple system for recording memorable quotes, significant thoughts. I read and read and read...but how could I ever retrieve, synthesise, analyse this mass of thinking? How would I even remember certain key points as they disappeared under the constant input I was subjecting myself to?
[...]I began to feel overwhelmed by the material coming in, by its sheer volume, and also by the existential challenge much of what I was reading presented to my own understanding of who I am and how I had come to think of myself in the way I did. About 15 months in I began to have heart palpitations. These were extremely alarming.. Sometimes at night, I would wake up, aware that my heart had skipped several beats, and with a sense of struggling for breath. Often, after having one of these experiences, I would sit up in bed and feel panic. The sensation of my heart skipping a beat, or suddenly racing, was very scary. And it was also shaming – something I didn't talk to with anyone in case they would think I was being ridiculous, or that I should give the research up if simply reading books was giving me such high levels

of stress. When I finally decided I had to stop reading and start 'creating', an incredible tightness across my chest and a heavy 'band like' feeling across my forehead. I was sat in my study, with hundreds of quotes/cards strewn across the floor, and a deep sense of foreboding. At that point I literally had no idea of how I was going to shape the literature I had read (subject-related and method/methodology-related) into a coherent, elegant, 'whole'. I remember groaning out loud at the prospect – as though I was involved in heavy physical labour ('Peter', written personal narrative about research, our markings)

This overwhelming experience continued until what Peter describes as him reaching a turning point. He tells about having to engage with something within himself 'which needed to be laid to rest before something new could emerge':

» Picking up each card and realizing that somehow I needed to understand how what was written on it related to everything else written on all the other cards felt like – and indeed was – a mammoth task. Nonetheless, **looking back, I do think that there was something incredibly powerful about almost wrestling with the information in actually engaging something within myself which needed to be laid to rest before something new could emerge.** Additionally, having physical 'bits' of information, as opposed to just bites of data on a computer, engaged me in a whole-person way that I don't think using some piece of qualitative data analysis software could ever have done. I felt more confident, I was developing a mind-map against which to cross-reference each additional story I heard **I had begun to interrogate those stories from a social constructionist angle,** seeing them as not just the personal creation of an individual but as emerging from within a particular social and historical setting.

When trying to represent our participants' accounts, we became inevitable co-creators, making decisions about what to include–and in what order and context. We wanted, as mentioned, to represent, for instance, Peter's account in full, as spoken by him, but chose to communicate our understanding of it with reference to what Gergen (1988) calls 'plot lines'. We read Peter's account as involving a progressive narrative turn, where Peter firstly reached tragedy but then moved away from it, towards a positive 'valued endpoint' characterised by new knowledge, deeper than expected and with an approach to 'not knowing' from a more considered, somehow 'owned' place:

» The palpitations did, however, continue right up until I made my final presentation. Then, amazingly and much to my relief, they stopped and have never returned. For me, they attest to the **reality that undertaking research into areas which are deeply meaningful and important to us as people, not just as academics, lays us open to challenge and struggle at very deep levels.** To my mind, they represent an existential struggle with fundamental concepts or building-blocks of what it means to be human; a far-from-easy letting go of aspect of life which have felt like certainties and an opening up to anxiety and learning to live with it without the need to simply resolve it. Fundamentally, my embodied experience – the pain and the fear – have left me much more aware of how easily we/I seek solid ground to live on, when actually there may be no such solidity. **Learning to live with uncertainty and possibility** is potentially liberating, but also deeply challenging. From that perspective, my journey continues, but what I learnt from my research (and strangely, it's much more about the literature review than it is about my participants' stories) continues to guide me and enlighten me. ('Peter', in parts from Bager-Charleson, du Plock and McBeath 2018)

The feelings of being lost, isolated and emotionally vulnerable were shared, and it felt appropriate to also look for themes in each participant account and across the group. Some separate themes were gathered into clusters, for instance 'seeking supportive coping strategies', within which some discrete coping strategies were identified as:

- Reconnecting with therapy practice
- Research journal
- *Supervision*
- Personal therapy
- Embracing discomfort
- Developing 'other mediums' to help to go 'where words wouldn't go'

How Many, How Often?

In comparison to this narrative-thematic study, our two subsequent studies (Bager-Charleson, du Plock, McBeath 2018, McBeath, Bager-Charleson, Abarbanel 2019) became guided by questions about 'How many?' and 'How often? I am mentioning those studies here to illustrate the shift of focus. Study number 2 was a mixed methods study aimed at training organisations within and outside the UK. The study generated data from an online survey ($n = 92$) and interview ($n = 9$)-based narrative-thematic analysis. Some key questions were: How do therapists describe their relationship to research? What amount of formal research training do therapists have? To what extent do therapists feel that their own research is valued? How do therapists perceive research—what sort of activity is it? To what extent does research inform therapists' clinical practice?

We found, for instance, that therapists rated the 'not knowing' as a significant source of understanding in their clinical practice; when asking how therapists generated knowledge in their practice a majority rated embodied, visceral and usually unspoken and unmeasurable forms of knowledge as particularly significant means of knowledge (◘ Fig. 2.3).

The high proportion of therapists referring to 'not knowing', ambivalence and unspoken forms of knowledge could then be compared and open for speculation about how their view of clinical knowledge might relate to their research interests. ◘ Figure 2.4 captures the response.

Our third study (McBeath, Bager-Charleson and Abarbanel 2019) focused, in turn, on therapists' involvement in academic writing. We were interested in how, if at all, they accessed others' and disseminated own research within the wider academic community through articles. The survey ($n = 248$) showed that over 80% of

2

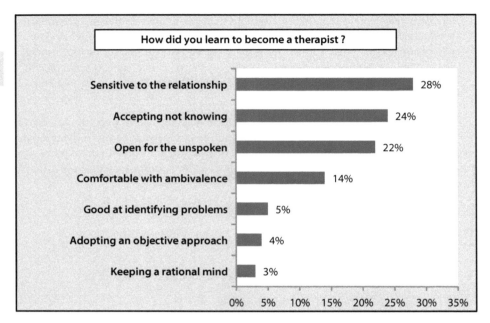

Fig. 2.3 The role of ambivalence and not-knowing in therapy. (Adapted from Bager-Charleson, McBeath, du Plock 2019)

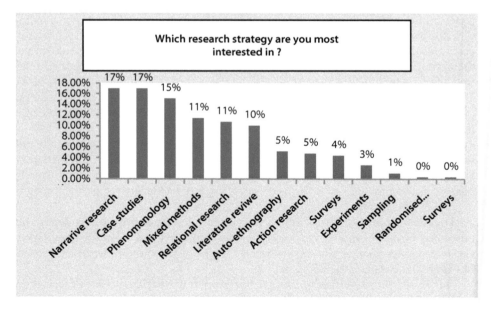

Fig. 2.4 Therapists' preferred research interests. (Adapted with permission from study Bager-Charleson, McBeath and du Plock 2019)

participants described their clinical practice as informed by reading published material, but nearly a third of respondents (32%) expressed a lack of confidence about writing for publication. Many therapists had engaged in academic writing before; this reason accounted for 22% of all responses. A further 20% accounted for fear of rejection.

Research Validity

The examples above illustrate how different research approaches can add to and complement the exploration. In our case it felt helpful to go both deep and broad. This can, however, as suggested in the previous chapter, involve having to address some conflicting epistemological positionings.

One of the many reasons that mental health and emotional wellbeing is so difficult to research lies in our historical and socio-cultural disagreement about what the *mind* 'is' and how we understand 'it'. Evidence-based research often refers to qualitative research as less trustworthy than research which follows the scientific model, RCT (random control trial)-based research in particular.

Some of the key standards within qualitative research relate to the extent to which it addresses *'specificity'* and *'reflexivity'* (Banister et al. 1994, p.21, my marking). In quantitative and scientific research 'specificity' often refers to being *different* to what is 'normal' or expected; sometimes it is used synonymously with being *'peculiar'* in the sense of being strange or odd. The earlier mentioned idiographic focus puts the unique at the forefront, often focusing on what makes us different rather than on what is 'normal' in the sense of the same and shared by many. This turns some of the natural scientific criteria for validity on its head. Whilst research validity and reliability in scientific research depends on objectivity and replicability, a qualitative research study can never be exactly replicated since the unique interplay of experiences forms the basis of the study. It should, however, be possible to trace and validate a qualitative research study, in terms of its interpretive stages. And this puts reflexivity and the issue of the positioning of the researcher at the forefront. Ultimately, qualitative research focuses, as suggested, on the experience or representation of something, rather than on a 'thing-in-itself'. Some regard the ambivalence and complexity surrounding experiences as interesting and significant. They seek, as Rupert King illustrates in the next chapter, to 'dwell *with* the mystery'. Others turn to explanations and clarity. A key figure in quantitative research, René Descartes, refers to a dwelling with the mystery of experiencing as 'being like madmen… not knowing whether we are awake or asleep' (1641/2011, p.22). Descartes (1596–1650) was a realist who sought a reality 'out there', independent of our minds. He was also a 'rationalist', aiming to explain through reason inspired by mathematics and geometry. Returning to the term epistemology, which derives from the ancient Greek words 'episteme', meaning 'knowledge', and 'logos', meaning 'rational', we can see how what is regarded as rational or not will vary depending on our starting point about reality. The Cartesian use of doubt became a means to find certainties by eliminating what could be subjected to doubt. Descartes (1641/2008:24) hoped to '[demolish] everything completely and start again right from the foundations ... to establish anything at all in the sciences that was stable and likely to last'. Descartes (1641/2008:23) writes, 'Arithmetic and geometry and other subjects of this kind, which deal only with the simplest and most general things ... contain something certain and indubitable. For whether I am awake or asleep, two and three added together is five, and a square has no more than four sides. It seems impossible that such transparent truths should incur any suspicion of being false' (Descartes 1641/2008:23).

At the other end of the 'ontological' debate about what we find real and regard as our focus of enquiry have been the Idealists, like the philosopher Berkley (1685–1753) who coined the phrase 'esse est percipi', 'to exist is to be perceived', and approached 'objects' purely as collections of sensations appearing in our minds; everything which we hold as reality literally ceases to exist the moment we leave the room.

Since then, phenomenology, interpretivism, constructivism and social constructionism have developed to explore the area of shifting, changing experience—usually with a shared critique of the Cartesian dualist stance.

Phenomenology

Phenomenology plays a crucial role in qualitative research. Phenomenology raises questions such as 'What is this kind of experience like; how does the lived world present itself to the client?' Van Manen (2017) asserts that 'the challenge of phenomenology is to recover the lived meanings of this moment without objectifying these faded meanings and without turning the lived meanings into positivistic themes, sanitized concepts, objectified descriptions, or abstract theories' (p.813). We can see this resonating with the kind of knowledge we often look out for in therapy. Therapy often revolves around 'truths' which 'do not have the property of extension or tangibility', as Symington (1986) puts it; 'it cannot be measured but it does exist':

> » Most psychological realities do not have the property of extension or tangibility; a dream, a hallucination, a belief, a thought. Truth is a reality of this nature. It cannot be measured but it does exist; the fact that is it difficult to define does not detract from this. (p.17)

Phenomenology aims to explore experiences from a subjective point of view. The early phenomenologist Husserl (1859–1938) spoke about what he called 'intentionality' to highlight a relationship between an 'intentional' act, ranging from perception, thought and emotions to social or linguistic activity, as directed to an object. Husserl (1960/1999:77) writes, 'The world, with all its Objects ... derives its whole sense and its existential status ... from me myself'. Merleau-Ponty (1999) echoed this, suggesting that 'everything I know about the world, even through science, I know of the basis of a view which is my own ... We must not wonder, then, if we really perceive a world. Rather, we must say that the world is what we perceive' (p.82, 86). Merleau-Ponty became a proponent of existential phenomenology which aimed for an in-depth, *embodied* understanding of human existence.

We will return to the issue of epistemological stances, to see how constructivism has grown from an interest in individual meaning makings, and social constructionism from focusing on how relational, cultural and social aspects both construct and convey interpretative frameworks, as we explored earlier. We will, however, also explore critical realism and mixed methods to see how deep, idiographic understandings might sometimes complement rather than be in conflict with broad nomothetic forms of knowledge for a trans-methodological approach to the complexity of human beingness, emotional wellbeing and mental health.

How to Do Phenomenology?

Perhaps needless to say, qualitative research takes a lot of time and effort. The analysis stage is particularly consuming, as suggested earlier in our narrative study (Bager-Charleson, di Plock and McBeath 2018). Narrative research focuses, as suggested (and explored later), on peoples' narrated experiences. The Interpretative Phenomenological Analysis (IPA) is a popular approach within phenomenology today. It shares an overriding phenomenological aim of getting 'close to the participant's personal world' (p.53), as if entering their world or standing in their shoes, but it is also interested in how, who, why and to whom people tell their experience.

IPA interviews typically include questions aimed to 'explore sensory perceptions, mental phenomena (thoughts, memories, associations, fantasies) and, in particular, individual interpretations' (Pietkiewicz and Smith 2014, p.11). Contrary to the descriptive phenomenology (Giorgi 2009), IPA asserts that it is impossible to fully experience the world from another's perspective, and the way experiences travel from one person to another is part of the focus of the study. Research is therefore approached as 'a dynamic process with an active role for the researcher in that process [where] access depends on … the researcher's own conceptions; indeed, these are required in order to make sense of that other personal world through a process of interpretative activity' (Smith and Osborne 2016, p.53).

IPA typically aims for purposive sampling based on the criterion that the research question is relevant and of shared significance for selected participants. The idiographic focus, for example the interest in each unique experience, means that the number of participants in small IPA (and phenomenology in general) is not driven by a nomothetic interest in generalisations; the focus is more on what makes people unique than on what they share and have in common. Having said that, IPA involves considering themes, and clusters of themes, from each case which will eventually be related to the others as part of the analysis.

The analysis starts with an initial aim for researchers to 'totally immerse themselves in the data or, in other words, try to step into the participants' shoes as far as possible' (Pietkiewicz and Smith 2014, p.11). It approaches the participants' accounts several times, expecting each reading and recording-listening to offer new insights, starting with immersion followed by new layers of 'framings' to gradually formulate emerging themes and then begin to look for connections and groupings of themes together 'according to conceptual similarities' (Pietkiewicz and Smith 2014, p.12).

This can be done using NVivo software or manually, using pen and paper for comments and themes in the margin, followed by listing major themes and subthemes with short transcript extracts highlighted by line number for easy tracing.

2

> ► **Example**

Integrative Therapists' clinical experiences of personal blind spots. An Interpretative Phenomenological Analysis, by Paula MacMahon

This study uses Interpretative Phenomenological Analysis to explore relational-integrative psychotherapists' lived experience of a personal blind spot in their therapeutic work. The five female participants aged between 42 and 60 years of age have between 2 and 20 years clinical experience. Each participant was interviewed on two separate occasions, with a period of 1 month between interviews. The inductive approach of IPA sought to capture the richness and complexity of participants' lived emotional experiences. Three superordinate themes and seven subthemes emerged from the interviews: Feeling the pressure; Facing a Blind Spot – the 'missing piece' and A Curious Kind of Settling. Theme one explores participants' difficulties with personal exposure and a loss of self-awareness when personal issues are triggered by client work. It also describes maladaptive coping skills such as avoidance, employed to cope with feelings of vulnerability. Theme two describes the process of facing a personal blind spot where participants recognise the impact of their personal needs and history on the therapeutic relationship. Theme three describes how participants develop an expanded sense of self-awareness and capacity to be present to their clients' concerns through self-compassion and by learning to tolerate difficult affects. The findings suggest that unprocessed fears about personal exposure and shame impact on therapists' ability to be emotionally responsive to their clients' needs. The study recommends that continued research be undertaken into resilience towards shame, so that therapists can work at greater relational depth. Some aspects of these findings can be found in previous research on countertransference with participants of varying experience and varying therapeutic modalities. Given the centrality of the therapeutic relationship as a vehicle for successful therapeutic outcome (and the current lack of improvement in outcomes), research that furthers our understanding of therapists' emotional resilience and personal efficacy can help guide training and supervision. ◄

IPA adopts a 'double hermeneutic' stance to peoples' lived experiences, which as mentioned involves understanding more about the way that people not just experience but also *interpret* and *communicate* pre-understandings when referring to experiences. How experiences are adapted through narratives and 'stories' about selves and others is an area of particular interest for narrative research.

Narrative Research

Narrative research draws on pace, emphasis and rhythm of the spoken words to communicate the narrative structure, meaning and emotional impact. It also focuses on how our narratives both convey and produce personal as well as cultural layers of understandings about self and others. Our narratives and stories about our own and others' experiences are approached as paths into how people arrange information (prioritising, emphasising, ordering, etc.) and interpret (making good, bad, right, wrong, etc.) these experiences and events. Our stories, in other words, not only communicate what has happened, but also how values, beliefs and experiences guide our interpretations of events and experiences.

Reflection

The speaker's pauses, repetitions, silences, emphases and so on help to communicate how the narrative is constructed. Stanza is an impactful way of capturing the emphasis and rhythm of the spoken word. Try to think of an own recent example, akin to the one below.

Example: Ruth enters the third session with her coat on; she keeps it on when she says:

'I really enjoyed our last session. I feel safe here, not like everywhere else I'm scrutinised and judged'.

Afterwards, the therapist is left ambivalent over mixed messages. She prepares for her supervision by recounting some of what Ruth said in stanza to better capture her sensed meaning of the words:

'I feel safe here

not

like everywhere else

I am scrutinised

and

judged'.

Narrative Research

Polkinghorne (1988) positions narratives at the heart of psychotherapy.

'Psychotherapy and narrative have in common the construction of a meaningful existence. When they come to the therapeutic situation, clients already have life narratives, of which they are both the protagonist and author [arranged into plots] (p.25) Polkinghorne also emphasises the power of re-authoring stories about ourselves and others; 'one's past cannot be changed [but] the interpretation and significance of these events can change' (p.25).

Personal and Cultural Values About Self and Others

Narrative research has in turn played an important role in the development of postmodern and social constructionist thinking, which emphasises how narratives both give form to shared beliefs and transmit values. Polkinghorne (1988) sums up the significance of narratives on both a personal and a cultural level:

[N]arratives perform significant functions. At the individual level, people have a narrative of their own lives, which enables them to construe what they are and where they are headed. At the cultural level, narratives serve to give cohesion to shared beliefs and to transmit values (p. 14).

Narrative research explores how narratives or stories convey complex patterns about identity construction influencing social discourses, highlighting how 'meanings depend on who is speaking' (Arvay 2003, p. 165). Absence of narratives is, first, a significant obstacle for any sharing, discussing and exploring of certain experiences.

Absence of Narratives About Self

The example below shows another study, by the therapist Mirjam, who develops therapeutic support for survivors of sex trafficking. *Not* having narratives to refer to experiences is one of the obstacles to understanding, healing and reaching new meanings.

► Example

Psychological Work with Survivors of Sex Trafficking: A Narrative Inquiry of the Impact on Practitioners, Mirjam Klann Thullesen (2019):

This study contributes to the limited body of psychological literature in the field of human trafficking through presenting new and applicable understanding about the impact on psychological practitioners of working with women survivors of trafficking for sexual exploitation. Underpinned by feminist postmodern values this study is shaped as a story of resistance against the marginalisation and oppression of women's voices. In taking a narrative inquiry approach to exploring both the singular and common experiences of impact, four women practitioners were interviewed, twice each. The design was collaborative, incorporating analysis and feedback between interviews, as well as drawing on poetic representation taken from interview segments. Each participant worked in different, often multifaceted roles, as psychologist, psychotherapist, counsellor and expert witness, yet all are psychologically trained. The three core aims of the study were, firstly, to expand understanding about the individual experiences of personal and professional impact. Secondly, to highlight the support required for practitioners working with survivors of trafficking for sexual exploitation. Through giving voice to practitioners, the third aim was to provide a new body of evidence in this much under-researched area, contributing towards improving clinical effectiveness. Across the four narratives, five different subject areas were identified: A personal philosophy, rite of passage, boundaries, protective factors, and knowers and not-knowers. These headings gave rise to a discussion of how practitioners are impacted in the immediate, on a psychological, social and embodied level, as well as longer-term. The underlying personal philosophies of practitioners emerged as both motivating and protective in the work. Pertinent was also how the impact of the work changed at different points in a person's career, the initial rite of passage representing a particularly challenging time in terms of impact and learning about boundaries. The individual understanding gained from the four narratives led to concrete output in the form of a template for a practice-based manual of recommendations, for application with organisations and individuals offering services to survivors of trafficking. ◄

Dominating Presence of Narratives

There are, second, several examples of how the *presence* of certain dominating narratives has impacted our therapeutic practice, ranging from narratives about 'hysteria' to 'gay aversion' therapy which illustrate Aguinaldo's (2004:132) exploration of narratives surrounding 'health' and 'illness' that highlight examples of how narratives surrounding slaves have conveyed meanings and uphold certain powers. Drapetomania was, for instance, a term used for 'mental illness' to describe the cause of enslaved Africans escaping captivity. 'Healthy' black men were thus 'once conceived as those who remained subordinated by white supremacist rule. Political resistance to that rule (e.g., black slaves fleeing white supremacy) was viewed as a form of sickness – drapetomania ... "Health", like "truth" – and thus, validity – can be used as a means to maintain unequal social relations' (p.132). The case study below illustrates further a valuable perspective on 'power' in the therapeutic relationship. The concept of 'intersectionality' offers a significant framework to explore power from multiple dimensions and angles, as described by the counselling psychology doctoral student Sabina Kahn below.

► Example

Research to reflect on practice, by Sabina Kahn

This autoethnographic study explores how my personal narratives about oppression, due to my intersectional socio-cultural and political positioning within my personal milieu, relate to my experiences of power in the therapy room, both as a therapist and a client. What happens when I – an older, lesbian woman of Indian descent and an Islamic religious background, born and raised in South Africa under the system of Apartheid – I am faced in the therapy room with another (client or therapist), who I view as differentially situated within the power structures that shape the societies we occupy? Does my subjective social and cultural positioning and level of awareness of my place/s in the social hierarchy, affect the way I conceptualize the psyche and its operation? Does it affect the way I experience my therapist, as a client, or the way I approach and understand my clients, as a therapist? Does it enhance that view or obstruct it? Beyond these issues, the research considers what might be re-enacted in the therapy process itself when the therapist is a member of or strongly identifies with a privileged and dominant group and the patient is/does not – and vice-versa.

Taking the position that identity is intersubjective – that my own multiple identities, and consequently my access to power in its many forms, are fluid and emerging in relationship – the research sought, through a single participant autoethnographic design to discover how my own own subjective socio-cultural positioning, ideological commitments and personal values might impact on the therapeutic relationship. My life narratives about intersectionality and experiences of power in the therapy relationship both as a therapist and as a client were therefore elicited through semi-structured face-to-face interviews in conversation with a trusted and willing critical research friend. As a therapist who has herself occupied various subordinate social and political positions and who has herself been taught to distrust and reject her own perceptions in order to capitulate to the perception of what [can be described] as dominant cultural beings [...] I am deeply aware of the very real possibility that I too, as a counselling psychology and psychotherapy trainee – and in this sense, myself a dominant cultural being – could become so immersed in […] the "authoritarianism" of my own world view that I may not only universalize that view but also become oblivious that I am doing so. Thus, Interactive conversations were also carried out with 2 co-participant therapists from my personal/ social network, who share my beginnings in a particular historical, socio-cultural and political milieu in South Africa to explore similarities or differences in our experiences of power in our relationships to the other and the clients we work with. ◄

We have looked at two forms of research which focus on understanding lived experiences, to develop therapeutic support. Both Phenomenology and Narrative Inquiry typically build on small groups of participants, with an interest in each unique case and the interplay of factors which may be specific to that person, in the context of her family background, gender, time and socio-cultural setting.

Research Reflexivity

In interpretive research, the researcher's experiences of others' experiences become a natural part of the study. Reflexivity 'asks' us, as Stuart and Whitmore (206:157) put it, 'to examine the process of how what we see and understand in a situation is influenced by our own subjectivity'. Subjectivity as used in the broadest sense (Stuart and Whitmore 206:157) involves:

- Cognitive and theoretical constructions
- Embodiment (ethnicity, gender, social position, sexual orientation, ability and age)
- Biography
- Values
- Ethics
- Emotions.

The concept of reflexivity originates from attempts to critically review the researcher's 'situatedness' (Haraway 1988) and positioning within a study to always link knowledge to the knower. There are now several definitions of reflexivity; Finlay and Gough (2003, p.6) refer to different 'reflexive variants', such as:

- *Introspective*
- *Intersubjective*
- *Collaborative and*
- *Socio-politically informed* 'variants' to reflexivity.

The 'variants' or reflexive approaches are interlinked and all involve the aim to 'explore the mutual meanings involved in the research relationship' (Finlay and Gough 2003, p.6), for example how knowledge is linked to the knower, and 'meanings depend on who is speaking' (Arvay 2003, p.165).

As we saw earlier, phenomenological approaches like IPA emphasise the importance of referring to how the researcher's framings impact the interpretations; the researcher cannot objectively 'access' someone's experiences.

Reflexivity on Introspection

This approach to reflexivity uses the researcher's 'introspection' as a route into 'a more generalised understanding' (Finlay and Gough, 2003, p.6) about something. Autoethnography, phenomenological and heuristic research are examples of approaches where reflexivity draws on the researcher's *introspective* reflections, for instance as documented in researchers' poems, artwork, diaries, autobiographical logs and personal documents. We will see examples of this in the two following chapters. The reflexive documents play a crucial role in research validity and reliability, not so much to highlight biases but to evidence how 'both participants' and researchers' interpretations of phenomena are taken into account in the process of analysis' (Pietkiewicz and Smith 2014, p.7). A qualitative study cannot, as suggested, be replicated, but it should be possible to trace the researcher's line of inferences and decision making.

Intersubjective Reflexivity

Psychotherapy offers 'a very particular kind of relationship and a very particular kind of space in which we hope that new meanings can be made and new stories told, stories that may make life more liveable through an enrichment of meaning', as Bondi (2013, p.4) asserts. And qualitative research often remains consistent with this approach to knowledge. Hollway (2009) and Bondi and Fewell (2016) write about the importance of 'experience near' research about 'actual people' instead of aiming for a distancing, neutral research role. In intersubjective reflexivity the self-in-relation to others becomes 'both focus and object of focus' (Finlay and Gough 2003, p.6). Hollway and Jefferson (2000) suggest, for instance, that 'impressions that we have about each other' are often 'mediated by internal fantasies which derive from our histories of significant relationships' (p.93). 'Intersubjective reflexivity' adopts a sharpened focus on the *interaction* between participants and researchers and refers to that as part of the findings. The 'free association' (Hollway and Jefferson 2000) interview and the 'infant-observation' (Bicks 1997, Datler et al. 2012) model are used as examples of reflexive approaches where transference and countertransference are becoming significant means to generate 'data' and new 'knowledge' in research. Psychosocial research brings projection, transference and countertransference to the forefront. It addresses how 'unconscious intersubjective dynamics' (Hollway and Jefferson 2000, p.93) affect how 'we are influenced by our emotional responses' also in research. Holloway and Jefferson (2000) conclude that '[Psychosocial research] adopts a theoretical starting point [to] construe both researcher and researched as anxious defended subjects, whose mental boundaries and porous where unconscious material is concerned' (p.43).

The focus on emotions is surprisingly unusual even in therapy-related research, often ultimately guided towards improving our knowledge about emotional well-being. There are some welcome exceptions. Boden (2016), Denzin (1984/2009), Orange (1996, 2009), Spry (2001), Josselson (2011, 2013, 2016), Willig (2012) and Rennie and Fergus (2006) offer different perspectives to explore researchers' rela-

2

tional, emotional or embodied responses during research, including during the data analysis stages. Within the framework of Grounded Analysis, Rennie and Fergus (2006) refer to 'embodied categorization' as 'an approach to interpretation in which subjectivity is drawn on productively' (p.496). Van Manen (1990), Todres (2007), Anderson and Broud (2011), Gendlin (1997, 2009) and McGinley (2015) contribute with further theory about how to incorporate emotional and embodied responses into research. McGinley (2015) defines, for instance, 'embodied understanding' as an understanding which includes the knower's 'moods, affect, and atmosphere' (p.88) as sources of knowledge. Gendlin (1997) writes about the significance of 'staying with' the 'body-feel' as part of generating new knowledge. Tordes (2007) emphasises paying attention to a 'felt sense' as part of the analysis and writes about 'participatory experience' with an interest in how emotions are being evoked in the researcher.

Reflexivity as Social Critique

The introspective and intersubjective approaches to reflexivity focus in this sense on underlying *personal* meanings, whilst reflexivity focusing on social critique 'openly acknowledge[s] tensions arising from different *social positions* …in relation to class, gender and race' (Finlay and Gough 2003, p 12). Aguinaldo (2004) refers, for instance, to an 'epistemological straitjacket' dictated by a historic, narrow idea about 'truth' suitable for people traditionally in power. Smith (1999) resonates with this, arguing for a 'decolonization of research' to explore 'reality' from hitherto marginalised viewpoints linked to gender, culture and socio-economical aspects. As Spry (2001) suggests, the traditional, dominating Cartesian dualism can 'sever the body from academic scholarship' (p.724). Spry refers to an 'enfleshment', asserting that the 'the living body/subjective self of the researcher [is] a salient part … to study the world from the perspective of the interacting individuals' (p.711). Ellington (2017) resonate with feminist and post-structuralist theory about 'embodiment in research' and writes, 'Research begins with the body. Although some researchers remain unconscious of it (or deny it) embodiment is an integral aspect of all research… I am a body-self making sense with, of, and through other embodied people and our social worlds' (p.196).

Theoretical Reflexivity

Across all reflexive approaches is an aim to address and be transparent about the 'ambiguity of meanings [and] how these impact on modes of presentation' (Finlay and Gough 2003, p.12). Resonating with the role of social critique, the mixed methods researcher Hesse-Biber (2015) stresses the importance of critically considering *theory*. She regards mixed methods and pluralistic research as potential bridges across disciplines, assuming we are interested in expanding our understandings. She draws our attention to what role this discipline plays in a larger research context of *whose 'reality' is being represented, and why?* Which discipline speaks loudest, and which/whose knowledge building processes may be silenced as a result? These are some of the questions which Hesse-Biber (2015) addresses as she reflects on how 'each discipline needs and has its own set of reified concepts that help to facilitate communication within disciplinary communities, and these concepts become the building blocks of knowledge in any discipline' (p.172).

The building blocks can, however, also become walls and sources of dominance and divides. In their book about reflexivity, Alvesson and Skoldberg (2002) critique the remaining dominance of Cartesian reductionism with regard to how 'male domination has produced a masculine social science built around ideals such as objectivity, neutrality, distance, control, rationality and abstraction [undermining] alternative ideals, such as commitment, empathy, closeness, cooperation, intuition and specificity' (p.3).

Reflexivity 'requires an overt recognition of how a researcher's standpoint' (Hesse-Biber 2015, p.175) helps us to critically reflect on our discipline in the context of who 'gets to carve out and determine what knowledge becomes legitimated'? To what extent does this process serve specific ends? What is lost? What is gained, for whom? Who gets to challenge, reconstruct and reframe certain given concepts?

Activity

Hesse-Biber (2015) writes:

Dialogue and reflexivity within and across research inquiry communities of sameness and difference can provide the ground for coming together to identify, challenge, and negotiate the range of out across methods and methodological differences and thereby providing the possibility of innovation and negotiation and a vibrant mixed methods community of practice. (p.174)

Return to your initial list of interests. How might they fit into the research referred to in this chapter? Consider your interest and/or problem in the context of some of the concepts referred to in this and the previous chapter, for instance idiographic or nomothetic research interests.

- What are your experiences from research so far?
- What might you build further on and improve to actually *enjoy* doing research?
- What kind of support might you need for that?

We hope that each chapter will add to your ideas and allow you to build on what you already might wonder and be curious about.

Summary

Qualitative research focuses on the *experience* or representation rather than on a 'thing-in-itself'. An interest in the unique interplay of experiences approaches every person as special and interesting in their own right. In this chapter, we considered how 'specificity' and 'reflexivity' form important aspects of qualitative research instead of aiming for objectivity or replicability. This focus often resonates with therapists and their interest in the unique combination of the contributing factors of each client, ranging from biography, life stage and gender to their socio-economic and cultural contexts. It also resonates with the significance of therapist self-awareness, and the emphasis on considering the practitioner's positioning, response and input in the interaction and interpretation. The chapter also considers different research areas and interests, suggesting an openness to learning from other perspectives to approach issues in the field of mental health and emotional wellbeing.

References

Aguinaldo, J. P. (2004). Rethinking validity in qualitative research from a social constructionist perspective: From "is this valid research?" to "what is this research valid for?". *The Qualitative Report, 1*(3), 127–136.

Alvesson, M., & Skoldberg, K. (2002). *Reflexive methodology*. London: Sage.

Banister, P., Burman, E., Parker, I., Taylor, M., & Tindall, C. (1994). *Qualitative methods in psychology: A research guide*. Buckingham: Open University Press.

Boden, Z., Gibson, S., Owen, G. J., & Benson, O. (2016). Feelings and intersubjectivity in qualitative suicide research. *Qualitative Health Research, 26*(8), 1078–1090. https://doi.org/10.1177/1049732315576709. qhr.sagepub.com.

Bondi, L., & Fewell, J. (2016). *Practitioner research in counselling and psychotherapy. The power of examples*. London: Macmillan Palgrave.

Castonguay, L. G., Nelson, D. L., Boutselis, M. A., Chiswick, N. R., Damer, D. D., Hemmelstein, N. A., Jackson, J. S., Morford, M., Ragusea, S. A., GowenRoper, J., Spayd, C., Weiszer, T., & Borkovec, T. D. (2010). Psychotherapists, researchers, or both? A qualitative analysis of experiences in a practice research network. *Psychotherapy: Theory, Research, Practice Training, 47*(3), 345–354.

Descartes, S. (1641/2008). Meditations on first philosophy. In J. Cottingham (Ed.), *Western philosophy: An anthology* (2nd ed.). Oxford: Balackwell.

Finlay, L., & Gough, B. (2003). *Reflexivity – A practical guide*. London: Blackwell.

Gendlin, E. T. (1997). *A process model*. New York: The Focusing Institute.

Gendlin, E. T. (2009). What first and third person processes really are. *Journal of Consciousness Studies, 16*(10–12), 332–362.

Giorgi, A. (2009). *The descriptive phenomenological method in psychology*. Pittsburgh: Duquesne University Press.

Gergen, K. (1988). *An invitation to social constructionism*. New York: Sage.

Haraway, D. (1988). Situated knowledges: The science question in feminism and the privilege of partial perspective. *Feminist Studies, 14*, 575–599.

Hesse-Biber, S. (2015). Mixed methods research: The "Thing-ness" problem. *Qualitative Health Research, 25*(6), 775–788.

Hollway, W. (2009). Applying the 'experience-near' principle to research: Psychoanalytically informed methods. *Journal of Social Work Practice, 23*, 461474.

Josselson, R. (2011). *"Bet you think this song is about you": Whose narrative is it in narrative research?* Fielding Graduate University: Available at Journals.hil.unb.ca/index.php/NW/article/download/18472/19971. Accessed 21 Nov 2012.

Merleau-Ponty, M. (1999). The phenomenology of perception. In M. Friedman (Ed.), *The worlds of existentialism: A critical reader*. New York: Humanities Books.

Orange, D. M. (1996). *Emotional understanding: Studies in psychoanalytic epistemology*. New York: Guildford Press.

Orange, D. M. (2009). *Thinking for clinicians: philosophical resources for contemporary psychoanalysis and the humanistic psychotherapies*. Abington: Routledge.

Polkinghorne, D. P. (1988). *Narrative knowing and the human sciences*. New York: Suny Press.

Ritchie, J., Lewis, J., Nicholls, M. N., & Ormston, R. (2014). *Qualitative research practice* (2nd ed.). London: Sage.

Rennie, D. L., & Fergus, K. D. (2006). Embodied categorizing in the grounded theory method. *Theory and Psychology, 16*(4), 483–503.

Spry, T. (2001). Performing autoethnography: An embodied methodological Praxis. *Qualitative Inquiry, 7*(6), 706–732.

Symington, N. (1986). *The analytic experience*. London: Free Association Books.

Tordes, L. (2007). *Embodied enquiry. Phenomenological touchstones for research, psychotherapy and spirituality*. London: Palgrave Macmillan.

Van Manen, M. (2017). But is it phenomenology? *Qualitative Health Research, 27*(6), 775–779.

Willig, C. (2012). *Qualitative interpretation and analysis in psychology*. Maidenhead: OU Press.

Doing Phenomenological Research. Dwelling with the Mystery

Rupert King

Contents

© The Author(s) 2020
S. Bager-Charleson, A. McBeath (eds.),
Enjoying Research in Counselling and Psychotherapy,
https://doi.org/10.1007/978-3-030-55127-8_3

3

After reading this chapter, you should be able to:
- Have an understanding of phenomenology;
- Recognise why phenomenology is not simply a methodology but is also an epistemological framework for researchers;
- Have the skills to frame a research question for a phenomenological inquiry.
- Be aware of the need to remain open to a phenomenon without rushing to resolve ambiguities by naming it too soon;
- Feel able to articulate the researcher's lens;
- Be encouraged to use phenomenological writing in research.

Researching Lived Experience

Researching lived experience is like setting sail on a vast ocean–there are many possibilities and it can be perilous. Therefore choosing the right methodology is crucial. Phenomenology is a powerful tool in qualitative research. It provides a creative approach to investigating complex issues, within a strong philosophical framework, and a means of analysis. Unfortunately, there is no single phenomenological methodology–there are many (Finlay 2011). When considering phenomenology, thoughtful deliberation is required before selecting the most appropriate method, which is often not the same as the most popular.

This chapter is an invitation to dwell, to take a step back and consider those issues critical to the selection of a suitable phenomenological methodology.

The aim is to provide the researcher with an overview of phenomenology, not to discuss the specifics of phenomenological methodologies. I will discuss details of my own research to help illustrate certain points. After weighing up these considerations I hope the reader will be furnished with the necessary insights to choose the right phenomenological methodology for their project.

Phenomenology

» "That which shows itself and at the same time withdraws is the essential trait of what we call the mystery" (Heidegger 1969, p. 55).

The phenomenal world is imperfect, incomplete and ambiguous. What lies before us is the mystery. As meaning-making beings we are faced with the endless task of interpreting lived experience. How we experience the world is similar to looking through a fog; those elements in the foreground of awareness take on striking prominence while background elements remains unknown. The tree in the foreground (◘ Fig. 3.1) is disproportionately vivid and dominates the image, while the other trees fade seamlessly into the background and we are left wondering what lies beyond. It is fair to say we never get a clear or complete picture.

Perhaps the best place to start understanding phenomenology is by looking at *intentionality*, a term coined by Brentano. Intentionality is a concept that states: *con-*

■ **Fig. 3.1** Dwelling on the mystery of experience. Phenomenology assumes a relational and directional nature of consciousness

sciousness is always conscious of something. Zahavi writes, "One does not merely love, fear, see, or judge, one loves a beloved, fears something fearful, sees an object, and judges a state of affairs" (Zahavi 2019, p. 68). Recognising the relational and directional nature of consciousness is the first step in any phenomenological inquiry, for whatever the searchlight of awareness falls upon becomes illuminated, growing in significance, and inevitably something new is uncovered or something familiar is reconstellated. The intentional relationship is the source of lived experience.

In truth, phenomenology is more than a methodology; it is an approach to life – 'a style of thinking and being' (Romanyshyn 2007, p. 88). It is about staying open and allowing the phenomenon to be seen. As Heidegger states, "Thus we must keep in mind the expression 'phenomena' signifies that which shows itself in itself" (Heidegger 1927/1962, p. 51) and "…'phenomena' are the totality of what lies in the light of day or can be brought to the light" (Heidegger 1927/1962, p. 51). At the same time other aspects of our worldview fall into shadow, becoming hidden and covered up, usually those things closest to us: "This Being can be covered up so extensively that it becomes forgotten and no question arises about it or about its meaning" (Heidegger 1927/1962, p. 59). Heidegger called the dialogue between what is revealed and concealed *aletheia* (Heidegger 1993). For Heidegger the essence of phenomenology is *unconcealment* and whatever is revealed will remain partial and a mystery. "There is much in being that man cannot master. There is but little that comes to be known. What is known remains inexact, what is mastered insecure" (Heidegger 1993, p. 178).

The fog of our worldview clouds our perception and in turn shapes how we understand the world. In other words we are informed by our preconceptions and prior experiences. In phenomenology this is called the natural attitude. The attempt to overcome the effects of our natural attitude is called *bracketing*. Whether we are truly able to bracket our natural attitude has been questioned. "I am now convinced that this wonderful term 'bracketing' is simply an illusion, a comforting idea that bears no relation to reality" (Adams 2014,p. 2). Even so, an awareness of our natural attitude, what we bring to the process, is a crucial aspect of phenomenological inquiry.

What is the goal of phenomenological research? Van Manen states, "The aim of phenomenology is to transform lived experience into a textual expression of essence" (van Manen 1990, p. 36). From this description three characteristics of phenomenological inquiry can be identified: the **source** of the inquiry–a description of lived experience; the **expression** of the inquiry–a textual reflection on the experience (and the phenomenon); and the **object** of the inquiry–the phenomenon under investigation whose meaning and essence is being elucidated. The phenomenologist seeks a tentative understanding, through description, in order to reach a possible essence–for it can only ever be *an* understanding of the phenomenon and not *the* understanding due to the incomplete nature of the phenomenal world. Seeking a final resolution to the meaning of lived experience is a common pitfall in phenomenological research. "The mistake we do is that we make definite what is indefinite" (Dahlberg et al. 2008, p.7).

At the heart of phenomenology is a tension between description and interpretation.

Heidegger (1927/1962) describes being human as *Being-in-the-world*, an embedded existence–always part of the world. By acknowledging this 'life-world' stance he recognised the futility of any subject/object split. In other words we cannot extricate ourselves from the phenomenon we choose to research or the interpretations we make. What I am describing is 'interpretive or hermeneutic' phenomenology (e.g. the work of van Manen). This is different to the Husserlian approach of 'descriptive' phenomenology (e.g. the work of Giorgi). In descriptive phenomenology the emphasis is on bracketing and the aim is to achieve an empirical description of the phenomenon, that is, one less contaminated by the natural attitude. "The major task of this meaning of phenomenology is to describe carefully what is given without presuppositions and then use this concrete description as a basis to methodically determine the essence of that experience" (Giorgi 2018, p. 26). Drawing this distinction between Husserlian (descriptive) and Heideggerian (interpretive) phenomenology might be an over-simplification. However, it is intended to help the researcher to navigate the plethora of writings on phenomenology and to gain some purchase on understanding.

How to describe the process of undertaking phenomenological research? It is the process of becoming totally immersed in your topic, the wonder of discovery, the richness of descriptions, the passions and frustrations that are evoked, and finally the enormous sense of satisfaction as things are revealed and a sense of harmony is achieved. The opening line of 'Hokusai Says', a poem by Roger Keyes, encapsulates my experience of doing phenomenology.

Hokusai Says

» Hokusai says look carefully.
He says pay attention, notice.
He says keep looking, stay curious. Hokusai says there is no end to seeing.
He says look forward to getting old. He says keep changing,

you just get more who you really are. He says get stuck, accept it, repeat yourself as long as it is interesting.

He says keep doing what you love…………….. (Williams 2015: 0.07–0.48).

In practical terms phenomenological inquiry offers a wealth of options, starting with the nature of the phenomenon to be studied (the gamut of human emotions, situations, concepts and objects). This is followed by the ways in which these can be explored (dialogues, transcripts, written reflections, anecdotes, poetic imagery, paintings and dance movement), combined with the variety of methodologies that can be employed. Finlay identifies six categories of approach: Descriptive empirical, Hermeneutic interpretative, Lifeworld, IPA, First-person and Reflexive-relational (Finlay 2011, p. 88–91). But beyond specific approaches, at the heart of phenomenology is a sense of wonder, the ability to dwell in the clearing of awareness and to allow phenomena to show themselves.

"To practice phenomenology is always to be surprised by the epiphanies of experience, by the extraordinary that bewitches the ordinary, by the invisible world that haunts the visible" (Romanyshyn 2002, p. xix).

When undertaking a phenomenological inquiry, there are real dangers. Once the inquiry has begun, it is easy to lose sight of the research question, or become overwhelmed by the volume of descriptions, or fail to bring about the phenomenological reduction. Attention to clarity of purpose and rigorous questioning throughout provide suitable countermeasures. The researcher must ensure their work is undertaken in a detailed, methodical fashion that will satisfy the rigours of academic scrutiny. The remainder of this chapter will discuss some of the ways in which these dangers can be kept to a minimum.

An Embodied Stance

Phenomenological research is not simply a case of selecting the right methodology. In a meta-review of 88 phenomenological studies, Norlyk and Harder (2010) noted the importance of clarifying the relevant philosophical principles being used and how these are implemented in the study. As researchers we are required to articulate an epistemological framework, select and implement a recognized methodology, and finally to embody a phenomenological attitude towards the work. All three aspects, when aligned, give the research a depth and authenticity that simply does not happen when merely applying a phenomenological methodology.

► Example

To illustrate this point I will draw on my own doctoral research, entitled **The Clearing of Being: A Phenomenological Study into Openness in Psychotherapy** (King 2017).

- **Epistemological/Philosophical**: The phenomenon I chose to explore was *openness*. Readily acknowledged but rarely understood, openness, as a concept in psychotherapy, invites further attention. This ineffable topic, much like *nothingness*, lends itself to phenomenological inquiry, where from lived experiences and texts I hoped to bring new meaning to openness in psychotherapy. The first step was to find an appropriate philosophical context in which to ground my research and give it credibility–to articulate my epistemological stance. I returned to primary sources and in particular the later writings of Martin Heidegger (Heidegger 1982, 1993; Braver 2009). This is a somewhat esoteric collection of works where Heidegger foregoes normal discussion in favour of imagery and poetic description. Amongst these later works I found a single line that provided me with a starting point. "In the midst of beings as a whole an open place occurs. There is a clearing" (Heidegger 1993: 178). This quote had a significant impact on me and illustrates what van Manen describes as: "..the reader must become possessed by the allusive power of text – taken, touched, overcome by the addressive effect of its reflective engagement with lived experience" (van Manen 2002, p. 238). Heidegger's line spoke to me as a psychotherapist, capturing as it does *Being-in-the-world* as a kind of openness and receptivity.

Engaging with these primary texts was crucial as they were a source of inspiration; they provided an epistemological framework and in the later stages helped contextualise my findings. "It is important to note that there is a significant amount of time spent reading and reflecting upon primary source texts in phenomenology" (Churchill 2018, p. 209).

— **Methodological**: I chose hermeneutic phenomenology (van Manen 1990, 2014) as my methodology as it fits with my epistemological view of the interpretative nature of *Being-in-the-world*. It also places an importance on hermeneutic engagement with texts, while at the same time acknowledging the role of writing as an expression of the phenomenon being studied: "we engage phenomenological research as both a form of inquiry and a writing practice" (Adams and van Manen 2017, p. 781). There is no specific method for doing hermeneutic phenomenology (Laverty 2003; Finlay 2011). However, there are guidelines (van Manen 1990) that can inform and structure the inquiry. If there is strong foresight as to the nature of the phenomenon under investigation, then the researcher is not approaching the task with a *beginner's mind* (Suzuki 1999). It is worth repeating Heidegger's idea of unconcealment (*aletheia*)– the inquiry will reveal new awareness.

  » "Phenomenology is more a method of questioning than answering, realizing that insights come to us in that mode of musing, reflective questioning, and being obsessed with sources and meanings of lived meaning" (van Manen 2014, p. 27).

Hermeneutic phenomenology as a methodology places an emphasis on questioning, reflection and considered elucidation. In this sense it accords well with Heidegger's invitation to let 'the phenomenon itself… set us the task of learning from it while questioning it, that is, of letting it say something to us' (Heidegger 1993, p. 442). In order to achieve this we must allow ourselves to become open to the lived experience, to be touched by it.

— **Personal**: I trained as an existential psychotherapist; a fundamental tenet of this approach is the embodiment of the phenomenological attitude towards the client (Spinelli 2007). The intention is to prevent the therapist from jumping ahead of the client and foreclosing exploration of their worldview. "The therapist remains temporarily open to any number of alternatives, neither rejecting any one as being out of hand, nor placing a greater or lesser degree of likelihood on any of the options available" (Spinelli 2007, p. 115). Likewise, as a researcher I had to ensure the same stance of openness towards the process of inquiry, text descriptions and analysis. Interestingly, as a therapist I have few problems with the phenomenological attitude, but as a researcher I quickly discovered it was easier to talk about openness than to embody it. The following anecdote proves this point. It was written while under time pressure to meet a deadline.

» I'm grappling with my topic, it seems just out of reach, I cannot see it. I hear it - whispering to me, teasing me. The frustration is driving me crazy. I cannot see the wood for the trees, too many ideas, too much reading. I have become trapped in Dante's wood. There are no paths - only brambles, thorns and fallen trees. Yet my topic keeps calling me. I fumble around in this shadow-world disorientated. Dry branches snap – loudly, harshly, intrusively announcing my stuckness. I rush at any and every opportunity. However these false trails lead me deeper and deeper into a tangled mass of undergrowth. The impending deadline encircles me like twilight.

Into this desperation comes a moment of clarity, a shaft of dappled light penetrating the dense canopy. Rather than rushing for answers and resolution I stop, breathe and allow an opening – the fertile void. I take a step back, try to contain my anxiety and allow things to settle. Here in this haunted forest there is no need for the ego of doing – only being. A kind of presence that shelters and allows, that does not jump to change things or rush to interfere. After a while I begin to move, slowly, one step at a time. I walk towards the light and step into a clearing of awareness. (King 2017, p. 134–135) ◄

I have described how three dimensions, epistemological/philosophical, methodological and personal, interconnect throughout the research process. "In order for qualitative research to pursue embodied understanding, it requires procedures that show phenomena in both experientially evocative as well as structurally coherent ways" (Todres 2007, p. 28).

Activity
- Can you place your research in a philosophical or epistemological context/tradition?
- Do you understand what your chosen methodology requires of you?
- Can you summarise, in a paragraph, the stance you will take towards your research topic?

Articulating the Research Question

This is possibly the most critical part of the process because everything flows from the right research question. Think of it as a guiding star by which you navigate across the ocean of your research. Lose sight of that star and your vessel quickly begins to drift off course.

"Every inquiry is a seeking. Every seeking gets guided beforehand by what is sought" (Heidegger 1927/1962, p. 24). Returning to my research: I was seeking an understanding of openness in psychotherapy. It was guided by my insights as a psychotherapist and curiosity as a researcher. I was drawn to understanding a quality of *open presence* achieved in the therapeutic relationship. This was my horizon of understanding at the outset of the research.

At the beginning of *Being and Time* (1927/1962) Heidegger poses a question – what is the meaning of Being? This is perhaps the ultimate phenomenological inquiry. He explains that his inquiry involves the idea that 'what is asked about is Being' (Heidegger 1927/1962, p. 25) and 'what is to be found out by the asking – the meaning of Being' (Heidegger 1927/1962, p. 26). Building on Heidegger's philosophy (Heidegger 1927/1962, p. 24–28), Churchill describes teaching phenomenology by acknowledging that there are three elements to any inquiry: What is asked about? [*Gefragte*]; What is interrogated? [*Befragte*]; and What is asked for? [*Erfragte*] (Churchill 2018, p. 210). I believe this is a helpful way for researchers to engage with their research topic and formulate their question. Relating these three elements to my research:

- What is asked about? – Openness in psychotherapy
- What is interrogated? – Psychotherapists' lived experience
- What is asked for? – An understanding and essence of open presence

"What is asked for" is the research phenomenon, which awaits elucidation through the inquiry. In my research it was rather loosely described as 'open presence'. "The research phenomenon itself is something that we cannot know quite so clearly at the beginning of an investigation; it is easier to talk about the situation, this is the 'lived experience' that we wish to have described for us" (Churchill 2018, p. 210). At the core of any phenomenological question is a seeking–a curiosity about *how* something is experienced, rather than a need to define *what* something is. If the researcher is able to formulate a research question by identifying these three elements, then the guiding star is set fair for the journey ahead.

Articulating the right research question will help to differentiate between the experience [*Gefragte*] and the phenomenon [*Erfragte*], which can all too easily become merged. "There would appear to be much confusion of thought here regarding the nature and relationship of 'experience' and 'phenomenon'. Indeed despite talk of seeking one through the other, for most of these researchers they are clearly interchangeable terms" (Crotty 1996, p. 17).

Activity

If you have chosen phenomenology as your methodology, what is the lived experience being investigated?

Are you able to identify

- what is asked about?
- what is interrogated?
- what is asked for? (this will remain relatively unknown)

Remaining Open to the Phenomenon

» "It is a matter of describing, not of explaining or analysing" (Merleau-Ponty 2002, p. ix).

Do you have a clear idea of your research phenomenon from the outset? If so, what, then, is being researched? It is all too easy to become fixed on what the phenomenon is rather than allowing it to emerge through inquiry. "[T]he 'subject' of phenomenological research (the 'about which') is something implicit that begs to be made explicit by the researcher" (Churchill 2018, p. 211).

Earlier I mentioned the tension between descriptions and meaning. It is through phenomenological reflection and description of lived experience that the Erfragte–*what is asked for*–emerges. Making meaning manifest while staying open to the ongoing process of description is the ultimate task of phenomenology. In reality, however, when faced with the uncertainty of making explicit the essence there is a tendency to rush and name things, as the following anecdote shows. It was written while on holiday in Japan, midway through the analysis phase of my research.

» I'm sitting on the temple steps, looking down on a strange configuration of stone pillars and raked sand. A Zen garden, then again it could be a children's playground or an installation by a trendy artist. These thoughts circulate in my mind and mirror the Karesansui (dry stone garden) in front of me (◧ Fig. 3.2). It is early morning and the temple has just opened. I follow the ripples in the sand and my mind wanders, imagining the stone pillars whispering to each other. Are they engaged in some erudite discourse on Buddhist doctrine? Or perhaps they are simply gossiping about the abbot. Soon even these thoughts evaporate and my mind empties. I sit in silence, occasionally being interrupted by the soft padding of other visitors walking behind me. Openness as Emptiness comes to mind. How can this be emptiness when there is sand, pillars and moss? Not sure - obviously I need to spend many more hours in Zasen (meditation). Maybe the emptiness I experience in these rocks and gravel is an invitation to Openness. I experience a powerful sensation inviting me to present – simply to be. My mind is floating freely on these flights of fancy when suddenly I'm hit by unmistakable noise; the sensation is like being woken up from a deep and restful sleep unexpectedly. It is the squawk of a megaphone - to my left I see a large group of tourists being marshaled by a tour guide. They march imperiously along the covered walkway and stand inches from me. The tour guide begins her spiel.

'We are now on the eastern side of Tofukuji Temple. This beautiful Zen garden was created by famous 20th C Japanese designer Mirei Shigemori. The seven pillars represent the star constellation of the plough or big dipper. They are believed to have been recycled from the monks' toilet block! [group laughter]'.

In that moment my contemplation of Openness in the Zen garden shatters. The tour group moves on crushing the fragments of my thinking under foot. What is it about our need to explain everything? I'm left feeling deflated and robbed. I can no longer look at the garden in the same way. I am wondering whether to stay or go. Then I spy another group making its way down the walkway. I am reminded of van Manen "In the act of naming we cannot help but kill the things that we name" (2002: 239). It is time to move on and find another object to contemplate. (King 2017: 129–130).

⬛ Fig. 3.2 The Naming of Things

What did I learn from the temple experience? How easy it is to name things in order to elevate the anxiety of not-knowing. However, in doing so we reify the elusive essence, which we seek. Only by cultivating openness can we resist the urge to name too quickly. If we remain open we can achieve a more nuanced understanding of the phenomenon. "Each new path embarked on in phenomenological inquiry intends to draw nearer to the phenomenon itself and to the inceptual clearing of wonder" (Adams and van Manen 2017, p. 783).

Explicating the Researcher's Lens

The agenda we have for our research can be pervasive. "Rejecting the possibility of being a neutral investigator, I need to describe clearly my own research trajectory…" (Du Plock 2016, p. 86). By acknowledging this trajectory, through written reflection, a picture develops as to why *this* topic is meaningful. Thus we gain an understanding of how this significant aspect might impact the research. In terms of interpretive/hermeneutic phenomenology it is less about bracketing and more about being open and acknowledging what we bring to

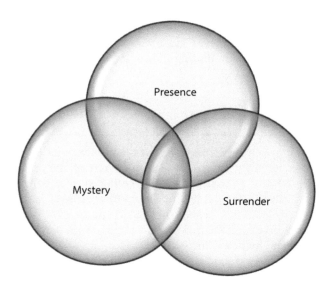

◘ Fig. 3.3 Meeting point between approaches in phenomenological inquiry

the research. "Many phenomenologists – particularly those with hermeneutic sensibilities – prefer to move beyond the idea of bracketing per se and discuss the phenomenological attitude more broadly as 'openness'" (Finlay 2011, p. 77).

In terms of my research, I spent many weeks dwelling with the data (Finlay 2013), which took many forms: hermeneutic engagement with philosophical texts, participants' interview transcripts and my own written reflections. From the analysis three key themes emerged: a quality of (presence), to let things be (surrender) and receptivity towards not-knowing (mystery). What of the essence of openness? I worked towards building up an impression of openness rather than a definition. In one final attempt to hold the line between description and definition I collected these qualities together and represented them (◘ Fig. 3.3).

Openness

For me this encapsulates the essence of openness; the decision to represent it in this way was inspired by a photograph of a clearing, where dappled light and shadows overlapped on the forest floor. *It captures the elusive qualities I associate with openness.* This insight was the culmination of a detailed process of careful deliberation using multiple sources: texts, interviews, reflections, anecdotes and photographs, which contributed to the revealing of an essence of openness (King 2017). "The phenomenologist is a witness and not a critic of experience, and for a phenomenologist what appears matters first before one asks what it might mean" (Romanyshyn 2002, p. 120–121). We can only be a witness if we are able to loosen our grip on the agenda for the research. Making this agenda explicit is the first step in letting it go. The next step is accepting that our research will never be complete. "Ultimately, whatever meanings are articulated in research, much more remains unsaid and our findings always remain provisional, partial and emergent" (Finlay 2013, p. 189).

3   Phenomenological Writing

In whatever manner we choose to explore the phenomenon of our research, eventually there is the need for a written reflection as part of the process of analysis. As I have stated, the aim of writing is to evoke the essence of the phenomenon without trying to capture and reify it. The two anecdotes in this chapter are examples of how *"to write is to reflect; to write is to research"* (van Manen 2014: 20), and putting these experiences down on paper, while I was in the midst of grappling with them, helped clarify the essence of 'stuckness' and 'naming' respectively. "A phenomenological anecdote is not intended to serve as an illustration but as an evocative example of a possible human experience" (Adams and van Manen 2017, p. 788).

It is worth considering your feelings towards writing–do you enjoy it? Does it come naturally to you? If your responses to these questions are less than fulsome then acknowledge them. However daunting it may be, try not to be deterred from undertaking a phenomenological inquiry. The key to writing is practice. Just write staying as close as possible to the phenomenon, give your thoughts freedom and keep your inner critic in check (Cameron 1992, 2004). The author Ray Bradbury summed it up by saying: "For if one works, one finally relaxes and stops thinking. True creation occurs then and only then" (Bradbury 1996, p. 147).

Activity
- Write a short piece describing, as richly as possible, your research topic without directly naming it. Give yourself permission to be as creative as possible. Sit in wonder and create space (openness) to allow the phenomenon to reveal itself in the clearing.
- Write a short piece describing why the topic matters to you.
- What are your beliefs, assumptions and attitude towards the research?

These considerations are by no means comprehensive or complete. They are based on my epistemological framework, personal experiences of conducting a phenomenological inquiry at doctoral level and a wish to share learning. I hope this chapter has provided food for thought and a challenge to preconceptions and that it helps to clarify your intentions. Most importantly, I hope it has inspired you to consider phenomenology as a research methodology.

Summary

Phenomenology is a powerful tool for qualitative research. It provides a creative approach to investigating lived experience and meaning, within a strong philosophical framework. Unfortunately, there is no single phenomenological methodology–there are many. As a result confusion arises with regard to the 'how' and 'what' of using phenomenology in research. This chapter is an invitation for the reader to step back and consider those issues critical to the selection of a suitable phenomenological methodology. The chapter was designed to encourage a greater understanding of phenomenology, to formulate an appropriate research question, to dwell with the mysteries of exploring lived experience, and to feel confident in writing about those experiences from a phenomenological standpoint.

References

Adams, C., & van Manen, M. (2017). Teaching Phenomenological Research and Writing. *Qualitative Health Research, 27*(6), 780–791.

Adams, M. (2014). *The Myth of the Untroubled Therapist*. London & New York: Routledge.

Bradbury, R. (1996). *Zen in the art of writing*. Santa Barbara: Joshua Odell Editions.

Braver, L. (2009). *Heidegger's Later Writings*. London: Continuum.

Cameron, J. (1992). *The Artist's Way*. London: Souvenir Press Ltd.

Cameron, J. (2004). *The Sound of Paper*. London: Penguin Books.

Churchill, S. D. (2018). Explorations in teaching the phenomenological method: Challenging psychology students to "grasp at meaning" in human science research. *Qualitative Psychology, 5*(2), 207–227.

Crotty, M. (1996). *Phenomenology and Nursing Research*. Melbourne: Churchill Livingstone.

Dahlberg, K., Dahlberg, H., & Nystrom, M. (2008). *Reflective Lifeworld Research* (2nd ed.). Lund, Sweden: Studentliteratur.

Du Plock, S. (2016). 'Bibliotherapy and beyond: research as a catalyst for change in therapeutic practice. In *Goss and Stevens Making Research Matter* (pp. 85–105). London & New York: Routledge.

Finlay, L. (2011). *Phenomenology for Therapists*. Chichester: Wiley & Sons Ltd.

Finlay, L. (2013). Unfolding the Phenomenological Research Process: Iterative Stages of "Seeing Afresh". *Journal of Humanistic Psychology, 53*(2), 172–201.

Giorgi, A. (2018). *Reflections*. Colorado Springs: University Professors Press.

Heidegger, M. (1927/1962). *Being and Time. (trans. Macquarrie & Robinson)*. Oxford: Blackwells Publishing Ltd.

Heidegger, M. (1969). *Discourse on Thinking*. New York: Harper & Row.

Heidegger, M. (1982). *On the Way to Language. 1st Paperback*. New York: Harper Collins Publishers Inc.

Heidegger, M. (1993) *Basic Writings*. (ed. D. Farrell Krell). San Francisco: Harper Collins Publishers Inc.

King, R. (2017). *The clearing of being: a phenomenological study of openness in psychotherapy* [doctoral thesis Middlesex University http://eprints.mdx.ac.uk/22643/].

Laverty, S. (2003). Hermeneutic Phenomenology and Phenomenology: A Comparison of Historical and Methodological Considerations. *International Journal of Qualitative Methods, 2*(3), Article 3. Available from: http://www.ualberta.ca/~iiqm/backissues/2_3final/pdf/laverty.pdf [Accessed 10/9/2015].

Merleau-Ponty, M. (2002). *Phenomenology of Perception*. London & New York: Routledge Classics.

Norlyk, A., & Harder, I. (2010). What Makes a Phenomenological Study Phenomenological? An Analysis of Peer-Reviewed Empirical Nursing Studies. *Qualitative Health Research, 20*(3), 420–431.

Romanyshyn, R. (2002). *The Ways of the Heart*. Pittsburgh: Trivium Publications.
Romanyshyn, R. (2007). *The Wounded Researcher*. Louisiana: Spring Journal Inc.
Spinelli, E. (2007). *Practicing Existential Psychotherapy*. London: Sage.
Suzuki, S. (1999). *Zen Mind, Beginner's Mind*. Boston & London: Weatherhill.
Todres, L. (2007). *Embodied Enquiry*. Basingstoke: Palgrave Macmillan.
van Manen, M. (1990). *Researching Lived Experience*. Albany: State University of.
van Manen, M. (2002). *Writing in the Dark*. Ontario: The Althouse Press.
van Manen, M. (2014). *Phenomenology of Practice*. Walnut Creek CA: Left Coast Press Inc.
Williams, M. (2015). *Hokusai Says* by Rogers Keyes read for The Mindfulness Summit available on Youtube *https://www.youtube.com/watch?v=zkTvAi9UdLw* [accessed 12/10/2018]
Zahavi, D. (2019). *Phenomenology the basics*. Abingdon: Routledge.

Doing Qualitative Research with Interpretative Phenomenological Analysis

John Barton

Contents

© The Author(s) 2020
S. Bager-Charleson, A. McBeath (eds.),
Enjoying Research in Counselling and Psychotherapy,
https://doi.org/10.1007/978-3-030-55127-8_4

Doubt is not a pleasant condition. But certainty is absurd.
—Voltaire (1770)

🔘 Learning Goals

After reading this chapter you should be able to:

- Appreciate the subjective nature of qualitative research in general and Interpretative Phenomenological Analysis (IPA) in particular;
- Understand the rationale for an IPA study;
- Describe the values, underlying philosophy and epistemological principles of IPA;
- Describe the process of carrying out an IPA study;
- Know a little more about disability;
- Feel encouraged and inspired to embrace the subjectivity of carrying out a piece of IPA research and make it your own.

Introduction

One afternoon at the Metanoia Institute, it was my turn to make a presentation to my peers, outlining my doctoral research project. I was nervous. "Sometimes the idea is right in front of your face," first-year tutor Paul Hitchings had advised. But my idea felt too close. Charcot-Marie-Tooth (CMT) is a hereditary neuromuscular wasting condition named after the three neurologists who identified it in 1886. It is an unfashionable affliction that turns its chosen few into people who are ungainly, clumsy and slow. Few people have heard of it—it is bereft of celebrity spokespersons—and it often comes with a lot of intrafamilial shame and blame. It isolates and excludes, and it only ever deteriorates. It affects every aspect of one's way of being in the world, and the only constant is change as the unstoppable condition unfurls. People with CMT suffer in silence.

My presentation to the group went well. But afterwards, in the discussion, I was choked up and momentarily unable to speak, because what was happening was simply revelatory: People were talking about CMT!

Many years later, my dissertation was complete: an investigation into the lived experience of progressive physical disability through the voices of people with CMT. I am one of those people. I have CMT. This was therefore a piece of "insider research" (Rooney, 2005: 6). On the one hand, I was highly motivated to carry out this work, and attuned and empathic to others who share the condition. But on the other, I brought to it my own unique experiences and attitudes—the danger was that I might see and hear myself rather than my research participants.

The experience of progressive disability is my life, in every minute of every day. Nine days before I presented my research proposal to the approval panel, in September 2013, I was diagnosed with an entirely unrelated and better-known chronic incurable degenerative neurological condition: Parkinson's. The diagnosis was devastating. But ... there was no escaping the strange synchronicity of its timing, which I chose to see as some weird kind of cosmic thumbs-up for my research, an affirmation, a benediction. Parkinson's greatly amplified the importance to me and my life of my research. It was a very long, challenging, complicated and uneven journey. It is of profound importance in my acceptance of ill-health, an accelerated individuation process, and an existential and spiritual midlife transformation. I'd just turned 50 when I was diagnosed with Parkinson's. In many ways, this is when I began to live.

Methodology

My undergraduate research on depression in children adhered to the prevailing positivist, quantitative logic of the British university system of the 1980s. Aside from providing instructions on how to fill out a questionnaire, it did not involve talking to any children. It was an unedifying and rather pointless experience.

Quantitative research, it is true, has made many useful contributions to psychology but in general our species refuses to conform to a worldview that seeks to understand and explain the human condition in terms of hard science, biological determinism, statistics, mental health questionnaire scores and diagnostic labels.

Impartial scientists are fallible victims of the very thing that they seek to deny: human subjectivity. Time and again, published research produces findings that conform to researchers' biases, sponsor preference or cultural difference, or are career-enhancing, or politically self-serving.

Fortunately, psychology's historic philosophical approach was not defeated by positivism. A descriptive, subjective, phenomenological psychology lives on, requiring for Merleau-Ponty "a foreswearing of science," which he regarded as "always both naïve and at the same time dishonest" (1945: ix).

I was interested in hearing other people's experiences of progressive disability, their understandings and interpretations in their own words. This led me towards a qualitative, phenomenological method. Counselling psychology has witnessed a flourishing of postmodern methodologies, giving rise to a great diversity of approaches, topics and findings (Ponterotto, 2005).

Qualitative research rejects objectivity as not only not possible, but also not desirable. The unique histories, qualities and biases of the researcher and participants are not denied; they are embraced, as are constructivist and social constructionist approaches which claim no grand narratives or fixed absolutes, and instead see reality as temporary, partial, local. For McLeod, "the primary aim of qualitative research is to develop an understanding of how the world is constructed" (2001: 2).

IPA: The Marriage of Hermeneutics and Phenomenology

If I were to take a traditional, Husserlian phenomenological approach, I would attempt to bracket my own experiences of CMT and Parkinson's and seek to understand with objectivity the unique experiences of my research participants—I would be attempting to get to the essence of those experiences, what Husserl called "the things themselves" (Husserl, 1927; Smith et al., 2009: 12).

For Husserl's erstwhile student Heidegger, however, such bracketing was seen as impossible; indeed for Gadamer, the very attempt is manifestly absurd (in Laverty,

2003). In Heidegger's eyes—and my own—one cannot separate one's self; one cannot be an impartial, objective "scientific" observer. Instead, the researcher's own subjectivity and interpretations are embraced. This is the essence of hermeneutics.

Husserl advanced the idea that "experience is of a system of interrelated meanings" (1913/1998), but for Heidegger those meanings are highly contextual. Humans are "thrown" into existence, he wrote, and must adapt to and be shaped by their unique environments. We cannot be divorced from our *Befindlichkeit*—our subjective, felt sense of ourselves in the world (Heidegger (1927/1962); Gadamer (1975/1991); Stolorow, Atwood and Orange (2002).

Through self-reflection, the hermeneutic researcher becomes aware of their own biases and assumptions, not in order to bracket them off, as a Husserlian phenomenological researcher might do, but to make them a central part of the interpretative research process. Writes Laverty (2003): "The overt naming of assumptions and influences as key contributors to the research process in hermeneutic phenomenology is one striking difference from the naming and then bracketing of bias or assumptions in phenomenology."

Hermeneutics and phenomenology thus appear at first glance to be at odds with each other. "Hermeneutic phenomenology" may seem like an oxymoron. But the twin approaches can be reconciled; both can be viewed as "integral, complementary aspects of any satisfactory way of knowing about human existence" (McLeod, 2001: 59). Phenomenology is what Heidegger saw as a "fore-understanding" to hermeneutic enquiry (ibid).

Interpretative Phenomenological Analysis (IPA) is the offspring of this unlikely union between hermeneutics and phenomenology, conceived in 1996 (Smith et al., 2009: 4) and now reaching respectable adulthood. Writes Smith: "IPA requires a combination of phenomenological and hermeneutic insights. It is phenomenological in attempting to get as close as possible to the personal experience of the participant, but recognizes that this inevitably becomes an interpretative endeavour for both participant and researcher. Without the phenomenology, there would be nothing to interpret; without the hermeneutics, the phenomenon would not be seen" (ibid, 2009: 37).

IPA is well suited to the study of the idiographic experiences of a homogenous group of people with a shared circumstance, for understanding how people perceive the "particular situations they are facing, how they are making sense of their personal and social world. It is especially useful when one is concerned with complexity, process, or novelty". It has been widely used for exploring issues in the personal, specific experience of health and illness; indeed health psychology was where IPA first found its voice (Brocki and Wearden, 2006).

Research methodologies, too, are subject to interpretation. Larkin, Watts and Clifton (2006) suggest that IPA is best regarded as a research perspective rather than a discrete research method. For my research, I broadly followed the principles of IPA. I choose not to swallow blindly any strictures and protocols, however, nor indeed any qualitative methodology since such "schoolism" would violate my belief in human meaning-making and knowledge. Instead I offer my interpretation of IPA. I eschew terminology that has positivist reverberations—"data," "coding" and "validity" are examples; another is referring to oneself in the third person—in favour of language that is more congruent with an inclusive, integrative approach.

My Interpretation of IPA

I have an old wise dog, Daisy, who often sits with one ear up and one ear down. She listens to the world and she listens to herself. Daisy (image 4.1) gets through life—with dignity and aplomb—by combining phenomenology and hermeneutics (■ Fig. 4.1).

Similarly, in my former career as a journalist, I came to appreciate that the best writers are those who harvest information from the world through extensive reporting, but who then knowingly combine it with their own experience and interpretations. The use of their subjectivity is deliberate, reflective and transparent.

And in my work, too, as an integrative psychotherapist, I choose not to practise in either a solely phenomenological or a hermeneutic way but rather to fuse these approaches. I tend to emulate advocates of interpretative, psychodynamic and existential methods that help the client clarify and shape their story and experience of life (e.g. Frankl, 2004/1946; Boss, 1963; Yalom, 1980; Bugenthal, 1999), as opposed

■ **Fig. 4.1** My dog, with dignity and aplomb

to those who favour a more purely phenomenological, client-led stance (e.g. Laing, 1960; Spinelli, 2007; Van Deurzen, 2012). Indeed, besides research, I believe IPA could also be usefully developed as a specific integrative therapeutic approach.

The epistemic position of pure phenomenology is that there is an objective reality that can be known and understood through science and reason. Pure hermeneutics, by contrast, sees human understanding and knowledge not as fixed "out there" realities waiting to be unearthed but instead as socially constructed and a matter of interpretation. Nietzsche wrote in 1887: "It is precisely facts that do not exist, only *interpretations*" (in Kaufmann, 1954: 458). Hermeneutics is born of a relativist ontology: each person is seen as inextricably embodied and embedded in a particular historical, social and cultural context.

I see no reason to exclude either position. Like Daisy, I don't deny a realist epistemology—there are some truths and there is a real physical world; "facts" indeed do exist. But I also believe that to understand the psychology of human beings, it is meanings and meaning-making that need to become the focus of attention. There are no absolute truths—human knowledge instead is a dynamic, social construction born of cognitive schemes and embodied interactions with diverse environments (Polkinghorne, 1992: 147). I am thus perhaps best described as a "critical realist" (Maxwell, 2012). I believe, as Lynch states, "that there is an objective order and meaning to reality, but that our knowledge of it is always partial (contextual and local, rather than universal)" (1996: 146).

We humans do our best, but we each have a particular and highly circumscribed apparatus with which to understand our lives. Our "doors of perception" (Huxley, 1954) are only partially open. We cannot be expected to know the truth of the universe any more than an ant can be expected to read the book upon whose open page it walks. This reflects my spiritual viewpoint that there are greater truths that we cannot know, only glimpse. I put my faith in the mystery and uncertainty of life.

Qualitative research thus embraces uncertainty—what the poet Keats referred to as a "negative capability" rather than an "irritable reaching after fact and reason" (Voller, 2010)—because there is no certainty.

I believe that it is in the subjective interplay and tension that exists between phenomenology and hermeneutics that truths—as opposed to *the* truth—are discerned, truths that are rather more modest, provisional and contextual than anything purporting to be factual. I am thus very much drawn to IPA, a rich, engaging process that with humility respects and honours the inherent complexity, changeability and mystery of human life. Indeed, its focus on understanding and making sense of experience (Smith, 2018) is the very essence of an existential life: a human search for meaning.

I also was encouraged and guided by van Manen's four interconnected and interacting aspects of hermeneutic phenomenological research (1984: 39):
(a) Turning to a phenomenon which seriously interests us and commits us to the world.
(b) Investigating experience as we live it rather than as we conceptualise it.
(c) Reflecting on the essential themes which characterise the phenomenon.
(d) Describing the phenomenon through the art of writing and rewriting.

I could have used one of various phenomenologically informed narrative methods of enquiry (e.g. Ricoeur, 1981; Polkinghorne, 1988), but these would tend to require a bracketing and diminishment of my own testimony. At the other extreme, I could have taken a solely autoethnographic approach (Etherington, 2004; Denzin, 2013), but that would have imprisoned me in my own experience of progressive disability. I very much wanted to reach out and connect with others who might similarly feel alienated and disconnected by CMT.

I see hermeneutic phenomenology as an organic, live conversation between the therapist and client or researcher and research subject—a "double hermeneutic" (Smith et al., 2009). "The process of interpretation is dynamic and iterative, engaging the concept of the hermeneutic circle in an interplay between parts and whole and between the interpreter and the object of interpretation" (Shinebourne, 2011). The circle then encompasses the reader, who will bring their own context and subjectivity to bear in their interpretation of the work and their contributions to the wider conversation.

But social science research is messy (Law, 2004), founded on human subjectivity and choice, defined as much by what is left in as what is left out: "What is being made present always depends on what is being made absent" (ibid, 83).

Hermeneutics and phenomenology are not always easy dance partners. Writes van Manen: "As soon as we turn to reflect on an experience that we have in this very moment, we inevitably immediately have stepped away from or out of the living sphere or sensibility of the livedness of lived experience. The instant of the moment we reflect on a lived experience, the living moment is already gone" (2017: 832). Warns Polkinghorne: "People do not have complete access to their experiences... People do not have a clear window into their inner life" (2005: 138). Participant self-reports can be banal or limited.

I felt that there were things I wanted to say. Moustakas (1975, 1994) extolled the virtues of the use of self in the research process. A critical realist is inherently quite a different animal from an "objective," "scientific," "bracketing" researcher. The critical realist is a critic, intentionally political, believing "that a discernable reality exists, but that this reality reflects the oppressive influence of social, political, and historical factors. The researcher's role is both interactive and proactive, with the explicit goal of facilitating change and emancipation from restrictive social conditions" (Havercamp and Young, 2007: 268).

My experiences of CMT and progressive disability are just as valid as those of my research participants, and formed part of the work. I felt a growing desire to include a chapter on my experience, to tell my story—my illness narrative.

Such an approach, however, is unorthodox. To explore this further I contacted IPA founder Jonathan Smith himself. He was a couple of miles away, across town, and he very graciously agreed to meet me to discuss my project. In my experience, well-known psychologists and therapists can be extremely helpful and encouraging when approached directly with questions.

I met Smith in his office in Birkbeck and he was very generous with his time and enthusiasm. He echoed the above concerns.

"There's a danger that your experience could completely flood this research and drown out your participants," he said. "They have to come first. But in principal I have no ideological problem with your approach. If you present your participants' accounts first and this is then followed by what is clearly signaled as your own personal account in a separate chapter, I can see that can offer a useful extra perspective" (cited, private conversation).

We talked more broadly about IPA—including whether it had potential as a therapeutic modality—and I left feeling encouraged and emboldened.

Participants

Qualitative research generally aims for depth rather than breadth. IPA research is usually carried out with a small, homogenous group who all have experience of the phenomenon under investigation; Smith et al. (2009) recommend between three and six participants.

My main selection criteria obviously were that participants must have CMT. I wanted participants who had been diagnosed at least 10 years ago, and consider themselves disabled, such that their symptoms, history and experiences with CMT are rich and significant. The final lineup of participants was six women with ages ranging from 25 to 68.

Ethics

To be a participant in a piece of qualitative research—as I have been—can be a challenging, demanding and upsetting experience. It's much easier to fill out an anxiety inventory, for instance, than to talk about your anxiety in a long face-to-face interview with a stranger. There are thus moral and ethical questions to be considered. Conducting this kind of research carries a great risk of doing harm to people, and researchers thus bear a great responsibility and duty of care. The nature of IPA research is open-ended and organic, without fixed methods and protocols, and complex and unexpected issues can arise. State Strawbridge and Woolfe: "many situations are vague and uncertain, decisions must be made, actions taken and accounted for" (2010: 14). Ethical guidelines are a helpful but crude map for navigating these challenging waters, which the researcher must do with sensitivity, a grounding in humanistic values and plenty of critical reflexivity (Etherington, 2004; Josselson, 2007). And supervision. The emotional depth of qualitative research is both its greatest strength and its biggest challenge.

Interviews

The standard (but not only) method that IPA employs to elicit first-hand experiences of a phenomenon is in-depth semi-structured interviews with a small number of research participants (Smith et al., 2009).

The IPA interview process is itself a blend of hermeneutics and phenomenology. The researcher prepares a list of open-ended questions based on their interpretation of the research enquiry and what they imagine the participants' experience might be. Smith et al. (2009) recommend starting with broad questions—my first question was the simple invitation: "Tell me about your CMT"—before narrowing the focus to specific areas. But the list of questions is not rigidly adhered to. It is important to listen, to follow up when there appears to be more to say, to open up the space for the participant's phenomenality. For researchers and journalists alike, this active and reactive interplay between questions and answers, with one ear up and one ear down, lies at the heart of good interviewing.

I elected to conduct two interviews with each participant—an initial interview lasting ideally at least 60 minutes and then a follow-up interview a few weeks later with the intention of exploring participants' experience in greater depth. The second interview also gave participants time to reflect on the first, as well as another fresh opportunity to tell their story. This is important since fatigue is a very common symptom of CMT, and symptoms can fluctuate depending on mood, stress, sleep and diet.

I also asked a colleague to conduct two interviews with me. As well as informing my own CMT story, the self-interview also helped to identify my own biases and preconceptions and thus develop a clearer understanding of my participants, as well as providing me with helpful insight into being an interviewee, informing my interview questions and how I might best conduct the interviews. I wanted to make my interview questions as free from implicit assumptions and biases as possible, and I wanted my participants to feel comfortable and relaxed.

The six participants spoke at great length and in great depth about their experiences with CMT. The recorded interviews totalled 22 hours and 38 minutes of testimony.

I found the interviews to be extraordinary encounters. None of the participants had spoken about CMT in such depth before; three of the six had never discussed their feelings about CMT with anyone. Additionally, the fact that I too have CMT generated an enormous sense of kinship. The interviews were not just a meeting of minds but of bodies too, bodies that shared the same peculiar kind of brokenness. These were deeply intersubjective, embodied encounters. Merleau-Ponty wrote: "It is through my body that I understand other people" (1945: 186); it was through the shared physical vulnerability wrought by CMT that I and my participants connected. I interpreted "interview" in the true, original sense of the word: both parties were "seeing each other." I felt fully present as myself, and available to the interviewee; together we co-created an egalitarian space of "reciprocal mutual influence" (Stolorow and Atwood, 1992: 18). I view intersubjectivity as a largely unconscious, embodied process (Gallese, 2015), one that emerges from the interaction between my subjectivity and that of the client, with both being altered by the dynamic. This is my understanding of a dialogic attitude (Buber, 1958; Hycner, 1993). I experience it as an altered, higher state of consciousness.

Quality

Quantitative research goes to great lengths to observe rigorous quality control procedures and to use large sample sizes, statistical protocols and peer review, all in the name of ensuring objectivity and validity. How is qualitative work to be judged?

What validity, reliability, truth or meaning is there to be found in a researcher's subjective engagement with a small sample of participants?

McLeod (2001: 183) suggests three considerations. First is the work grounded in epistemological principles—does the research remain faithful to an underlying authentic and coherent philosophy and associated values and literature? Second are quality control standards observed: clarity and detail of procedures, what the researcher actually did and the process of recruiting participants, for example. Relatedly, how transparent, open and reflexive is the researcher about their own background, qualities, biases and personal engagement with the research topic? And third, is the report any good—is it interesting, compelling or useful?

For some, the flexibilities and ambiguities that are inherent in the process of IPA call into question its worth as an academic endeavour. A recent review of IPA's alleged "promiscuity" described it as "the black swan of qualitative research" (Dennison, 2019). Missing the point, Giorgi (2010) bemoaned IPA for being insufficiently prescriptive in how it should be executed, not replicable and not "scientific." This is akin to complaining that Picasso's portraits of Dora Maar don't much look like her. In art as in research, this is the challenge of postmodernism: the old "rules" no longer apply, and anyone who is faced with a piece of work must decide for themselves whether or not it has merit.

For a piece of qualitative insider phenomenological research such as this, Rooney argues that rather than considering validity and trustworthiness, more helpful terms might include "authenticity, credibility and understanding" (2005: 5). Yardley advocates the following principles as a guide to quality: sensitivity to context; commitment and rigour; transparency and coherence; impact and importance (2000).

I believe my deeply personal involvement in this project did not detract from it; rather, it carries "the potential to increase validity due to the added richness, honesty, fidelity and authenticity of the information acquired" (Rooney, 2005: 7).

Analysis

In a research workshop at the Metanoia Institute during my training, I played a 12-minute segment of one of my research interviews, with participant "Mary," to my colleagues with the intention of then conducting a data analysis exercise using the transcript. Mary's voice filled the room. We were all moved by her anguish at having to give up her beloved hiking. At the end of the segment, with half the room in tears, it felt preposterous to reduce Mary's powerful testimony to a deconstruction of words on paper. We abandoned the coding exercise. Instead, we discussed Mary, and the raw emotion of loss.

This experience crystallised my ideas about what constitutes "data" in qualitative research and how understanding and meaning are to be pursued. One of the appealing aspects of IPA for me is that it is ideographic as opposed to nomothetic; it drills down deep into the fullness of an individual, exploring and celebrating the unique peculiarities and infinite variety of the human experience rather than seeking out or upholding norms. This involves a commitment to a thorough analysis of the participants' testimonies (Pietkiewicz and Smith, 2014: 8).

I decided to consider my interviews from a variety of "altitudes": at the highest, with the widest lens, were the interviews themselves, descending and narrowing to the audio recordings of the sessions, the transcripts, and finally right down to the granular line-by-line scrutiny and coding process.

After each interview I wrote free-flowing, unstructured notes about my impressions, reflections and feelings surrounding the encounter. This process was repeated when, two years later and wishing to re-engage with the project, I listened to the audio recordings again. In the meantime I had had all 12 interviews transcribed (owing to the volume of recordings and my hand tremor and weakness, I felt unable to do this myself). I read through the transcripts, writing further notes.

I find the traditional characterisation of the process of "coding" can be somewhat prescriptive: an attempt to add an element of apparent positivism and objectivity to the proceedings by those who feel uncomfortable about the qualitative nature of their research. IPA does not use the terminology of codes or coding (Smith, 1996). Nevertheless, to complete the process of analysis, I conducted an in-depth analysis of the text that essentially was a coding exercise. Saldana defines a code as "a word or short phrase that symbolically assigns a summative, salient, essence-capturing, and/or evocative attribute for a portion of language-based or visual data" (2009: 3). Codes can be clustered together into patterns which can be considered alongside earlier reflections.

My engagement with and reflections and writings on interviewees, recordings and transcripts, as well as my own experience, contributed to what Gadamer called a "hermeneutic circle" (in Laverty, 2003) on which this project turned. The dance around the hermeneutic circle is a complex one. Smith et al. warn that the process "will not be a linear one, and the experience will be challenging" (2009: 80).

For van Manen, the purpose of phenomenological enquiry and research is to arrive at "meaningful insights"; this is "not conducted through sorting, counting, or even systematic coding efforts. Rather, phenomenological inquiry proceeds through an inceptual process of reflective wondering, deep questioning, attentive reminiscing, and sensitively interpreting of the primal meanings of human experiences" (van Manen, 2017: 819). He describes what he calls a "nonmethodical method" (ibid: 820): sometimes insights, meanings, understandings and other epiphanies arrive only once the quest to unearth them is abandoned.

Considering multiple viewpoints, stages of interpretation and shifts of the camera lens allowed meaningful overarching themes to come into sharp focus. I found this to be an organic, iterative process. My immediate response to the interview subjects and the interviews themselves, coupled with my own experience, suggested several possible broad, overarching themes. The in-depth scrutiny of the transcribed interviews, on the other hand, identified a comprehensive list of all possible themes worth considering. These subthemes coalesced into groups that influenced and were influenced by the initial list of overarching themes. This back and forth dialogue crystallised four main themes: loss, discrimination, identity and growth, each with attendant subthemes, some of which were used and some not—in general I favoured subthemes that best reflected participants' lived experience. On countless discarded pages of scribbles, the four main themes eyed each other nervously at first, then began to interact and make sense of each other, before finally taking their positions: four pillars of disability around which an imperfect house of understanding was constructed.

The nature of the response to the first three fundamental pillars of living with CMT, loss, discrimination and identity, dictates the extent to which the fourth, growth, can happen—it can inhibit growth or sometimes accelerate it. However painful and traumatic the loss, however acute the level of discrimination, however impacted the identity, there is always the possibility of choice—of choosing growth over safety; of choosing life over a kind of death. Of choosing ability over disability. My dissertation also offers 12 clinical recommendations for anyone providing psychological support for people with CMT and other disabling conditions, and further, proposes an integrative "two worlds" model as a way of looking at the current situation with regard to disability, which may be described as a kind of social apartheid. The able-bodied live in "abled world," a land of growth, a land of potential hope and glory. The disabled by contrast inhabit "disabled world," which can be a place of solidarity, support and political activism, but also a place of lack, victimhood and powerlessness. I support the ideal of "one world" but currently the two worlds are separated by two porous yet enduring borders: a hard political border and a soft psychological border. Much progress has been made in dismantling the former—the work of the social model of disability in demanding a less disabling environment with improved access, opportunity, representation and power. But we will never all live together in one world, where individual strengths are valued and vulnerabilities are supported and catered for, until the disabling internal psychological barriers are removed. Both disabled and able-bodied people can be guilty of two-world thinking. This only changes when we meet, greet and get to know each other.

Making it your Own

In producing a qualitative dissertation, there is a tension between adhering to the academic and institutional traditions, protocols and strictures that are traditionally observed, and taking a postmodern approach that embraces the subjectivity of the enterprise. Too much qualitative research in my opinion seems to be conflicted, practically apologising for itself and presenting itself at least partially still clad in the constricting vestments of positivism.

Therapists understand that apologising for oneself and trying to squeeze into other people's ill-fitting clothes, ideas and rules for living is a recipe for unhappiness. Qualitative research is thus partly an enquiry, exploration and celebration of the authentic self of the researcher. I believe this revelation transforms the research process. Suddenly the researcher fully inhabits their work. The weighty, super-ego-driven project becomes injected with id, ideas, identity, idiosyncrasies. There is room for creativity, playfulness, vitality. The sun comes out from behind the clouds.

Qualitative research is best when it is authentic, from the heart as well as the head, and enjoyable. Here are six suggestions to help that process:

1. Love your research. Choose something you care about. If you don't, no one else will either, and it will be a long, hard slog. Talk through your ideas out loud—your voice will betray any inner doubt. Your unfolding relationship with your research is a central part of your research. This relationship should be constantly monitored and explored—in your reflections, your research journal, tutorials, peer groups, supervision and therapy. If you and your research aren't getting along, be curious about why. What is your connection to different parts of your research? If your research could speak—perhaps on the sofa in a couples counsellor's consulting room—what would it say about you?

2. Relatedly, be a reflexive researcher. Etherington writes, "The judicious use of our selves in research needs to be essential to the argument, not just a 'decorative flourish' for it to be described as reflexivity" (2004: 37).

3. Write in your voice, not someone else's. Good writing is authentic and accessible. The novelist Elmore Leonard used to write something, read what he had written, then cross out anything that sounded like "writing" and write those bits again (Leonard, 2007). I've met a number of trainee therapists who can speak with eloquence and passion about their clients but who lose all their fluency and confidence on paper. Their writing becomes tortured and unintelligible. It's possible to be scholarly yet also engaging and clear. I have little patience for academic writing that is deliberately obfuscatory, dense, boring or littered with unnecessary insider jargon.

4. Use images. While academic journals may be constrained in the use of art and photography by budgetary or ideological or logistical realities, in your own student research projects you are operating under no such restrictions.

5. Change channels. Whatever its literary and visual merits, a doctoral thesis that exists solely as a leather-bound volume in the bowels of an academic library or on the author's shelf is academic in both senses of the word; it is practically irrelevant. We live in an age of short attention spans—shorter than goldfish, apparently (McSpadden, 2015)—and a proliferation of outlets and platforms, soundbites, tweets and video clips. If you want to tell the story of your research, there are many different ways to do it. I made a 6-minute film about my doctoral research that included segments of my participant interviews (with their permission). I opened my viva with it—this not only afforded me a little time to catch my breath, but also allowed the participants' voices to fill the room, bringing the project to life.

6. Play. We tend to think of research as serious, worthy, important, something a million miles from anything so frivolous as play, but we turn our back on playfulness at our great peril. Even psychoanalysis, according to Winnicott (1991), is a form of play, and the same could be said of research. Play can help us understand ourselves and our world. It increases our engagement and apprecia-

tion of life. It subverts the rules and shows us new ways of doing things. It helps us cope. It helps us grow. It helps us live.

Question yourself and be rigorously transparent about the ways in which you and your research are blessed but also unavoidably biased, compromised and constrained by their own parameters. Your "truths" may not be universal. You are not only learning about your topic, you are learning about you.

In my case, progressive disability is a deeply personal, embodied, ever-present process that impacts everything I do. I cannot be objective about what Merleau-Ponty calls my "lived body" (1945). There were other contextual factors. I conducted this research during a midlife period of immense personal change, yet also, following a successful career, from a position of relative economic stability. As a white British heterosexual male, I carry the "invisible rucksack" of privilege (Tuckwell, 2006: 208). In so much research whiteness in particular is often taken for granted—"a veil, a norm, a neutral zone in which all is apparently possible" (Lago, 2006: 202). My participants were all female. Historic patriarchal power relations between men and women inevitably form part of the set decoration to this research. Clearly there are gender differences with regard to disability (e.g. Coleman, Brunell and Haugen, 2015).

Phenomenological research in particular demands good writing—van Manen says phenomenology is "a poetizing project: it tries an incantative, evocative speaking, a primal telling, wherein we aim to involve the voice into an original singing of the world … We must engage language in a primal incantation or poetizing which hearkens back to the silence from which the words emanate" (1984: 39).

My photographs, paintings and other visuals appear throughout my doctoral dissertation. Even if they were purely decorative I believe they would heighten the experience of reading the thesis and enhance understanding. Schnotz (2005), for example, highlights the benefits of multimedia learning. Further, I believe that images can pack an emotional punch in the way that words don't. Words and cognitions rattle around in the neocortical "human" brain; powerful imagery and emotion perhaps belongs to the more mammalian, limbic system where they are more likely to endure (Lewis, Amini and Lannon, 2001).

Images are increasingly being used in phenomenological research, as a means of communication for both researcher and researched (e.g. Goble, 2013; King, 2017). Indeed, rather than justify the use of imagery in a qualitative research thesis, one might instead challenge the prevailing orthodoxy that makes it a rarity. Why wouldn't a deeply personal piece of qualitative insider research use meaningful imagery? If anything, this is a return to an earlier tradition of psychology, before it took a positivist turn, when imagery was very much part of the discourse. This is best exemplified by Jung's paintings, symbols, iconography and mandalas that often accompanied his written words, which I seem to return to, over and over.

◘ Fig. 4.2 A zebra abandoned by his able-bodied herd

In the introduction to *The Red Book: A Reader's Edition*, Shamdasani writes of that rich period, the first few decades of the twentieth century: "Psychologists sought to overcome the limitations of philosophical psychology, and they began to explore the same terrain as artists and writers. Clear demarcations among litera-ture, art, and psychology had not yet been set; writers and artists borrowed from psychologists, and vice versa" (2009: 2).

My dissertation opens with a photograph of a zebra (◘ Fig. 4.2) I took some years ago, during a walking safari in Botswana.

The zebra was lame. Abandoned by the rest of his able-bodied herd, he stood alone in a clearing, waiting for the inevitable moment when he would be attacked, killed and eaten by a predator, most likely a lion. He was entirely vulnerable. Yet I also felt that this magnificent animal seemed calm and dignified. There was a sense of acceptance. It was a raw image of disability, perhaps more powerful than the ensuing 40,000 words, and it has stayed with me as I come to terms with my own physical impairments.

Play is something to do away from your research so that you can come back to it refreshed. But also introduce playfulness into your research. Imagine all your research participants meeting each other at a party. Imagine performing your viva in mime. Imagine you are a talk-show host and the topic of your research is a guest. Write a sonnet, haiku or song about your research.

And when you're writing, cut loose from how you imagine academics should be and have fun. Something that was enjoyable and engaging to write is more likely to be enjoyable and engaging to read (although of course, there's no guarantee).

Writes Michael Rosen: "Our concept of play in the West is often bound up with the idea that play is inseparably connected to childhood, while adulthood is connected to seriousness and responsibility…In fact, I believe play is key to helping us develop and reach our full potential" (Rosen, 2019: 21).

Activity
1. Think about a significant experience in your life—something that happened to you. How would you describe it to a sympathetic, caring friend? What happened? How did it affect you? Can you break it down into themes? What did it teach you about you and your world? How would you deepen your understanding of the experience with an IPA study?
2. To be a good reflexive researcher, you need to understand that you see the world from your own unique vantage point. So ask yourself where you are coming from. How would you detail what Heidegger calls *Befindlichkeit*—

> your subjective, felt sense of yourself in the world? And how might that impact the research that you do?
> 3. One example of adding play to a research design: An IPA study investigating the experience of pain (Kirkham, Smith and Havsteen-Franklin, 2015, cited in Smith, 2018: 12) invited participants first to draw their pain, and the drawings were used as a focus for the interviews. Get a sheet of paper and fill it with creative and playful ideas that could be part of your research, or of your thinking about your research, or your life away from your research.

Summary

In this chapter the author tells the story of his doctoral research journey, from choice of subject (the lived experience of progressive disability) to the choice of IPA as a methodology, to the finished dissertation. IPA was chosen because its marriage of phenomenology and hermeneutics was in accord with the author's philosophy and experience as a psychotherapist, journalist and dog owner, and because its ideographic approach lends itself well to a deep exploration of a profound and significant individual experience of human life such as ill-health. The author highlights the epistemological underpinnings of IPA, explains his own interpretation of IPA, and takes us through the process of his research, including interviewing and analysis of the data at different "altitudes." Finally, the author suggests six ways to make this kind of research more authentic and enjoyable.

References

Boss, M. (1963). *Psychoanalysis and daseinsanalysis*. New York: Basic.

Brocki, J. M., & Wearden, A. J. (2006). A critical evaluation of the use of Interpretative Phenomenological Analysis (IPA) in Health Psychology. *Psychology and Health, 21*, 87–108.

Buber, M. (1958). *I and thou*. Edinburgh: T. and T. Clark.

Bugenthal, J. F. T. (1999). *Psychotherapy isn't what you think: bringing the psychotherapeutic engagement into the living moment*. Phoenix: Zeig, Tucker & Theisen.

Coleman, J. M., Brunell, A. B., & Haugen, I. M. (2015). Multiple forms of prejudice: How gender and disability stereotypes influence judgments of disabled women and men. *Current Psychology, 34*(1), 177–189.

Dennison, M. (2019). IPA: The black swan of qualitative research. *Qualitative Methods in Psychology Bulletin, 27*: Spring 2019

Denzin, N. K. (2013). *Interpretive autoethnography*. London: Sage.

Etherington, K. (2004). *Becoming a reflexive researcher: using our selves in research*. London: Jessica Kingsley.

Frankl, V. E. (2004/1946). *Man's search for meaning*. London: Rider.

Gallese, V. (2015). Which neurosciences and which psychoanalysis? Intersubjectivity and bodily self: notes for a dialogue. *The Italian Psychoanalytic Annual, 9*, 189–203.

Giorgi, A. (2010). Phenomenology and the practice of science. *Existential Analysis, 21*(1), 3–22.

Goble, E., 2013. Dwelling between word and image: Using images in phenomenological writing. *Spectrums and Spaces of Writing*, 33-46

Havercamp, B. E., & Young, R. A. (2007). Paradigms, purpose and the role of literature: formulating a rationale for qualitative investigation. *The Counseling Psychologist. March, 35*(2), 265–294.

Husserl, E. (1927). *Phenomenology. Encyclopedia Britannica* (Vol. 17, pp. 699–702).

Huxley, A. (1954). *The Doors of Perception*. London: Chatto and Windus.

Hycner, R. H. (1993). *Between person and person: Toward a dialogical psychotherapy*. Gouldsboro. Me.: Gestalt Journal Press.

Josselson, R. (2007). The ethical attitude in narrative research: Principles and practicalities. *Handbook of Narrative Inquiry: Mapping a Methodology, 21*, 545.

Kaufmann, W. (1954). *The portable Nietzsche*. New York: Viking Penguin.

King, R. E. (2017). *The clearing of being: a phenomenological study of openness in psychotherapy*. Doctoral dissertation: Middlesex University.

Lago, C. (2006). *Race, culture and counselling: the ongoing challenge*. Maidenhead: OUP.

Laing, R. D. (1960). *The divided self*. Harmondsworth: Penguin.

Laverty, S. M. (2003). Hermeneutic phenomenology and phenomenology: a comparison of historical and methodological considerations. *International Journal of Qualitative Methods, 2*(3), 21–35.

Law, J. (2004). *After method: Mess in social science research*. London: Routledge.

Leonard, E. (2007). *Elmore Leonard's 10 rules for writing*. New York: William Morrow and Company.

Lewis, T., Amini, F., & Lannon, R. (2001). *A general theory of love*. New York: Vintage.

Maxwell, J. A. (2012). *A realist approach for qualitative research*. London: Sage.

McLeod, J. (2001). *Qualitative research in counselling and psychotherapy*. London: Sage.

McSpadden, K. (2015). *You now have a shorter attention span than a goldfish. Time Online Magazine*.

Moustakas, C. (1975). *The touch of loneliness*. Englewood Cliffs, New Jersey: Prentice Hall.

Moustakas, C. (1994). *Phenomenological research methods*. Thousand Oaks, California: Sage.

Pietkiewicz, I., & Smith, J. A. (2014). A practical guide to using interpretative phenomenological analysis in qualitative research psychology. *Psychological journal, 20*(1), 7–14.

Polkinghorne, D. E. (1988). *Narrative knowing and the human sciences*. Albany: State University of New York Press.

Polkinghorne, D. E. (1992). Postmodern epistemology of practice. In S. Kvale (Ed.), *Psychology and postmodernism*. London: Sage.

Ponterotto, J. G. (2005). Qualitative research in counselling psychology: A primer on research paradigms and philosophy of science. *Journal of Counselling Psychology, 52*(2), 126–136.

Ricoeur, P. (1981). *Hermeneutics and the human sciences: Essays on language, action and interpretation*. Cambridge: Cambridge University Press.

Rooney, P. (2005). Researching from the inside—does it compromise validity? A discussion. *Level 3*, Issue 3, May

Rosen, M. (2019). *Michael Rosen's book of play*. London: Profile Books.

Schnotz, W. (2005). *An integrated model of text and picture comprehension. The Cambridge handbook of multimedia learning*. Cambridge: Cambridge.

Shinebourne, P. (2011). The theoretical underpinnings of interpretative phenomenological analysis (IPA). *Existential Analysis, 22*(1), 16–31.

Smith, J. A. (1996). Beyond the divide between cognition and discourse: Using interpretative phenomenological analysis in health psychology. *Psychology & Health, 11*(2), 261–271.

Smith, J. A. (2018). *Participants and researchers searching for meaning: conceptual developments for interpretative phenomenological analysis. Qualitative Research in Psychology*.

Smith, J. A., Flowers, P., & Larkin, M. (2009). *Interpretive phenomenological analysis: Theory, method, and research*. London: Sage.

Spinelli, E. (2007). *Practising existential psychotherapy*. London: Sage.

Stolorow, R. D., & Atwood, G. (1992). *Contexts of being: The intersubjective foundations of psychological life*. Hillsdale, N.J: Analytic Press.

Stolorow, R. D., Atwood, G. E., & Orange, D. M. (2002). *Worlds of experience: interweaving philosophical and clinical dimensions in psychoanalysis*. New York: Basic.

Tuckwell, G. (2006). Specific issues for white counsellors. In *Lago, C., Race, culture and counselling: the ongoing challenge*. Maidenhead: OUP.

Van Deurzen, E. (2012). *Existential counselling & psychotherapy in practice*. London: Sage.

van Manen, M. (2017). Phenomenology in Its Original Sense. *Qualitative Health Research, 27*(6), 810–825.

Voller, D. (2010). Negative capability. *Contemporary Psychotherapy, 2*(2).

Voltaire (1919/1770). Letter to Frederick William, Prince of Prussia, 1770 Nov 28. In: Tallentyre SG (ed.) *Voltaire in his letters*. New York: G.P. Putnam's Sons

Winnicott, D. W. (1991). *Playing and reality*. Psychology Press.

Yalom, I. D. (1980). *Existential psychotherapy*. New York: Basic.

Further Reading

Gadamer, H. G. (1975/1991). *Truth and method*. New York: Crossroads.

Heidegger, M. (1927/1962). *Being and time*. New York: Harper and Row.

Husserl, E. ([1913](1998). *Ideas pertaining to a pure phenomenology and to a phenomenological philosophy*. Dordrecht: Kluwer Academic.

Larkin, M., Watts, S., & Clifton, E. (2006). Giving voice and making sense in interpretative phenomenological analysis. *Qualitative Research in Psychology, 3*(2), 102–120.

Lynch, G. (1996). What is truth? A philosophical introduction to counselling research. *Counselling, May, 7*(2), 144–148.

Merleau-Ponty, M. (1945). *Phenomenology of perception*. London: Routledge.

Polkinghorne, D. E. (2010). Language and meaning: data collection in qualitative research. *Journal of Counseling Psychology, 52*(2), 137–145.

Saldaña, J. (2009). *An introduction to codes and coding. The Coding Manual for Qualitative Researchers*.

Shamdasani, S. (2009). Liber Novus: the "Red Book" of C.J.Jung. In Jung, C.G., Shamdasani, S.E., Kyburz, M.T. and Peck, J.T., (2009). *The red book: Liber novus*. New York: W.W. Norton & Co.

Smith, J. A., & Osborn, M. (2007). Pain as an assault on the self: an interpretative phenomenological analysis. *Psychology & Health, 22*(5), 517–534.

Strawbridge, S., & Woolfe, R. (2010). Counselling psychology: origins, developments and challenges. In R. Woolfe, S. Strawbridge, B. Douglas, & W. Dryden (Eds.), *Handbook of counselling psychology* (3rd ed.). London: Sage.

van Manen, M. (1984). Practicing phenomenological writing. *Phenomenology and Pedagogy, 2*(1), 36–69.

Yardley, L. (2000). Dilemmas in qualitative research. *Psychology & Health, 15*(2), 215–228.

Becoming a Narrative Inquirer

Kim Etherington

Contents

© The Author(s) 2020
S. Bager-Charleson, A. McBeath (eds.),
Enjoying Research in Counselling and Psychotherapy,
https://doi.org/10.1007/978-3-030-55127-8_5

☺ Learning Goals

After reading this chapter, you should be able to:

- Understand the meaning of 'narrative inquiry' and its appropriateness for counselling and psychotherapy research;
- Understand the historical and societal changes that have shaped its philosophy;
- Be able to situate yourself and your own stories in relation to the development of your personal philosophies that underpin your choice of methodologies;
- Understand how reflexivity adds value and rigour to research writing;
- Know the ethical issues and practices appropriate to using narrative inquiry;
- Understand the criteria that trustworthiness and rigour depend upon in narrative inquiry.

Introduction: Stories and their Impact on our Lives

I have always enjoyed stories: as a small child I spent many hours at the local library, sitting cross-legged on the floor beside the bookshelves, choosing books to borrow. I learned so much from the stories in those books: about people; about relationships; about the world and other ways of living.

» *What we learn from stories* When we listen to peoples' stories we hear about their values, beliefs, attitudes, their life experiences, their interpretations of those events and what has guided and influenced them. We hear about the relationships people have with themselves, with others, between and among people, contexts and cultures. We hear how people create meanings as they tell or reflect upon their stories; we hear their emotions, thoughts, and sometimes their hopes for the future. We hear the personal, family and cultural stories and how these are set alongside or brush up painfully against the societal discourses that shape our lives: perhaps stories of power, gender, religion, health; we hear the discourses that are promoted, allowed, and those that are silenced or dismissed. We might also hear stories of victimhood, resistance and resilience explicitly or implicitly located within these stories, or contradictory stories that reveal different aspects of the storytellers (or ourselves) as they unfold.

Having been born in Liverpool during the Second World War into an Irish Catholic family, stories, or 'yarns' as my parents would say, were all around us. My family were blessed with the 'blarney', the gift of eloquence supposedly gained by kissing the 'blarney stone', set into the battlements of Blarney Castle, Cork: an ancient tradition that millions of visitors from around the world follow, even today. Sometimes yarns would be started by one person and others would join in, adding something from their own particular point of view, stories evoking other stories. Sometimes stories were told through songs sung at family gatherings, around the piano in the 'front room' or accompanied by my brother's accordion. Those songs told stories about the fight for the Irish to remain free from British rule, or the execution of Kevin Barry, an 18-year-old medical student and first volunteer army member to be 'hung upon the gallows tree' by the English in 1920; or my mother's wistful songs about her home on the West Coast of Ireland, haunting melodies of exile, about watching 'the moon rise over Claddagh, and … the sun going down on Galway Bay'. The pictures created through those stories and songs are with me still, as I write these words today. It seems I've always felt the power of stories: the power to teach us; to pass on knowledge from one generation to another; to engage our emotions; to engage our curiosities; and to offer a sense of identity. Who do these stories tell me I am? An English child, with Irish parents singing songs and telling stories about 'the Bloody English' who 'took our land' and 'killed our young men at the crossroads at midnight'. Even more confusing was my knowing that the same father who told these stories enlisted in the British Army during the First World War, lying about his age to ensure he was old enough: a true patriot it would seem.

My Own Pathway to Becoming a Narrative Inquirer

Many counsellors and psychotherapists view research as an endeavour that is conducted in the ivory towers of academia and 'not for the likes of us' (Etherington and Bridges 2011), seeing research as something separate from their practice. Those ideas are usually based upon traditional scientific research. In this chapter I offer the idea that narrative inquiry is a relevant and appropriate and even *enjoyable* methodology for therapists who listen every day to their clients' stories of lived experience. I have begun this chapter with a short piece in the spirit (but not the letter) of 'autoethnography': a form of narrative inquiry that describes and analyses (graphy) personal experience (auto) in order to understand cultural experience (ethno). This seems like a good place to begin because as researchers we need to understand the beliefs we hold that guide our choices in research, how those beliefs were formed and what influences them to change over time. This knowledge helps us to position ourselves philosophically in our research endeavours. We need to ask: What is my view of reality–what can be known or what exists (ontology), and how do I know what I know (epistemology)?[1]

I too had started my counsellor training thinking that research was not for the likes of me but I was fortunate that my postgraduate diploma expected us to submit a small research project on a subject of personal interest. During the course I was employed as a Community Occupational Therapist, visiting disabled people at home to assess their needs and provide for their daily living requirements. At that time, in the 1980s, I met many disabled people who wanted and needed to talk about their feelings; about how their lives and their sense of self and identity were impacted by their experience of disability. That experience led me to train as a counsellor and guided my choice of topic for research: 'The Disabled Person's Act: the need for counselling'.

---

1 ▶ http://salmapatel.co.uk/academia/the-research-paradigm-methodology-epistemology-and-ontology-explained-in-simple-language/.

At that time my view of what it meant to be a researcher was shaped by being married to a biochemist for over 25 years: he wore a white coat, wrote learned papers and presented them at international conferences, used test tubes and became excited by graphs and blobs on paper which meant nothing to me. So I did not see myself as a 'proper' researcher but I *did* search the literature, conduct a question-naire survey of 26 disabled people and interview 8 volunteers, in-depth: now I see that this *was* research in its full and even formal sense. Back then, however, we had no training in philosophy, methodology, methods or analysis: we had to find our own way–a baptism by fire indeed.

In 1990 I began an MSc in Counselling (Training and Supervision) and, once again, we were expected to produce a dissertation with no research training. My reading led me to discover *experiential research* (Heron 1971, 1981), *New Paradigm Research* and *Human Inquiry* (Reason and Rowan 1981), and, in turn, this led me to the work of Clark Moustakas on *Heuristic Inquiry* (1981) *and Heuristic Research* 1990). These people were introducing me to the idea of doing research *with* and not *on* people, and of using 'self' as a major tool in psychological research (although a whole movement, known as the Third Force, was emerging around this time that supported reflexivity in research in the field of humanistic psychotherapy).

I embarked with excitement on my first heuristic study: *The Father-Daughter Relationship and its impact on the lives of adult women*. However, even though Moustakas was trying to break away from traditional objective research, he was still heavily influenced by 'realist' and 'essentialist' notions of 'reality' and 'self'–as we might expect from someone of his time in the history of psychological research.

Moustakas' emphasis on the 'inward gaze', and belief that there actually was such a thing as an 'essence' of an experience, which had seemed so exciting to me when I first found it, was beginning to trouble me.[2] Essentialism is a philosophical theory ascribing ultimate reality to essence embodied in a 'thing' perceptible to the senses. In early Western thought Plato's idealism held that all things have such an 'essence'—an 'idea' or 'form'. I believed that although the inward gaze was neces-sary, it was not sufficient. My thinking up to that point had been influenced by my psychological training within a constructivist framework: that people see and inter-pret their 'problems' and the world through a personal belief system. But social constructionism (Burr 2003; Gergen 1999) was showing me that this was only half the story: that those very belief systems were shaped by the contexts and cultures of our lives, of the generations that came before us and the dynamic interactions between all of that. As my gaze moved between my inner and outer worlds I began to understand that realities and selves are socially constructed and continuously reconstructed in *response* to those lived experiences. Although these ideas were then new to counselling and psychotherapy, they had been long held by sociolo-

---

2 Essentialism: a philosophical theory ascribing ultimate reality to essence embodied in a 'thing' perceptible to the senses. In early Western thought Plato's idealism held that all things have such an 'essence'— an 'idea' or 'form'.

gists and anthropologists. These views challenged the notion of the 'autonomous bounded self' that most counsellors and psychotherapists (myself included) had taken for granted (McLeod 1997), which in turn shaped our thinking about change, healing and personal growth.

My interest in research had continued so I began to explore the possibilities of doing a PhD. Having been involved in training therapists and others to work with sexual abuse I decided to learn more about *men*'s experiences of abuse. This was in the early 1990s when society was beginning to acknowledge that females were abused by males, but the idea that males could also be victims of sexual abuse, or that females might be perpetrators, was new and in some circles unthinkable. I wanted to hear and tell the stories of the 'man in the street', rather than convicted offenders or those who had been diagnosed within the mental health system: the stories that had *not* been heard, told by the men themselves, in their own words. Thus began a powerful, sometimes lonely, and transforming journey.

I had not discovered narrative inquiry at that time but I wanted to gather, analyse and re-present 'local' stories of men who had been abused during childhood. I decided to explore those stories through the theoretical lens of patriarchy (Lerner 1986; Struve 1990) and male psychosocial development (Finkelhor 1986 and others) so I came to the stories with the knowledge gained from my reading, mainly from the USA, and with interview questions drawn from the theoretical frameworks mentioned above. This felt risky enough: I felt the need to hide to some degree behind theory and structure because I still had in mind the rules of positivism, that 'good' research, research that would be taken seriously, should be objective, use large cohorts, be represented by numbers, graphs and statistics. By the time I came to write my PhD (stories of 25 men–far too many I now realise), I believed that in the wider world of academia my subjectivity and reflexivity might be seen as a contamination of 'objectivity', which was still the taken-for-granted benchmark for 'good' research. But I did allow myself to use 'I' throughout and, looking back, I can see that this work was indeed reflexive as I struggled to balance those concerns with the powerful influence of the literature I was exploring from other disciplines in order to develop my *own* philosophy, my own way of understanding reality (ontology) and ways of knowing (epistemology), with which to guide my choice of methodology.

I called my PhD methodology 'feminine research', influenced by the writing of feminist researchers of the time (Stanley and Wise 1983; Kelly 1988; Oakley 1981). However, I had read that feminist research was conducted *by* women, *with* women and *for* women, so I believed I could not call my PhD methodology 'feminist': my work was with men, and for all of us. I did, however, hold the feminist beliefs about transparency, reflexivity, accountability, relationship, collaboration, and the recognition of power and inequality that has continued to influence and guide my work since that time. In my PhD dissertation I wrote:

» I value the quality of relationship between … the researcher and the researched, relating as a co-operative team, working towards the balance of meeting the needs of both …. The basic values that underlie this approach are that of respect for the person and equality, although it would be disingenuous of me to deny the inevitable inequality of the positions of power between researcher and researcher. (1994: 84).

It's hardly surprising that when I discovered narrative inquiry I began to enjoy research even more. The ways I wanted to conduct creative research had a name at last!

Following the publication of my PhD book I was approached by Mike and Stephen, brothers who had been sexually abused by their grandfather from very early childhood until the age of 18. They said that my book had given them the courage to seek help: that it had been difficult for them to find anything written about the sexual abuse of males, thus increasing their sense of alienation and isolation. We engaged in therapeutic work together (individually) and, towards the end of their counselling, they told me they would like to share their experiences of counselling with other men, to show how it was possible to heal.

Three years after our counselling relationships had ended Stephen, Mike and I began a different journey, to write about our experiences of each other and the processes of therapy we had engaged in (Etherington 2000). By this time I had discovered post-structuralism via the lens of *Narrative Means to Therapeutic Ends* (White and Epston 1990). This thinking subsequently fed into my therapeutic approach as well as my research, that stories are central to the process and products.

The work of other post-structuralist thinkers (Derrida 1981; Freedman and Combs 1996) showed how post-structuralism infers that words, conversations and ideas have no *absolute* or inherent meaning but rather that meaning is co-created between people from within the local, partial knowledge they have available at the time (Geertz 1973, 1983). This means that there are infinite possibilities for interpretation, leaving space for alternative stories/meanings to emerge. Foucault's work (1980) helped me to think about the relationship between power and knowledge and how a person can be limited by their ability to participate in discourses that constitute what is possible within a society at any given time (e.g. men being sexual victims, women being perpetrators). This thinking enabled me to approach the research with Mike and Stephen with curiosity and openness as we explored our experiences of their therapy and how, between us, we could tell those stories.

The creation of *Narrative Approaches to Working with Adult Male Survivors of Childhood Sexual Abuse* (2000) was an exhilarating and terrifying time for all three of us. For the first time I described my work as 'narrative': this was my 'narrative turn' which overlapped with my 'postmodern turn', which had been forming in my thinking over several years before I could name it. Jane Speedy, describing this point in her life as 'a very busy crossroads, in several dimensions', writes:

» My overarching description of this crossroads would be the place where the "narrative turn" (turn towards "story" as a metaphor for how human beings make sense of their lives and their world) meets the postmodern condition of uncertainties and incredulities towards universal truths. (2008:11)

Postmodernism overlaps and intertwines with post-structuralism and social constructionism as these changes were concurrently happening against a societal backdrop. Calling for an ideological critique of foundational knowledge and privileged discourses (grand narratives), it questioned notions of 'Truth', certainty and objective reality and put forward ideas of many possible truths, many ethics to live by, multiple cultures and many ways of organising our social worlds. It called for an appreciation of diversity which led to a growth of academic interest in 'local' knowledge, personal stories with possibilities for unexpected outcomes. Postmodernism views knowledge and meaning-making as co-constructed, thereby challenging Western ideas of the individual as an 'autonomous knower'.

These ideas have all contributed to a greater recognition of the importance of the relationships between the storytellers and the listeners/readers, and between the knower and what is known, and what each brings with them into the research relationship to create meaning and understanding of the topics under exploration.

All of the above influences have helped legitimise the reflexive use of 'self' in research, reflexivity being at the heart of narrative inquiry and, increasingly, other methodologies too: 'It [reflexivity] permeates every aspect of the research process, challenging us to be more fully conscious of the ideology, culture, and politics of those we study and those we select as our audience' (Hertz 1997, p. vi, ii).

Reflexivity

Reflexivity, sometimes called 'critical reflexivity' (Etherington 2016), has become an increasingly significant theme in contemporary social research and there is an ongoing debate about its meaning and value that runs across discipline boundaries, with some researchers wholly embracing this principle while others reject or question its value. John McLeod reminds us that: '...the subjectivity of the researcher does not command a privileged position. Personal statements made by researchers are themselves positioned within discourses' (McLeod 2001: 199). However, reflexivity is *more* than subjectivity: rather, reflexivity opens up a space *between* subjectivity and objectivity where the distinctions between content and process become blurred. The judicious use of our selves in research needs to be essential to the purpose, not just a decorative flourish.

Reflexivity is a dynamic process of interaction within *and* between our selves and our participants, *and* the 'data' that informs decisions, actions and interpretations, at all stages. We are therefore operating on several different levels at the same time.

Reflection

To be reflexive is to have an ongoing conversation with ourselves and others about our experience while simultaneously living in the moment. Hertz (1997) suggests that a reflexive researcher does not simply report facts or 'truths' but actively constructs interpretations of his or her experiences in the research, and then questions how those interpretations came about. This way we can produce transparent, reflexive knowledge that provides us with insights on the workings of the social and personal worlds under study along with insight on how that knowledge was created. This kind of transparency adds validity and rigour by allowing the reader to see how the contexts and culture in which the stories (data) are created and located shape the narrative knowledge, thereby allowing the reader/audience to judge for themselves its quality. For me and other like-minded individuals, these are ethical, moral and methodological issues (Frank 1995; Josselson 1996; McLeod 2001).

> **Activity**
> — Consider 'reflexivity' with some of *your own* values and beliefs in mind.
>
> The YouTube link below may help to bring reflexivity 'to life':
> ► https://www.youtube.com/watch?v=zBcBNKz0ESo Qualitative Conversations: about Reflexivity and 'Becoming a Reflexive Researcher': Kim Etherington with Kitrina

What Do we Mean by Narrative Inquiry?

Narrative inquiry has been described as an umbrella term for research that covers an array of theoretical forms, philosophical positions, methods and analytical practices (Mishler 1999). This diversity provides flexible and systematic ways of gathering, analysing and re-presenting complex material in storied forms that explains and describes human experience with much of its messiness and complexity still intact.

The various approaches that come under the umbrella of narrative inquiry include Life story research, Autoethnography, Life history, Biography/Autobiography, Collective Biography, and Auto/biography.

The diversity within different approaches to narrative inquiry reflects one of the basic tenets of postmodernity: that there is no one 'right way'. However, the extent of this diversity sometimes confuses and worries new researchers who are trying to find their own way, so in response to the invitation I received to contribute to this book I offer here an explanation of my own ways of thinking about and conducting narrative inquiry, bearing in mind that each time I undertake a new study something changes. I will draw on several of the studies I have undertaken to illustrate some of the issues.

Narrative Knowing

Narrative inquiry draws on what Bruner (1986) and Polkinghorne (1988) described as 'narrative knowing' as opposed to a 'paradigmatic' mode of thought. The latter draws on reasoned analysis, logical proof and empirical observation, and is used to explain events in terms of cause and effect, to predict and control reality, and to create unambiguous objective 'Truth' that can be proven or disproved. However, these methods do not help us to make sense of the complexity of human lives. On the other hand, narrative knowledge is created and constructed through the stories people tell about their lived experiences, and the meanings they ascribe to those experiences that might change and develop as their stories unfold over time.

Even within narrative paradigms there is an ongoing debate between those who approach stories as a 'window' onto a knowable reality, which can be interpreted by 'experts', and those who view stories as knowledge constructions in their own right.

Denzin (2014) reminds us that

» ... there is no clear window into the inner life of a person, for any window is always filtered through the glaze of language, signs and the process of signification. And language, in both its written and spoken forms, is always inherently unstable, in flux, and made up of the traces and other signs and symbolic statements. Hence there can never be a clear, unambiguous statement of anything, including an intention or a meaning. (p.14)

Why Use Stories for Research?

I do not offer stories as causal explanations or to make generalisations other than from the belief that the 'personal is the political...and the reverse is true - the political is personal'. I view stories as telling of 'a kind of life' (Scott-Hoy 2002) so they will reach readers on many different levels. I believe that in-depth, small-scale studies created by practitioners and students can result in 'intimate knowledge' that is 'likely to teach us more than distant knowledge' (Mair 1989: 4), allowing the reader to respond emotionally *and* intellectually.

Knowledge gained through stories is memorable and interesting. It brings together layers of understandings about a person's culture and context; their embodied engagement in events; their senses, emotions, thoughts, attitudes and ideas; the significance of other people; the choices and actions of the teller based on their values, beliefs and aims; metaphors, symbols and intuitive ways of knowing that create pictures that capture vivid representations of experiences. Knowledge gained in this way is contextualised, transient and partial, characterised by multiple voices, perspectives, truths and meanings. It values transformation at a personal level as well as subjectivity (McCormack 2004). The stories people tell of their experiences depend upon their audience, the context in which they tell those stories and the purpose for which they are being told. Stories told in therapy will be told differently from those told to GPs or to researchers, for example.

Stories have meaning beyond the local and personal context[3]; stories resonate and outlast their telling or reading, and sometimes have unintended consequences. They change us in ways we may not always anticipate because they

---

3   ▶ https://www.youtube.com/watch?v=zBcBNKz0ESo: Qualitative Conversations: about Reflexivity and 'Becoming a Reflexive Researcher': Kim Etherington with Kitrina Douglas and David Carless (2009).

can move us emotionally, change our attitudes and opinions, and sometimes influence our future behaviours. Stories are powerful because they touch all our lives.

Healing Stories

Telling stories of lived experience can have a 'recuperative role' (Frank 2000; Rosenthal 2003) for individuals, relationships and societies[4] and therefore becomes a moral act (Frank 1995). For Helen, whose family had tried to silence her, her participation in the narrative inquiry I undertook with people who had misused drugs (Etherington 2007a) became a means by which she met a long-standing need to have her stories witnessed and accepted by an empathic audience, and to have them used in ways that she believed were worthwhile. Other participants had also been silenced by family or cultural loyalties; by their own or other peoples' denial, minimisation or normalisation of painful events; or because they had no frame of reference or language for describing their traumatic experiences.

As therapists we help people piece together their stories, to have them witnessed, accepted and understood: as researchers, as well as bearing witness to participants' lives, we provide a platform from which those stories can reach others, and thereby potentially contribute to a field of study concerning many. Additionally, this kind of work can challenge the 'grand narratives' and 'taken-for-granted assumptions' about the causes of, attitudes towards and judgements about others whose lives are little understood.

Becky, another participant in the study mentioned above, told me how good it felt when she heard my transcriber's[5] response to her story:

>> Oh, yes. I think it was really nice to hear that she didn't judge me. I think that's really important to hear. She said [that]…if other people could hear [my story] then maybe people will be less intolerant. Lots of times I've been told: "Just pull your socks up, why can't you stop it". I was told by a GP: "If you come here again and say that you've used heroin I will take your kid away." So there was no understanding there at all. Then that just makes it more isolated and lonelier and more shame based … attitudes like that don't help: they just reinforce that idea that you're just a bad, bad person to the core, and I don't believe that I am. (Etherington 2007b)

---

4   For example: The documentary Kathy Come Home written by Jeremy Sandford and directed by Ken Loach (1966). This story of one woman's experience of homelessness was debated in parliament and MPs William Shearman and Ian Macleod led a campaign highlighting the plight of the homeless, which directly led to the charity Crisis being established in 1967.
5   It was usually the case that I did my own transcribing but in this instance I didn't – this being the only piece of research for which I had received funding.

Selves and Identities

Narrative inquiry can lead to understandings of how our socialisation and life choices have impacted on the creation of our selves and identities, recognising the importance of locating individuals within their local environments, and how these, in turn, are situated within, and influenced by, wider historical and sociocultural contexts (Mishler 1999). These perspectives have steered me away from viewing identity as 'fixed' towards viewing identities as constructed, constantly reconstructed, constituted through interpersonal processes and 'performed' through the stories that we tell. Narrative inquiry is particularly suitable for those interested in the process of 'becoming': examples of this are shown in my book *Becoming a reflexive researcher: using ourselves in research*' (Etherington 2003).

Autobiographical recollections told by participants in narrative inquiries create a 'remembered self' (Neisser and Fivush 1994). Research has shown that certain kinds of self-narratives may originate from 'scripts' found in interactions between parents and children early in life which are internalised as children develop speech and language. The internalised stories contribute to how a person perceives themselves, and to the identities they construct.

Concepts of identity have been explored by a variety of narrative researchers over the years, recognising that the stories are a means by which both the researcher and the storyteller are richly informed, and identities are formed:

> » If you want to know me, then you must know my story, for my story defines who I am. And if I want to know **myself**, to gain insight into the meaning of my own life, then I, too, must come to know my own story (McAdams 1993:11).

In stories we can hear how people construct (and reconstruct) their sense of self and identity and their subjective meanings as the stories unfold, whilst bearing in mind that stories are *reconstructions* of the person's experiences, *remembered* and told at a particular point in their lives, to a particular researcher/audience and for a particular purpose, all of which will have a bearing on *how* the stories are told, *which* stories are told and how they are presented/interpreted. The stories presented are not 'life as lived' but the researcher's re-presentations of those lives as told by participants.

> » For each of us ... a multitude of discourses is constantly at work constructing and producing our identity. Our identity therefore originates not from inside the person, but from the social realm, where people swim in a sea of language and other signs, a sea that is invisible to us because it is the very medium of our existence as social beings. (Burr 1995: 53)

Ethics in Narrative Inquiry

Although reflexivity is recognised as a useful tool for ensuring rigour, improving the quality and validity of research and recognising the limitations of the knowledge that is produced, it is less often considered as a tool for ensuring ethical research (Etherington, 2007c; Guillemin and Gillam 2004). The link between narrative inquiry, reflexivity and ethical research seems to lies in transparency. When the reader is shown the interactions between researchers and participants, they can observe the behaviours involved in respecting the autonomy, dignity and privacy of participants and the risks of failing to do so; the 'ethically important moments' that might have occurred; and the means by which they are ethically negotiated (ibid). Ethical conduct in these instances relies on awareness of the need to recognise and talk about the potential dilemmas raised by the research and our openness to engage in 'the ebb and flow of dialogue' (Helgeland 2005:554). Ethical considerations for reflexive narrative researchers will also include the need to remain aware of and sensitive to cultural difference and gender (Cloke et al. 2000; Denzin 1997). This would mean being sensitive to the rights, beliefs and cultural contexts of the participants, as well as their position within patriarchal or hierarchical power relations, in society and in our research relationships.

Traditionally, as ethical researchers we have been expected to think about informed consent: the right to information concerning the purposes, processes and outcomes of the study (related to fairness); the right to withdraw at any stage (related to autonomy); and confidentiality (to protect the right to privacy and 'do no harm'). These ideas are usually held within guidelines or codes of ethical practice. However, many researchers are now asking if 'dutiful ethics' are sufficient for research that upholds the values of human worth and dignity, when 'it may not be possible to satisfy both the demands of the ethical guidelines and those maintaining standards for conducting research' (Helgeland 2005: 553), if we do not also take into account the demands of the context (Denzin 2014; Villa-Vicencio 1994).

Relational Ethics of Care

Narrative ethics are usually most concerned with the ethical issues raised when we use our own or other peoples' stories for research, the main concerns being related to confidentiality, anonymity and informed consent–which might be hard to achieve when the research is an unfolding process that cannot be fully known before the research begins and therefore needs to be an ongoing process. This chapter does not allow space for in-depth discussion of these ethical issues so here I recommend the eighteen richly informative chapters on ethical approaches to Narrative and Life Story research (Goodson 2017).

An important consideration within research relationships is 'an ethic of care' (Gilligan 1982; Ellis 2007, 2017) which requires that we pay close attention to how we are with participants during every stage of our relationship. This means that we view dutiful ethics as the minimal setting for moral and ethical conduct, while 'care' requires that we act in ways that are over and above those obligatory minimums (Ellis 2017).

All of this requires trust and openness in research relationships: mutual and sincere collaboration, where we view research relationships as consultancy; sharing ownership of data with participants, thereby undermining the bias of dominant paradigms and opening up their assumptions to investigation (e.g. that the professionals are the experts); the storyteller having full voice, but the researcher's voice also being heard; reflexive engagement throughout; tolerance of ambiguity; valuing signs, symbols, metaphors; and using whatever 'data' sources are available.

Reflexive relational ethics pays attention to the balance required between our own needs as researchers and our obligations towards, care for and connection with those who participate in our research (Gilligan 1982). It requires not only that researchers acknowledge and reflect on these obligations but that we also put them into practice through striving for mutual understanding and dialogue.

> ► Example

An example of Relational Ethics of Care in action: We join the conversation towards the end as we spoke about anonymity, considering whether or not they might use their real names......

Kim: We don't have to decide today - these are just things I wanted to flag up - to begin that process of awareness of what [doing] this might mean. For instance - does Stella [wife] know about this book [to Stephen]?

Stephen: Yes.

Kim: Stella will want to read it?

Stephen: Presumably – yes.

Kim: What might Stella feel when she read some things that....

Stephen: Mmm. Perhaps I'll need to talk to her.

Kim: Yes, that's one way, and maybe there are things we might not be able to put in the book ...?

Mike: I had thought of Stella as being a person who would know who I was.

Kim: Yes, of course. What about Ellen – what about your kids [to Mike]?

Mike: Well – they would want to read it if they knew of its existence I suppose. I hadn't thought that I would tell them – having said that - they could find out...

Kim: The other thing... a possible dilemma – was the idea of 'secrets' - the need to keep a secret.

Mike: Meaning that it would be healthier for me to tell them?

Kim: Not necessarily, but I don't want to re-create a situation in which you are forced to keep a secret again that might feel in some way not comfortable or ...

Stephen: I think I have to bear in mind that it would not be appropriate for my children to read it *now*, but that in the future it might be. I'll have to bear that in mind.

Kim: Right – so when we are writing or reading this, we'll have to be doing that through lots of different eyes.

[Pause].

Mike: Yes, what you've done for me now, is to show me how complicated the anonymity side of it is going to be.

Stephen: Yes, I was looking at it in a too narrow way.

Mike: Yes, it's about other people as well as us...

[Long pause - in which I am wondering if I should offer them an explicit opportunity to withdraw at this stage].

Kim: You might change your mind altogether.

Stephen: No. I've been thinking about the reasons for doing it and maybe the reasons for not doing it. What I said already is - I think that to re-look at it again from this perspective will help me; the other thing is, I want to help other people in the same situation, people who are victims. People like you are doing so much to help. I really want to give some of that back - I want to help. This is my chance. It was chance that you lived near enough for me to have counselling – even if it was quite a journey. I felt very fortunate and I don't think I've put anything back and I want to....

Kim: You don't have to put anything back.

Stephen: No, but I want to. (Etherington 2000, adapted from chapter 22). ◄

Gathering Stories

Stories can be gathered in a variety of creative ways, for example unstructured interviews, conversations, written stories, journals, diaries, video diaries, metaphors, poems, symbols, life-lines, masks, identity boxes, photographs, drawings–to name a few (Etherington 2000, 2003).

In my work with Mike and Stephen we had many conversations: some were exploratory (as in our first meeting (above box) to consider what the book might look like and the potential ethical issues involved); some were more focused–as in the conversations I had with them separately about their experiences of therapy, our therapeutic relationships, their experiences of beginnings and endings, significant moments and other areas of interest to us; and final conversations concerning how they had experienced the research journeys we had shared during the creation of the book. Both men generously gave me permission to use their journals, written during the period of therapy, in whatever way I thought useful for the purposes of the book. These were used for Part 1: *The Clients' Stories* where the power of their experiences shone through in their own words. They also gave me written stories, letters and poems. I used poems I had written over many years during my own therapy and metaphorical 'fables' and 'allegories' to capture some of the less tangible qualities of our experiences. These were some of the many and various 'data' sources used.

A researcher decides on the topic she[6] wants to explore, identifies who might be in the best position to answer her questions and invites them to join her. In the invitation she will spell out what she wants to learn more about and if the person she is contacting would want to join her in her quest. She has some ideas that this might be a person who knows more about it than she does, or that this person who might also like to find out more about the topic. When I undertook my study of *Trauma, drug misuse and transforming identities* (2003) I contacted drugs agencies and posted adverts in *Therapy Today* inviting people to tell me their stories. On first contact–usually by phone or email–I asked them what had attracted them to the project. That way I found out how they recognised that the title and description of the focus of my research applied to them. I did not define 'trauma' or 'drug misuse' or 'transformation': rather they simply explained to me this was their story. On our first meeting I began by repeating my focus and simply asked 'Where does your

---

6   Here I choose to use the feminine rather than the clumsy device of he/she.

story begin?' That was usually enough. Further questions such as 'What happened then?' or 'How old were you?' or 'Was anybody else there at the time?' were related to historical contexts and enabled the 'thickening of the stories' (Geertz 1973); questions such as 'How did you make sense of that'? or 'What did that mean to you?' or 'How did you know that?' or 'Why do you think that happened?' invited an organic co-construction of meaning, whilst also keeping the focus on what the participant was telling me. These questions were related to culture, context and meaning-making, giving details of values, beliefs, habits and so on.

5   Narrative Conversations

A narrative researcher begins from a 'curious, not knowing' position (Anderson and Gehart 2007) and focuses on questions that help the storyteller tell their stories.

Thus the research conversations are dynamic, organic, dialogical processes. Questions emerge as the researcher strives to understand participants' descriptions of their experiences, and to clarify and check if she is clear about what the person wishes to convey. In this dialogic process (Martin 2007) the researcher can include her own questions as they arise and/or additional clarifications can be made later through email, phone contact or further meetings. It is important that the reader has some access to the researcher's voice to judge their part in the co-construction of knowledge.

Analysing Narratives

There are different ways of analysing narratives: some focus on the storied content of the transcribed conversations; others focus on evocation and resonance (Ellis 1995; Ellis and Bochner 1996; Denzin 2014; Richardson 2000, 2001); others focus on poetic-mindedness or talk that sings (Speedy 2008), all of which contributes to meaning-making (Etherington 2003, 2007a). By creating a narrative synthesis we can bring all of this together.

Some tension exists in the field of narrative inquiry between cognitive-orientated analytical methods and affective-orientated methods of synthesis, as noted by Alan Bleakley (2005), Professor of Medical Education in the UK. He points out that a science-orientated medical education may privilege analytical methods over approaches that encourage a synthesis. This of course also applies in other fields where rationality and logic are privileged over empathy, intuition and narrative knowing. He draws attention to Polkinghorne's work (1995) concerning the 'analysis of narratives: thinking *about* a story' and 'narrative analysis: thinking *with* stories'.

As a postmodern social constructionist, influenced by post-structural thinking, I view stories as socially situated knowledge constructions in their own right that value messiness, differences, depth and texture of experienced life (narrative analysis), whilst also valuing opportunities to look across the stories for similarities and differences (analysis of narratives). From this latter position (which I sometimes talk about as 'standing on the top of a hill from where I can view the breadth as well as the depth) I have seen unexpected and important details. An example of this was when looking across the stories of people who had misused drugs and noticing–for the first time–that *all* of them had been exposed to alcohol, in childhood or very early adolescence (Etherington 2007a).

As stated above, I see analysis (meaning-making) occurring throughout the research process rather than being a separate activity carried out after 'data collection' (Gehart et al. 2007). The emphasis is on co-construction of meaning between the researcher and participants. While being involved in, listening to, reading and transcribing the conversations, researchers can take in what is being said and compare it with their personal understandings, without filling in gaps in understanding with 'grand narratives' (e.g. theories), but rather inquiring about how pieces of the stories make sense together. The process of 'data gathering', 'transcribing' and 'analysis' thereby becomes a continuous harmonious and organic process.

For example, in Part 2 of my study *Trauma, drug misuse and transforming identities*, I first paid attention to and analysed each person's narrative on its own terms, and created an individual narrative (narrative analysis) from the transcribed co-constructed conversations. These narratives were written in a way that 'shows' rather than 'tells about' participants' lived experience: the narratives I constructed from our conversations showed the connections between how society, grand narratives and the behaviour of adults around them contributed to their childhood traumatic experiences and how that had shaped their construction of a drug misuser identity. The narratives also showed ways participants found to reconstruct a new sense of self and identity through healing and transformative experiences and relationships. The narratives therefore needed very little interpretation. They also showed some of my own part in our conversations, in order to be transparent about the relational nature of the research, and the ways in which these stories were shaped through dialogue and co-construction, as well as providing a reflexive layer with regard to my own positioning.

In Part 3: *Thinking across the stories*, rather than looking for 'themes' or similarities (which tends to eliminate anything that does not fit within the theories from which the themes are drawn), I searched the stories for similarities *and* differences, as described above. I am interested in thinking *with* stories, rather than *about* them. Arthur Frank (1995) says:

> » To think **about** a story is to reduce it to content and then analyze that content. Thinking **with** stories takes the story as already complete …. (p.23)

I made some further interpretations as I thought *with* the stories, using the storytellers' own words alongside my own personal and theoretical responses. In these ways I made meaning both within *and* across the stories.

My re-presentations of participants' lived experiences were sent to each person with an invitation to respond in any way: perhaps to correct anything that did not feel true to their own sense of lived experience or to comment in any other way–so these narratives were also co-constructed.

The above form of analysis treats stories as knowledge per se which constitutes 'the social reality of the narrator' (Etherington 2004:81) and conveys a sense of that person's experience in its depth, complexity, richness and texture, by using the actual words spoken.

Narrative *re*-Presentations

My descriptions above show the blurring between analysis and re-presentation, and the blurring between gathering the stories and analysis. The stories are *re*-presented in ways that preserve their integrity and convey the concrete, irreducible humanity of each person.

The 'crisis of representation' (Denzin 2005) created by postmodernism has led researchers to gravitate to forms of inquiry that are diverse and creative. This may be via any creative means of verbal or visual expression. Combining stories with creative expression may facilitate deeply reflective multi-layered visual, cognitive, emotive and embodied ways of knowing that are much richer, fuller and more holistic than the written word alone. However, written words can be variously presented: in poetic forms (Gee 1991; Richardson 2000, 2001; Speedy 2008 and others), metaphor, allegory, stories, fictional narrative and song (Douglas and Carless 2005). Visual and creative representations such as film and documentary making (Loach 1996; Jones 2013[7]; Douglas and Carless 2016); performances such as dance and movement (Spry 2001); drama (Clough 2002; Denzin 2014); and craft making such as tapestry, collage and knitting (Samuels 2011) can all be used to investigate and represent research, either by participant or researcher, or both.

Quality Criteria

We need to address quality criteria in order to ensure the acceptability and recognition of the rigour of Narrative inquiry. Many narrative studies subscribe to the criterion of verisimilitude[8] as a form of quality check. However, such a criterion does not fully or explicitly address the issue of quality or rigour. In evaluating narrative studies we need first to examine literature from the broader qualitative research field, which is too vast to address here, 'qualitative research' being a term that applies to a wide range of approaches that may lie somewhere between traditional, modernist, post-positivist studies (such as grounded theory or thematic analysis) and non-traditional, postmodern approaches, including narrative inquiry. I believe I can do no better here than to direct the reader to Norman Denzin's

---

7   Jones, K. (Exec Prod) (2013). RUFUS STONE (short film) Retrieved from ▶ https://vimeo.com/109360805.

8   Verisimilitude: the quality of seeming to be true or real (Oxford Dictionary). One way this can be achieved is by using the participant's own words and detailed sensory and embodied descriptions.

excellent chapter (5) in *Interpretive Autoethnography* (2014) and Jane Speedy's list of some of the criteria (2008: 55–58).

Reflections

Here I will ask you, the reader of this chapter, some of the evaluative questions that apply to reading narrative research (although this chapter, whilst written in a reflexive, narrative style, is not itself narrative research).

Drawing on Jane Speedy's list, some of those questions might be concerning:

Transparency: Have I made it clear why and how I came to write this chapter? Do I make the purposes, perspectives and positions that have informed the construction of this chapter available to you?

Trustworthiness: Does this text seem a truthful, credible account of my journey towards becoming a narrative inquirer? Does the work provide you with a sense of 'lived experience'?

Aesthetic Merit: Does the text succeed aesthetically? Is it written in ways that invite your interpretive responses? Is it satisfying and, *above all*, not boring?

Reflexivity: Have I been sufficiently transparent to help you judge the value of this work: how my personal history led to my interest in this topic; my pre-suppositions about knowledge in this field; how I am positioned in relation to this knowledge; how my gender and culture influence my positioning in relation to this topic; whether this text is partial, situated and contingent; and whether I show you how I know what I know?

Accountability: Do I make it clear which community's interests this work serves? Are ethical issues and issues of collaboration and power relations addressed? Does the contribution this chapter makes outweigh the ethical dilemmas for those mentioned, including myself?

Substantive and enduring contribution: Does this work contribute to a body of knowledge that adds to the field of qualitative research in counselling and psychotherapy generally, and narrative inquiry specifically? Will this text be of some lasting value in the field of counselling and psychotherapy research?

Impact and transformation: Does this work resonate with you? Does it affect you emotionally, intellectually, politically or in any other ways? Does it generate new questions? Does it move you to try some new ways of doing research? Move you to any other actions (e.g. training/supervising researchers)? Does it transgress some of your taken-for-granted assumptions? Has it changed you in any other ways? Does is show my own 'transformation' as a researcher?

However, I would like to reiterate Andrew Sparkes' warning (2002): that we must resist the temptation to 'seek universal foundational criteria, lest one form of dogma simply replaces another' (p.223). Undoubtedly, there will be new and different criteria emerging from thoughtful considerations of what might be required as we, society, the current state of knowledge and the world we live in change over time.

Enjoying Narrative Inquiry

As I have reflected on the processes of writing this chapter I have asked myself what I have enjoyed about narrative inquiry over the years: the first thing that comes to mind is relationship. As a practitioner-researcher, having always had a private practice alongside my academic role, I have been fortunate to engage professionally with many people in meaningful relationships: clients, supervisees, students, colleagues and participants, all of whom have enriched my life. My pleasure continues, even into my semi-retirement as I accompany masters and doctoral students on their research journeys, alongside my work with a few clients and supervisees. But most of all, I think of the people who have joined with me in my research endeavours and, in some cases, made them their own. By collaborating with me to explore the importance and meaning of their stories of lived experiences they have taken risks and given me their time and trust. Many of those stories have been about painful, traumatic events in their lives, some of which they have not spoken of before. However, our conversations have also included stories of resilience, resistance and transformation: indeed, sometimes people tell me that they have experienced our research conversations themselves as transformative and healing. Following a conversation with George, an ex-drug misuser, who had previously been in therapy for several years and was at that time a participant in my study, he emailed me saying:

» Just wanted to tell you how energised and positive I felt after our meeting … I heard myself saying things and expressing them in a way I had not noticed before.

I was intrigued to know more about how George understood his positive feelings. In a further email he elaborated:

» The context of research, rather than personal therapy, somehow faced me out into the world rather than inwardly toward myself ….There were similarities to therapy … but you remained focused on the specifics of the task at hand … without unduly or specifically delving into, or focusing on, my emotional state.

   I fully accepted for the first time that I had been sexually abused in my childhood … I think it may be to do with the "facing out into the world" that I mentioned above. I described the experience to my wife as, "Something moved, something changed". (Etherington 2009: 230)

Over the years, as I have collected and re-presented stories and written my own, I have been taken into new places that have challenged me and moved me on. The stories have touched my own, some of them overlapping and others that are clearly different: all of them have created a response in me.

   I have enjoyed the process of ongoing learning that my research offers to others: participants, fellow researchers and audience–even transcribers (Etherington 2007b). Jane Speedy refers to this as 'ethics of transformation and emancipation' (2008, p. 84). Additionally, the creative ways we use to re-present stories make them accessible, not only to academics in their 'ivory towers', but also to people who would not normally read research: those who value story, poetry, performance and other visual expressions.

Engaging in narrative inquiry has provided me also with the pleasure of being part of a community of like-minded people who share similar philosophical positions–sometimes drawing together to challenge and resist the force and influence of the dominant narratives of rationality and reason (left hemisphere of the brain) at the potential expense of the visual and intuitive strengths of the right brain and the power of 'betweenness' that allows something new to emerge in the gaps that lie between. As McGilchrist (2009: 97) notes: 'The model we choose to use to understand something determines what we find'.

Summary

As I draw to a close and read back over what I have written I realise that this chapter supports what others have said about how people make meaning of their lives by reflexively ordering them as life stories (Bochner 2014; Bruner 1990; Polkinghorne 1988, and others). Events from the past take on extraordinary meaning over time as their significance in the overall story of our lives is realised, depending on the stocks of knowledge we have available to us at any one time as we mature and learn. As I tell this stories of becoming a narrative inquirer during my eightieth year (a kind of reminiscence therapy!) I do so from a wider perspective than ever before, being able to place my experiences in the larger context of childhood and adult experience. With maturity we are able to stand back from the cultures and contexts that have shaped us and examine those influences. This has felt like another 'creative reengagement with my history' (White 2001: 66) that provides me with a degree of pleasure and satisfaction that I had not expected to feel–and I am grateful for that.

References

Anderson, H., & Gehart, D. (2007). *Collaborative therapy*. NY: Routledge.
Alan Bleakley, A. (2005). Stories as data, data as stories: making sense of narrative inquiry in clinical education. *Medical Education, 39*(5), 534–540.
Bochner, A. (2014). *Coming to Narrative: A Personal History of Paradigm Change in the Human Sciences*. New York and London: Routledge.
Bruner, J. (1986). Actual minds, possible worlds. Cambridge, MA: Harvard University Press.
Bruner, J. (1990). Acts of Meaning, Cambridge, MA: Harvard University Press, J. (2002) Making stories: Law, Literature and Life, New York: Farrar, Strauss and Giroux.
Bruner, J. (2002). *Making stories: Law, Literature and Life*. New York: Farrar, Strauss and Giroux.
Burr, V. (1995) An introduction to social constructionism. London: Routledge.
Burr, V. (2003). *Social constructionism* (2nd ed.). London: Routledge.
Carless, D and Douglas, K (2016) Arts-based research: radical or conventional? The Psychologist, 29. 350–353. ISSN 0952-8229.
Cloke, P., Cooke, P., Cursons, J., Milbourne, P., & Widdowfield, R. (2000). Ethics, Reflexivity and Research: Encounters with Homeless People. *Ethics Place and Environment, 3*(2), 133–154.
Clough, P. (2002). *Narratives and Fictions in Educational Research*. Buckingham: Open University Press.
Denzin, N. K. (1997). Interpretive ethnography: Ethnographic practices for the 21st century. London: Sage.
Denzin, N. K. (2005). *The SAGE Handbook of Qualitative Research*. Thousand Oaks, CA: Sage.
Denzin, N. K. (2014). *Interpretive Autoethnography* (2nd ed.). Urbana: University of Illinois: Sage.
Derrida, J. (1981). *Positions*. Baltimore: Johns Hopkins University Press.

Douglas, K., & Carless, D. (2005). *Across the Tamar: Stories from women in Cornwall*. Bristol, UK: Independently produced: Audio CD.

Ellis, C. (1995) Final negotiations: a story of love, loss, and chronic illness. Philadelphia: Temple University Press.

Ellis, C., & Bochner, A. P. (Eds.). (1996). Ethnographic alternatives book series, Vol. 1.Composing ethnography: Alternative forms of qualitative writing. AltaMira Press.

Ellis, C. (2007). Telling secrets, revealing lives: relational ethics in research with intimate others. *Qualitative Inquiry, 13*, 3–29.

Ellis, C. (2017). Compassionate Research: Interviewing and Storytelling from a relational ethics of care in. In I. Goodson (Ed.), *The Routledge International Handbook on Narrative and Life History* (pp. 431–445). Abingdon, Oxon: Routledge.

Etherington, K. (2000). *Narrative approaches to working with male survivors of sexual abuse; The Clients', the Counsellor's and the Researcher's Story*. London: Jessica Kingsley.

Etherington, K. (2003). *Trauma, the Body and Transformation: A Narrative Inquiry*. London: Jessica Kingsley.

Etherington, K. (2004). *Becoming a reflexive researcher: Using Our Selves in Research*. London: Jessica Kingsley.

Etherington, K. (2007b). Working with traumatic stories: from transcriber to witness. *International Journal of Social Research Methodology: Theory and Practice., 10*(2), 85–97.

Etherington, K. (2007c). Ethical research in reflexive relationships. *Qualitative Inquiry, 13*(7), 599–616.

Etherington, K. (2007a). *Trauma, Drug Misuse and Transforming Identities: a Life Story Approach*. London: Jessica Kingsley.

Etherington, K. (2009). Life story research: a relevant methodology for counsellors and psychotherapists. *Counselling and Psychotherapy Research, 9*(4), 225–233.

Etherington, K. (2016). Personal experience and critical reflexivity in counselling and psychotherapy research. *Counselling and Psychotherapy Research*. https://doi.org/10.1002/capr.12080.

Etherington, K., & Bridges, N. (2011). Narrative case study research: On endings and six session reviews. *Counselling and Psychotherapy Research, 11*(1), 11–22.

Finkelhor, D. (1986). *A Sourcebook on Child Sexual Abuse*. Newbury Park, California: Sage Pubs.

Foucault, M. (1980). *Power/Knowledge: Selected Interviews and Other Writings*. Brighton, UK: Harvester.

Frank, A. W. (1995). *The Wounded Storyteller: Body, Illness and Ethics*. Chicago: University of Chicago Press.

Frank, A. W. (2000). The standpoint of storyteller. *Qualitative Health Research, 10*, 354–365.

Freedman, J., & Combs, G. (1996). *Narrative therapy: The social construction of preferred realities*. New York, NY: Norton.

Gee, J. (1991). A Linguistic Approach to Narrative, in. *Journal of Narrative and Life History, 1*, 15–39.

Geertz, C. (1973). Thick Description: Towards an Interpretive Theory of Culture. In C. Geertz (Ed.), *The Interpretation of Cultures*. NY: Basic Books.

Geertz, C. (1983). *Local Knowledge*. London: Fontana.

Gehart, D., Tarragona, M. and Bava, S. (2007) A Collaborative Approach to Research and Inquiry, in H. Anderson and D. Gehart (eds.) *Collaborative Therapy: Relationships and Conversations that make a Difference*. (367-390). London: Routledge.

Gergen, K. J. (1999). *An Invitation to Social Construction*. London: Sage.

Goodson, I. (Ed.). (2017). *The Routledge International Handbook on Narrative and Life History: Abingdon*. Oxon: Routledge.

Gilligan, C. (1982). *In a Different Voice*. Cambridge, MA: Harvard University Press.

Guillemin, M., & Gillam, L. (2004). Ethics, Reflexivity and 'ethically important moments' in Research. *Qualitative Inquiry, 10*(2), 261–280.

Helgeland, I. M. (2005). 'Catch 22' of Research Ethics: Ethical Dilemmas in Follow-up Studies of Marginal Groups. *Qualitative Inquiry, 11*, 549–569.

Heron, J. (1981). A Philosophical Basis for New Paradigm, in Human Inquiry. In P. Reason & J. Rowan (Eds.), *A Sourcebook for New Paradigm Research* (pp. 19–35). N.Y.: Wiley and Sons.

Heron, J. (1971). *Experience and Method*. Guildford: University of Surrey.

Hertz, R. (Ed.). (1997). *Reflexivity and Voice*. London: Sage.

Jones, K. (2013). Infusing Biography with the Personal: Writing Rufus Stone. *#REATIVE. ØPPROACHES TO 2ESEARCH, 6*(2), 4–21.

Josselson, R. (Ed.). (1996). *Ethics and Process in the Narrative Study of Lives, vol 4*. London: Sage.

Kelly, L. (1988). *Surviving Sexual Violence*. Oxford: Polity Press.

Lerner, G. (1986). *The Creation of Patriarchy*. New York: Oxford Univ. Press.

Loach, K. (1996) *Kathy Come Home.*, BBC Films.

Mair, M. (1989). *Beyond Psychology and Psychotherapy: a poetics of experience*. London: Routledge.

Martin, V. (2007). Dialogue in the narrative process. *Journal of Medical Ethics: Medical Humanities, 33*, 49–54.

McAdams, D. (1993) The stories we live by: personal myths and the making of the self. New York: Morrow.

McCormack, C. (2004). Storying stories: A narrative approach to in-depth interview conversations. *International Journal of Social Research Methodology, 7*, 219–236.

McGilchrist, I. (2009). *The Master and His Emissary: The Divided Brain and the Making of the Western World*. US: Yale University Press.

McLeod, J. (1997). *Narrative and psychotherapy*. London: Sage.

McLeod, J. (2001). *Qualitative Research in Counselling and Psychotherapy*. London: Sage.

Moustakas. (1981). Heuristic Inquiry. In P. Reason & J. Rowan (Eds.), *Human Inquiry: a sourcebook for new paradigm research*. New York: Wiley and Sons.

Moustakas, C. (1990). *Heuristic Research: Design, Methodology and Applications*. London: Sage Publications.

Mishler, E. G. (1999). *Storylines: Craftartists' narratives of identity*. Cambridge, MA: Harvard University Press.

Neisser, U., & Fivush, R. (1994). *The Remembered Self: Construction and Accuracy in the Self Narrative*. Cambridge: Cambridge University Press.

Oakley, A. (1981). Interviewing women: a contradiction in terms. In H. Roberts (Ed.), *Doing Feminist Research*. London: Routledge and Kegan Paul.

Polkinghorne, D. E. (1988). *Narrative knowing and the human sciences*. Albany: State University of New York Press.

Reason, P., & Rowan, J. (Eds.). (1981). *Human Inquiry: a sourcebook for new paradigm research*. N.Y.: Wiley and Sons.

Richardson, L. (2000). Introduction - Assessing Alternative Modes of Qualitative Ethnographic Research: How do we Judge? Who Judges? *Qualitative Inquiry, 6*(2), 251–253.

Richardson, L. (2001). Poetic Representation of Interviews. In J. Gubrium & J. Holstein (Eds.), *Handbook of Interview Research*. Thousand Oaks, CA: Sage.

Rosenthal, G. (2003). The healing effects of storytelling: On the conditions of curative storytelling in the context of research and counseling. *Qualitative Inquiry, 9*(6), 915–933.

Samuels, E. (2011). *Artistic transformations of self: The use of arts-based narrative and autoethnography in a study of identity construction*. PhD thesis: University of Bristol, UK.

Scott-Hoy, K. (2002). The visitor: Juggling life in the grip of the text. In A. P. Bochner & C. Ellis (Eds.), *Ethnographically speaking: Autoethnography, literature, and aesthetics*. Walnut Creek, CA: AltaMira Press.

Stanley, L., & Wise, S. (1983). *Breaking out: feminist consciousness and feminist research*. London: Rutledge and Kegan Paul.

Speedy, J. (2008). *Narrative Inquiry and Psychotherapy*. UK. Palgrave Macmillan: Hamps.

Spry, T. (2001). *Performing Autoethnography: An Embodied Methodical Praxis in: Qualitative Inquiry, 7*, 706–732.

Struve, J. (1990). Dancing with patriarchy: The politics of sexual abuse. In M. Hunter (Ed.), *The Sexually Abused Male* (Vol. 1). New York: Lexington Books.

Villa-Vicencio, C. (1994). Ethics of responsibility. In C. Villa-Vicencio & J. de Grucy (Eds.), *Doing ethics in context* (pp. 75–88). New York: Orbis Books.

White, M. (2001). Folk psychology and narrative practice. *Dulwich Centre Journal, 2*(1), 37.

White, M., & Epston, D. (1990). *Narrative Means to Therapeutic Ends*. New York: W. W. Norton.

Doing Constructivist Grounded Theory Research

Elvis Langley

Contents

© The Author(s) 2020
S. Bager-Charleson, A. McBeath (eds.),
Enjoying Research in Counselling and Psychotherapy,
https://doi.org/10.1007/978-3-030-55127-8_6

🟡 **Learning Goals**

By the end of this chapter you should be able to:

- Understand some of the basic elements of constructivist grounded theory methodology and how these relate to research design;
- Have an understanding of constructivist grounded theory's philosophical background and history;
- Understand how constructivist grounded theory can be used effectively in counselling and psychotherapy research;
- Consider some key issues when determining whether to use grounded theory as a research methodology.

6 Introduction

Grounded theory, with its background in sociology, many different iterations and attention to methodological detail, may not initially appeal to the beginning researcher. However, if one can move beyond these initial factors, it can provide an elegant and relatively straightforward approach to developing new understandings or theories about the psychological world. In this chapter, I will provide a simple and practical introduction to constructivist grounded theory (CGT) using my own research on the impact of peer-led Hearing Voices Network Groups (HVNGs) (Langley, 2020) to illustrate its use in counselling and psychotherapy research. I hope to take you hand in hand, navigating past some of the pitfalls and dead-ends that I encountered as a beginning researcher and pointing out some of the milestones and key features of the landscape to hold in mind when you (hopefully) conduct this journey on your own. Along the way, we will discuss questions that I imagine might come up for you. I hope that some of these questions will be answered by the time you finish this introductory tour of CGT, but it is likely that there will be many more to ponder on, especially in relation to your potential research. If so, you are on the right track, because as we will see, considering the use of CGT in your research is very much about framing the right questions. Some of the questions we will consider include when to use CGT, whether CGT produces the type of knowledge you are seeking to create, whether your epistemological and ontological position fits the methodology, what factors to consider when sampling, and how to build a theory that has explanatory value. The next sections of this chapter discuss these areas of enquiry, as well as outlining the process of CGT research itself.

Constructivist Grounded Theory in Context

Grounded theory developed from Barney Glaser and Anselm Strauss' frustration with the 'grand theories' tradition of social sciences research, which often seemed to fit poorly with research data and real-life situations. Instead, their aim was 'the discovery of theory from data' that 'fit the situation being researched, and worked when put to use' (Glaser and Strauss 1967, pp.1–3). Grounded theory is set apart from other methodologies by this focus. Where quantitative research seeks to prove or disprove theories (hypotheses) and other qualitative approaches aim to describe or explore the essence of phenomena, grounded theory's goal is to generate theory through a comparative analysis of data and abductive reasoning, creating plausible explanations that can be expanded on and tested by future research. In the next sections we will look at the philosophical background of this approach and its utility in different research situations.

Epistemological and Ontological Foundations

In order to understand grounded theory, it helps to have some sense of the history of the methodology and its epistemological and ontological foundations. Otherwise, confusion can arise regarding which is the 'right' grounded theory. Grounded theory has undergone a number of different iterations following the divergence in thinking between its founders, who from the start came from different research traditions. Anselm Strauss' background was in the qualitative 'Chicago Tradition' while Barney Glaser first trained at Columbia University, which had a more quantitative approach. When they parted ways, Strauss (Strauss and Corbin, 1994; 1998) continued to embrace the constructed, positional nature of knowledge, while Glaser (Glaser, 1978; Glaser, 1992) argued for a more realist epistemological positioning, leading to different versions of grounded theory methodology. As a newcomer, it can seem daunting and possibly lead you to think you may be 'doing it wrong' when confronted with multiple versions of grounded theory in multiple texts. In fact, it is much more important to know *which* grounded theory methodology you are using, and *why*, including an understanding of where you sit ontologically and epistemologically. There is no 'right' version, but there is the possibility for muddled thinking in this regard. Because of this, it is helpful to know where you position yourself ontologically and epistemologically before conducting your research. The position you take will have implications for how you do your research, the way you apply your methodology and the quality criteria you use.

► Example

In my research on the impact of peer-led Hearing Voices Network Groups (Langley 2020), I grouped myself with grounded theory researchers who acknowledge the methodology's roots in the Chicago School pragmatist philosophical tradition, and its links with symbolic interactionism (Strauss and Corbin, 1998; Bryant and Charmaz, 2007; Charmaz, 2014; Strübing, 2007; Strübing, 2019). Pragmatism considers that the ontological nature of what is being studied is known by its effects only, with facts and values seen as linked (Hookway, 2012). Grounded theory's focus on process and action stems from this way of thinking (Strübing, 2019). Rather than focus on the essence of a phenomena itself, it aims to build theory about the processes and actions that define an area of enquiry: what is happening on a practical level. Symbolic interactionism (which evolved from within the pragmatist paradigm) in particular focuses on understanding the basic social processes inherent in situations and the interplay between personal and societally held meanings in determining how people understand situations and what actions they take (Blumer, 1969; Mead, 2015). This philospohical approach fitted well with enquiry into the processes of change in HVNGs and in my research I acknowledged the link and the role that it played in the focus of my theory.

Epistemologically, I took a constructivist stance, which led me to use Kathy Charmaz's (Charmaz, 2014) version of constructivist grounded theory (CGT) from among the different grounded theory methodologies available. Constructivism (as opposed to social constructionism, discussed in ▶ Chap. 1) can be viewed as an epistemological position that focuses mainly on the co-constructed nature of knowledge. Constructivist grounded theory applies this position to grounded theory methodology, reflexively considering the role of the researcher in co-creating the knowledge produced during the research process, as opposed to assuming that researcher knowledge is value free (Charmaz, 2014). As such, CGT values and requires reflexivity about the particular values, experiences and knowledge of the researcher in relation to the theory constructed and the research process. I find that this focus on reflexive thinking has utility in relation to counselling and psychotherapy research, mirroring the respect for subjectivity and reflexivity that is embedded in the practice of these traditions. It also seemed especially important to be aware of my role as a non-voice hearing professional researching voice-hearer led groups, since the subjectivity and first person experience of voice-hearers has often been devalued in pursuit of professional explanation (Romme and Morris, 2007; Calton et al., 2009). By taking a constructivist stance, I chose to acknowledge and be reflexive about my role in creating a theory about (and with) voice-hearers, rather than assume an 'objective' position. I hoped that by being explicit about this left room for further clarification and refinement of my theory by voice-hearers and other professionals. ◄

Choosing when to Use Constructivist Grounded Theory

So what then is the purpose of constructivist grounded theory in psychological research? When should it be used? Let's explore some of the cases in which CGT may fit particular research situations and purposes, in order to find out when it might work for you.

Open and Collaborative Discovery of Theory

As discussed in ▶ Chap. 1, a good fit between the research question and methodology is essential. In order to address the question of when CGT is a good fit, one needs to consider what kind of knowledge CGT leads to. Grounded theory, as a research methodology, has an explicit aim of building theory. CGT produces pragmatic, practical and useful *concepts*: theories grounded in the data. Therefore it works well when there is a possibility for open enquiry. It is a useful methodology when the topic of enquiry is not well known, when existing theories do not fit the data, or when new knowledge is being sought (Glaser and Strauss, 1967).

In CGT the final research topic need not be fixed: your analysis and interpretation of the data guides you to the final destination. Many research proposals do not allow for a change in the research question, so it is important to consider carefully what one wants to study and how you word this, so as to allow yourself enough flexibility to follow where your analysis of the data leads. If you are required to be specific, initial or pilot research can reveal interesting concepts to explore. However, as a CGT researcher you can always go back later and explore concepts that do not fit the scope of your current research. In this sense, data is never lost or old in CGT.

Partly because of this flexibility, CGT also works well in situations where participants can be involved in meaningful and transparent ways. It is valid and encouraged to be collaborative in the process of theory development: going back to participants for more clarification and exploration and using member-checking to engage them in theory development can increase the quality of your research (Charmaz, 2014).

Informing Future Research

Constructivist grounded theory has the potential to bridge gaps between qualitative and quantitative research. CGT is fundamentally a process of theory building. Without bringing the process of theory creation into the field of published research and grounding it in data, there is a danger that our theorising (especially in quantitiative research) will be biased towards our own worldview and assumptions. In quantitative terms, poor hypotheses lead to poor answers, and poor hypotheses come from poor theorising. Specifically, CGT can help quantitative researchers ask the right questions, questions that are grounded in a reflexive process; that arise from a disciplined and documented process of engagement with data; and that focus on social action and process.

This bridging function is especially important for counselling and psychotherapy researchers. As a psychological practitioner in clinical practice, I see that my clients' interpretations of their reality become the way they see the world. These ways of knowing, influenced (consciously or not) by cultural norms, language, relationships, personal and societal history, and issues of power (race, gender, sexual orientation, socio-economic status, etc.), *are* reality for those experiencing them. Equally, as researchers and clinicians we have particular ways of seeing the world that may differ from those of the people we are researching. If we engage in research that asks questions from our point of view only, we may miss the point entirely. CGT makes the process of theorising explicit, while providing a structure that enables us to base our theorieson detailed engagement with the people we want to help.

Reflexive Enquiry

As discussed above, constructivist grounded theory is a methodology that is intimately involved in a reflexive way of viewing the world through its acknowledgement of the construction of meaning (Charmaz, 2014) and the 'situatedness' of knowledge. This is not just considered in relation to research participants, but also the researcher: CGT seeks to enable reflexivity about how our own assumptions, worldview and situated experience influence the research process, including the role that culture, race, socio-economic status, gender identity and personal experience may play in the creation of different narratives and discourses. CGT also acknowledges the 'rich data' to be found in examining the researcher—participant relationship (Charmaz, 2014). This includes an acknowledgement and examination of how the non-verbal, verbal and situational cues, as well the implicit and explicit relationship (including power dynamics) between researcher and participant, influence the unfolding of knowledge that is voiced between them. As such, it is a useful methodology when this sort of reflexive enquiry adds value to the research.

For Exploring the Social Processes Through Which Meanings are Constructed

Rather than trying to capture an experience via number of static themes, grounded theory focusses on process and social action. Because of this, it lends itself well to an analysis of interactions between people, as well as the ways in which people make sense of the world. CGT researchers such as Kathy Charmaz have focussed their interest especially on participants' sense of self and the link between this and the wider relational realm, drawing on grounded theory's roots in Symbolic Interactionism as a 'theory-methods package' through which to analyse data (Charmaz, 2014). However, CGT research could equally work with a number of different lenses. The important element as a researcher is to be explicit about the particular interests and ways of viewing the data that you are bringing to the research and how CGT as a methodology fits with your approach.

Personal fit

Finally, it is useful to consider the fit between your own values and framework as a researcher and/or clinician, in order to see whether it is the right methodology for you. Some comfort with not knowing the final outcome, being open to new ideas and valuing different ways of viewing the world are probably helpful in conducting CGT. One has to be open to publicly presenting ideas that, after long hours of comparing, contrasting and coding multiple data sets, are by the nature of the methodology provisional and open to testing. It is also helpful to be interested in and comfortable with sharing your own reflexive process in the research, since this is part of the quality criteria linked to CGT methodology.

I chose CGT as a methodology for my research on the impact of peer-led Hearing Voices Network Groups (HVNGs) for a number of the reasons discussed above. First, it is an area of enquiry where I felt an open and collaborative approach to discovering theory was appropriate. The Hearing Voices Movement can be characterised as an example of an area where many existing theories and assumptions are rejected and people are involved in a collaborative process of making sense of their experiences in new ways. HVNGs arose from the wider Hearing Voices Movement (Romme and Escher, 1993) with the aim of offering 'a safe haven where people who hear, see or sense things that other people don't, can feel accepted, valued and understood' (English Hearing Voices Network, 2018). The Hearing Voices Movement rejects the medical model and positivist assertions about mental wellbeing (Corstens et al., 2014; Dillon and Longden, 2012; Romme and Escher, 1993; Romme et al., 2009). It places itself within a broader political frame and sees itself as a 'social movement', specifically advocating for the rights of people who hear voices, have unusual beliefs and/or see visions (Longden et al., 2013; Slade, 2009). The Hearing Voices Movement rejects the validity of the term 'schizophrenia' (Romme and Morris, 2007), instead adopting the term 'voice-hearer' as a descriptive label (Dillon and Hornstein, 2013; Woods, 2013). From this stance, they position themselves firmly against the idea that voice-hearing needs be a signifier of mental 'illness', or distress at all (Romme et al., 1993; (Boyle, 2013; Johnstone, 2012)). Instead, they focus on helping people who hear voices to accept their voices (rather than try to get rid of them) and create meaning around the voice-hearing experience through formulation-based approaches (Johnstone et al., 2018; Romme and Escher, 2000) and through Hearing Voices Groups (Dillon and Hornstein, 2013).

Second, grounded theory's focus on social process and meaning (Charmaz, 2014; Strübing, 2019) also fit the topic of my research. My first contact with a hearing voices group was through feedback from voice-hearers who had attended a peer-led HVNG hosted in the building of a charity I was managing. After listening to the impact that the group had on people, I became interested in finding out more about the patterns of growth people were describing and what the processes of change in peer-led HVNGs might be. This looked like a gap in current theory within the Hearing Voices Movement, as previous research had focused on voice-hearers' individual recovery journey, rather than processes in HVNGs (Romme et al., 2009; Romme and Morris, 2013). Choosing grounded theory as a methodology enabled me to theorise about the relationship between the group and the individual in those processes, as experienced via the shared meanings created in the groups. This topic also seemed to have the potential to become the basis for prompting future research, since there had been calls from within the Hearing Voices Movement for research in this area (Corstens et al., 2014).

Having reviewed various iterations of grounded theory (Glaser, 1992; Glaser and Strauss, 1967; Strauss and Corbin, 1998), I chose to follow Kathy Charmaz's (2014) constructivist grounded theory as my research methodology, since this approach best fit the nature of my research topic and my philosophical stance. Constructivism allowed me to consider both the various Hearing Voices Movement positions and diagnostic explanations of voice-hearing as constructed knowledge, with different individual and societal impacts. In contrast to earlier conceptions of grounded theory, data in CGT is seen as an outcome of research activity, not an objective starting point (Bryant and Charmaz, 2007). Therefore, through a constructivist frame, it was also possible to explore and discuss my role in the research, how my own discourse creates meaning and how this influences the research process. I wanted my participants to be involved in my theory construction, and called them co-researchers (a term I will use for them here also) to acknowledge their active role in doing that. I felt that this was important given the nature of power dynamics inherent in research in this area (Johnstone, 2012) and because the dialogue around hearing voices often excludes voice-hearers' own experiences and explanations of voice-hearing (Calton et al., 2009; Coles, 2013).

Finally, in terms of my own stance as a researcher, I saw parallels between a constructivist position and my own professional values. This also fit with the Hearing Voices Movement's stance on subjective knowledge and respecting a plurality of explanations for people's voices. The willingness to meet someone where they are, on their own terms, is a value deeply rooted in my clinical work. As a counselling psychologist, the profession's focus on the value basis of practice and subjective meaning and experience, rather than a value-free 'objective' enquiry (Woolfe, 2012), fit with my constructivist worldview as a researcher. Strawbridge and Woolfe (2003) highlight the foundation of counselling psychology as being rooted in the values of engaging with subjectivity, empathically respecting people's experiences as valid on their own terms and negotiating between worldviews, without assuming that one way of experiencing, knowing or feeling is automatically more valid. Therefore, my values as a practitioner and researcher sat relatively easily in relation to both the Hearing Voices Movement ethos and the methodology I chose. ◄

Activity
- Consider the fit between constructivist grounded theory and the research you want to embark on:
  - What kind of knowledge do you want to create?
  - What ontological and epistemological position do you want to take? (Does it fit with constructivist grounded theory, or does another methodology fit better?)
  - How well does CGT fit with your own values and worldview?
  - How well does existing theory fit your field of enquiry? Is there a need for new theoretical insights?
  - Is prompting further research something you find important?
  - How interested are you in exploring social processes and the construction of meaning in your research?
  - How comfortable are you personally about presenting a theory, as opposed to 'proving' your findings?

Doing Constructivist Grounded Theory

At its heart grounded theory methodology is an iterative process of 1) collecting data and analysing it via increasingly abstract coding strategies and 2) using 'constant comparison' between each source of data at each step of the analysis, in order to 3) develop a meaningful theory about what is being researched (Charmaz, 2014). In grounded theory, the process of collecting data, coding it and comparing it with other data leads to emergent *categories*, the elements of concern and focus within the data. These categories are built upwards using coding that starts very close to the data (data near) and becomes progressively more analytic and abstract as codes between and within data sets are compared, reviewed and updated at each step of coding. What grounded theory researchers look for when reviewing their initial coding are codes with *explanatory power*: codes that encapsulate and elucidate what is found in the data (Charmaz, 2014). The researcher then pursues the ideas these codes represent, making choices about subsequent sampling and data collection that allow them to test the utility and scope of them, and refining and developing them through subsequent coding. From this purposeful sampling strategy (called *theoretical sampling*), not only do categories emerge, but also *properties* of categories. Properties provide context and dimensionality: the what, why, when, who and how of categories (Glaser and Strauss, 1967). They fill out and explain categories, helping to create meaningful 'thick descriptions' (Geertz, 1973). Through this process, a theory that is grounded in data is developed. The next few sections of this chapter will take you through a step-by-step summary of how this is carried out.

Data Collection

In grounded theory, sources of data can be interviews, 'field research', group discussions, ethnographic data, body language, behaviour and interactions, or extant texts (Charmaz, 2014). In constructivist grounded theory, data is also considered a situated co-creation of knowledge between the researcher and subject. Not only do researchers bring their own ways of viewing the data to the research, based on many factors, but they are also acknowledged as active participants in the *creation* of data: the way they present themselves, the questions they ask (or don't ask), the smiles and encouragement given or not given all create moments where meanings can be shared, hidden, lost or discovered together. As practitioners in the field of counselling and psychotherapy, we already know from our clinical work the value of relationship in enquiry. It is not just that the relationship allows us to understand another, but also that relationships can allow individuals to understand, or discourage them from understanding, their own experience differently and express it in new ways. Constructivist grounded theory, with its roots in studying the relationships between meanings and social processes (Charmaz, 2014), allows for this knowledge and encourages reflexivity regarding the interpersonal, societal and intrapersonal aspects of the research process itself (see ▶ Chap. 1 for a detailed discussion of these areas of reflexive focus). In CGT, data is inherently linked to the meanings people create and the way in which they act. The process of uncovering and recording this is relational and CGT acknowledges it as such.

This approach not only shapes the way data is used, but also the way data collection methods have developed within the methodology. For example, in CGT, 'intensive interviews' take the place semi-structured interviews often do in other research methodologies. Charmaz, (2014, p.56) calls the intensive inteview technique 'a gently guided, one sided conversation that explores a person's substantial experience with the research topic'. Intensive interviews do not follow set interview schedules; this allows the focus of the interview to change over time as required, as the researcher follows the emergent ideas of their analysis, to allow category development (Charmaz, 2014), as well as allowing more responsiveness in relation to the interviewee's interests and areas of concern.

6

> ► **Example**

In my research (Langley, 2020) I used a mixture of intensive interviews, taped group discussions and field observations of the groups as my primary data sources. I conducted nine intensive interviews, with most interviews lasting roughly one hour. I aimed to conduct interviews where people were most comfortable. Most interviews took place in private rooms I rented, local to my co-researchers. Where it was possible, I rented a room in the same building that groups took place. I also attended three peerled hearing voices groups, with a total of eight visits. This provided me with observational data to allow comparison with individual interviews. I obtained consent from the second group I observed to tape the discussion during part of two sessions. Through this ethnographic method, I was able to see the construction of social process in action in the group (Blumer, 1969). I felt that this was important in order to provide rich data that supplemented and helped me understand what I was hearing in interviews, therefore increasing my 'theoretical sensitivity' (Glaser and Strauss, 1967, p.46). I was interested particularly in the correlation between what I understood people had said to me about hearing voices groups and my direct observations of the group process. Attending the groups allowed me to consider the underlying mechanisms of how groups worked directly (what people were doing and saying), as well as what voice hearers said about their experience of the groups. ◄

Data Analysis

Coding and Memo Writing

CGT employs an open coding strategy that moves from data near coding to the creation of more abstract and analytic codes (Belgrave and Seide, 2019). Gerunds (words ending in 'ing') are often used as a device to capture the active and process-driven elements of the data, reflecting grounded theory's emphasis on social action. At every stage of coding, each set of data is put through a process of 'constant comparison' (Glaser and Strauss, 1967) with other data. Incidents within the data are compared with other incidents, interviews compared with other interviews and so on. Comparison also takes place *between* levels of data; for example, a code generated during line-by-line coding might be considered in relation to its explanatory power in relation to a whole section of data. Through this process certain codes with explanatory power are 'elevated' to higher-level codes and refined, eventually becoming the categories and properties of a theory (Charmaz, 2014). Throughout coding, researchers write *memos*, mapping the process of coding and their reflections. Memos not only serve as a reflexive tool, but also as an aide-mémoire regarding thinking at each stage of comparison of data sets. They also provide a transparent way to record the process of your analysis. Memos often form the basis of theory construction and can take any shape or form that suits you (Charmaz, 2014).

Initial and Focused Coding

Different versions of grounded theory employ different specific coding strategies. Charmaz (2014) employs a flexible structure that may be of use to the beginning researcher in grounded theory, differentiating between *initial* codes and later *focused* codes. Your initial line-by-line analysis will probably provide you with hundreds of codes. Don't be dismayed. Through constant comparison, you will be able to see that many of them have a consistent theme, or flavour. One code may stand out as encapsulating a set of codes, or you may find that working through your thinking in memos allows you to capture the essence of what is being said in a different way. From this process your focused codes will emerge. Focused coding of your data using these codes then allows you to engage with it at a higher level, producing the categories and properties of your theory in the same way that comparing your initial coding built the foundation of your focused codes.

Theoretical Sampling

As each new piece of data is analysed and compared with previous sets of data, grounded theory researchers adapt their areas of focus and interest, as well as who they study, in order to pursue emergent/developing ideas. This purposeful and theory-led technique is called 'theoretical sampling' (Glaser and Strauss, 1967). This means that by following the ideas that seem to hold the most potential, the specifics of *who* and *what* is studied can change progressively over time. The aim of the process of collecting data is to create 'thick descriptions' (Geertz 1973) that not only describe, but have the power to explain. Therefore, the direction of analysis, who is recruited and sample size are not fixed, but instead are in service to theory development. For example, if the initial data suggests that people's experience varies because of a specific factor, or particular element of what is being studied turns out to be central to understanding the focus of the research, both sampling and the focus of data collection can be adapted.

Charmaz (2014) suggests that in the initial stages of coding and analysis a *homogenous* sample group can maximise potential for meaningful categories to emerge. Focussing in on areas of specific interest within this sample, including going back to participants to ask more about emerging ideas, and updating interview questions to explore these areas are valid parts of the initial stages of a theoretical sampling strategy. The properties of the categories that emerge from this process can be drawn out and made explicit by increasingly *heterogeneous* sampling. This can help to understand where categories endure, if they hold value, and how they change in relation to people with different experiences and in different situations. Gradually, following this process and the rules inherent in it, pursuing the ideas that arise from immersion in the data, a meaningful theory emerges.

Theoretical Saturation

Grounded theory researchers employ a criterion of 'theoretical saturation' in order to decide when to stop collecting and analysing data. Theoretical saturation means that the data is not yielding new information about the categories central to the theory being developed. It is important to understand that this does not mean that new data doesn't create new information (it always will), but rather that you have reached saturation regarding your categories when employing a heterogeneous sampling strategy, as described above (Charmaz, 2014). This means that new data has stopped providing more insight into the properties of your existing categories. Here, the matter of understanding the scope of your research comes into play. For example, what settings and population have you proposed to study? Are you aiming towards a 'substantive' theory with specific criteria relating to the area you have studied, or trying to establish a 'formal' theory of underlying mechanisms of social action, which can be applied in many settings (Glaser and Strauss, 1967)? Most grounded theory research will lead to substantive theories, at least initially, as a theory would need to be tested in many situations before approaching formal theory (Urquhart, 2019).

Activity
- Your research design should allow your analysis to flow easily, following the basic steps of the methodology you choose. Consider the following elements before submitting a CGT research proposal:
  - How can you give yourself enough room to follow points of theoretical interest as they emerge and engage in theoretical sampling?
  - Are there multiple data sources you could use?
  - What chances will you have to go back to participants in order to clarify and expand on points of theoretical interest?
  - How else will you engage participants (including but not limited to member-checking)?
  - How will you engage in reflexive thinking about your role in the research?

▶ **Example**

Recruitment

In my research I chose my co-researchers based on a theoretical sampling strategy. I followed Glaser and Strauss' (1967) advice to use sampling homogeneity at the start of the research process in order to form and understand tentative categories and use sampling heterogeneity later in the process to test theoretical saturation and contextualise emergent theorising. This included considering diversity regarding a number of demographic factors, for example race, gender and age, but also length of time attending HVNGs and differences in the voice-hearing experience and the actual group attended.

My criteria for choosing co-researchers were that they identified as people who hear voices and had attended at least two sessions of a hearing voices group that was peer-led (facilitated by people with lived experience of hearing voices) and was affiliated with/ listed by the English Hearing Voices Network. I did not apply any further selection criteria regarding diagnosis, history of using mental health services, positive/negative experiences with voices and so on, although I did include these questions in my interviews. This was because I wanted to be able to follow theoretical sampling across the full range of people who might attend peer-led HVNGs. I aimed to recruit participants in a variety of ways. I found, however, that all of my interviewees came forward following personal contact and my conversations with groups during my exploratory visits.

Initial coding

Initially, I coded line-by-line for the first four interviews and first group session transcript, in order to create initial codes (Charmaz, 2014). I also wrote memo-like notes next to my codes. I started this practice after reading Glaser and Strauss' (1967, p.108) recommendation to 'write memos on, as well as code, the copy of one's field notes'. Conducting initial coding in this way produced a lot of writing about the data and helped me to think about and develop my focused codes. At this stage I was not concerned with the large number of codes I generated. I was more concerned with coding for process and social action (Blumer, 1969) through use of gerunds, as per grounded theory methodology (Charmaz, 2014; Creswell, 2007). I was interested in the change mechanisms and outcomes in peer-led HVNGs, as experienced by the groups' participants. Here is a section of an interview discussing one of my co-researcher's early experiences in the group she attended, along with my initial line-by-line coding (◘ Table 6.1).

During this stage in the analysis, I started writing memos regarding my coding and group observations, as well as keeping field notes on the observations that I did not tape. Memoing allowed me to keep a higher-level record of my thinking and advance my theorising. For example, a short memo on the section above highlighted my thinking on the experience of 'feeling normal' (which had already become a repeating theme in the data) and its relationship to the other codes from the section that represented core processes in the groups (◘ Figure 6.1):

At this point of coding the data, I was particularly interested in how the social processes impacted on the meanings that people in the group held about themselves, as well as the voice-hearing experience, as this seemed to be a major part of the impact of the group. It seemed like the actions of the group (opening up, sharing similar experiences) prompted different ways of viewing oneself both as a voice-hearer (feeling normal) and in relation to others (belonging, solidarity, etc.). This early theorising became the basis for developing some of my focused codes and elements of my final theory.

■ **Table 6.1**   Initial line-by-line coding

Interview text	Initial codes
I just felt - it was- it was a safe haven. I felt I belonged. I felt - I was sitting there and people was talking and I'd think, 'I get it, I get it, and these people are gonna get *me*'.	Feeling safe Belonging Feeling solidarity through sharing similar experiences
And, did that change the way you see yourself at all and understand yourself?	
Yeah, as I'm *normal* in it, this group. I'm normal in that group, yeah. I hate using that word because I don't think any of us are normal, but on entering that door, I'm no longer mad - or we're a mad bunch. It's either way you look at it is-, yeah - and that's what I like. Yeah.	Feeling normal Rejecting constrictive norms No longer feeling mad Identifying with others in the group Subjectivising 'madness'
Yeah, yeah, yeah.	
And, I've sat there, I've cried, I've screamed. I don't know, I've sobbed. I've opened my heart up. I've - yeah, it's - and there's always at least eight people, nine people to give me the advice, 'yeah, I've been there, I've done that. Let's try this. Let's try that'.	Expressing emotions Opening up Having a consistent source of support Sharing similar experiences Receiving advice

Memo: feeling normal (all interviews)

Feeling normal is a reoccurring and important theme (see memos on stigma, and other social impacts of the voice-hearing experience for context).

The link between *belonging, solidarity, opening up, sharing similar experiences* and feeling normal is clear. Is feeling normal the outcome of these?

Feeling normal seems to be the internal perception of self that is changed by the social interaction in the group. The *social* element of identity is solidarity/*belonging*. The external *actions are sharing similar experiences* and opening up emotionally.

Subjectivising 'madness' is part of feeling normal. It's rejecting that the label 'mad' is objective

■ **Fig. 6.1**   Memo on the intial code 'feeling normal'

Focused coding

As my coding advanced I used incident coding (generating codes for whole sections of data dealing with a specific incident) as well as line-by-line coding. I developed my codes through constant comparison of different sections of the data, slowly refining the line-by-line codes and incident codes I had developed in different sections of interviews and group sessions. Through this ongoing, iterative and gradual process, which I recorded and aided via extensive memo writing, I was able to increase the level of abstraction and analytic power of my codes over time in order to develop a set of focused codes. I then re-coded my data using the focused codes I had developed, continuing to refine these codes into the *categories* and *properties* of my theory through ongoing constant comparison (Charmaz, 2014).

To illustrate part of this process, I provide some examples below of sections of transcripts from a number of interviews that helped me during the process of comparing my incident coding to develop the focused code 'making links', which I used as a code for the meaningful links people made about their voices as a result of attending HVNGs. These included understanding that their voices did not have physical bodies, that their voices spoke in metaphors, that voices related to the past, and other personally meaningful understandings:

Interview 2

I've understood that the voices aren't real. Like although I believe them and they feel real, I've realised that they're not real. They can't hurt me unless I hurt myself. So they have no body – they're just a voice.

Interview 4

A: You sit down [in the group] and listen - and they listen to me and I listen to them. And this time I understood the meaning of voices - [that they are] not real!

B: So before you came to the group -.

A: - I thought they were real people.

B: You thought they were real people?

A: Yeah. Yeah. I thought they were real people. I thought they were very, very real people.

Interview 6

A: I often get told by my voices a lot to kill myself, go and harm myself, and I'm not worthy, but [group facilitator] has turned around and said, 'Turn that negative into the positive and look at it. When they're telling you to kill yourself, no; it's time to change. Change something about yourself. Look at something different. Go and have a haircut. Go and do something different!'

B: A symbolic death?

A: Yeah, yeah, yeah.

Interview 8

You can develop insight in yourself, and sometimes, you can instil it in other people as well... Because I think [the voices] are, um, metaphorical and symbolic in, in, some senses. But I feel it's the mind protecting itself, by throwing up these voices which you listen to, and in that way, you're not listening to the pain that's in your heart.

If you're under stress, the triggers come out, and [the voices] will instigate hell with you, absolute hell, but I take that back to my past where I was in a hellish family. So, to me, it was - it was at the age of 22, 23 - it was quite clear to me that my upbringing was responsible for the way I feel now. And, I don't think I would have got that without the hearing voices group.

While each of these sections of transcript had a number of codes attributed to it from my initial coding at earlier stages (often describing the type of insights people related as a result of the groups), I was primarily interested at this point in identifying the key mechanisms of change in the group. Therefore, I developed 'making links' as a high-level focused code that could describe the *process* of change, regardless of the content of what was understood. Coding for process in this way helped me uncover the key elements of my final theory about the impact of the groups. ◄

Theory creation

Grounded theory studies in psychological research often present more than one category or main idea, while in other fields one category can take central importance. Whatever shape your theory takes, it should offer meaningful explanations that provide useful insight into the subject and fit the situation being researched (Glaser and Strauss, 1967). The main body of your findings should include a detailed exploration of the categories and properties that make up the theory being presented. This presentation should illustrate how the theory is grounded in the data, with relevant examples. Relationships between categories should be examined. The scope of the theory, including whether it is a 'substantive' theory or 'formal' theory (Glaser and Strauss, 1967) should also be mentioned. In the discussion section, your thinking around the theory should be made clear, as well as it's implications in relation to other research and the wider field of enquiry.

A theory of course, is more than a series of codes, categories and properties. It should aim towards explanatory power. In order to make this step, a final process of 'theoretical sorting' is helpful (Charmaz, 2014). This is a process of thinking about how the categories of your analysis fit together and reviewing your memos, in order to refine and develop your theory. Diagramming can also be helpful at this stage of theory construction and a graphical representation of relationships between categories and properties can clarify the key processes in your theory (Charmaz, 2014).

Considering the situatedness of researcher knowledge (Mruk and Mey, 2019), engaging participants in this process of theory construction (as well as at all stages) increases the trustworthiness of your research and is a common strategy employed to meet quality criteria in qualitative research (Charmaz, 2014).This can be a natural extension of discussions that took place during data collection, or could take the form of feedback on the initial versions of your theory. This kind of member checking (discussing emergent analysis with people who have taken part in the research) helps to ensure that people who took part have had their views accurately reflected in the final product, as well as have some ownership of the research (Charmaz, 2014). In research, the power differentials between the voice of the professional and those of the participats can be significant, so there is often an ethical, as well as methodological reason for this strategy.

▶ Example

Theory construction and member checking

After the coding described above, I went through a final stage of theoretical sorting and diagramming to determine the relationship between the final properties and categories of my theory. The categories of my theory were the broad outcomes that people spoke about as a result of being in the group. For the purposes of my theory, the core properties that I highlighted were the change mechanisms that led to these outcomes. In terms of the examples above, I theorised that the properties 'making links', 'normalising' (a later version of my initial code 'feeling normal') and 'contextualisation' (the process of contextualising one's own voice-hearing experiences in relation to those of others in the group) were all core processes of growth and emancipation in peer-led HVNGs that led to a fundamental shift in the way that voice-hearers understood their voices and the voice-hearing experience (my category 'understanding voices differently'). ◘ Figure 6.2 shows the mutual relationship between these processes.

During these final stages I also engaged in member-checking, going back to my co-researchers in the HVNGs to refine theoretical points and ensure that my interpretation of the data fit their lived experience. I felt that it was important to allow people as much input as they wanted, not just in co-creating the initial data and knowledge with me, but also the final product. In this sense, I viewed my member-checking as an emancipatory strategy, as well as a way to increase the credibility of my research (Harper and Cole, 2012).

◘ Figure 6.3 shows one of the final graphical representations I presented to illustrate my theory, outlining the relationship between the outcomes of attending the peer-led HVNGs I studied (my main categories from the analysis) and properties of these categories (processes and mechanisms of change that lead to these outcomes). In this diagram 'understanding voices differently' and the properties I have discussed are placed within the larger picture of outcomes and change processes that emerged from the data. In the findings and discussion sections of my research, I discussed the relationship between these processes and their link to existing theory. In this way I presented a theory that encompasses meaningful predictions and ideas about the impact of peer-led HVNGs, grounded in the data that emerged from my discussions with voice-hearers about their own experience and my direct observation of the groups in action. ◄

◘ **Fig. 6.2** 'Making links' etc. as a property of the category 'understanding voices differently'

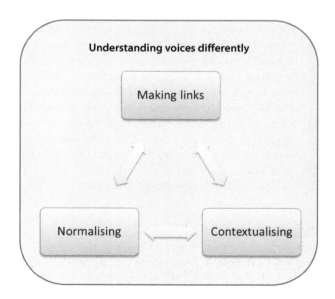

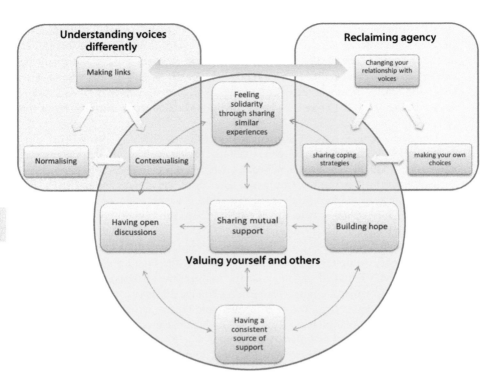

◘ Fig. 6.3   A graphical representation of change processes in peer-led HVNGs

Summary

In this ► chapter I have provided a short introduction to some of the main points of CGT, including some of its philosophical background and history, the basic elements of CGT data collection and analysis, and its role in qualitative research. In counselling and psychotherapy research, the worldview, meanings and actions of the people we study are of central concern. CGT provides a methodology for placing these elements at the forefront of theory development while presenting a clear and detailed approach to creating theory that is grounded in data. CGT also encourages reflexivity in relation to the person of the researcher and the co-constructed nature of research. These are elegant and useful elements of the methodology in a field where theory is so central to practice and yet where the process of its creation is often left implicit. I hope that this chapter will prompt you to read more and consider using CGT to develop theories of your own.

References

Belgrave, L., & Seide, K. (2019). Coding for grounded theory. In M. Bryant & K. Charmaz (Eds.), *The SAGE Handbook of Current Developments in Grounded Theory* (pp. 167–185). London: SAGE Publications.

Blumer, H. (1969). *Symbolic interactionism: Perspective and method.* New Jersey: Prentice Hall.

Boyle, M. (2013). The persistence of medicalisation: is the presentation of alternatives part of the problem? In S. Coles, S. Keenan, & B. Diamond (Eds.), *Madness contested: Power and practice* (pp. 3–22). Ross-on-Wye: PCCS Books.

Bryant, A., & Charmaz, K. (2007). Grounded theory in historical perspective: an epistemological account. In A. Bryant & K. Charmaz (Eds.), *The SAGE handbook of grounded theory* (pp. 31–57). London: SAGE Publications.

Calton, T., Cheetham, A., D'Silva, K., & Glazebrook, C. (2009). International schizophrenia research and the concept of patient-centeredness: an analysis over two decades. *International Journal of Social Psychiatry., 55*(2), 157–169.

Charmaz, K. (2014). *Constructing grounded theory*. London: Sage.

Clarke, A. E. (2005). *Situational analysis: Grounded theory after the postmodern turn*. Thousand Oaks, C.A.: Sage.

Coles, S. (2013). Meaning, madness and marginalisation. In S. Coles, S. Keenan, & B. Diamond (Eds.), *Madness contested: Power and practice* (pp. 42–55). Ross-on-Wye: PCCS Books.

Corstens, D., Longden, E., McCarthy-Jones, S., Waddingham, R., & Thomas, N. (2014). Emerging perspectives from the hearing voices movement: implications for research and practice. *Schizophrenia bulletin, 40*(Suppl 4), S285–S294.

Creswell, J. (2007). *Qualitative inquiry & research design* (2nd ed.). Thousand Oaks, California: SAGE Publications.

Dillon, J., & Hornstein, G. A. (2013). Hearing voices peer support groups: a powerful alternative for people in distress. *Psychosis, 5*(3), 286–295.

Dillon, J., & Longden, E. (2012). Hearing voices groups: creating safe spaces to share taboo experiences. In M. Romme & S. Escher (Eds.), *Psychosis as a personal crisis: An experience-based approach* (pp. 185–198). Hove: Routledge.

English Hearing Voices Network. (2018). *Hearing Voices Network: Hearing Voices Groups.* Available at: https://www.hearing-voices.org/hearing-voices-groups. (Accessed: 14th December, 2018).

Geertz, C. (1973). *The Interpretation of Cultures*. New York: Basic Books.

Glaser, B. G. (1978). *Theoretical sensitivity*. Mill Valley, C.A.: Sociology press.

Glaser, B. G. (1992). *Basics of grounded theory analysis: Emergence vs forcing*. Mill Valley, C.A.: Sociology Press.

Glaser, B. G., & Strauss, A. L. (1967). *The discovery of grounded theory: Strategies for qualitative research*. London: AldineTransaction.

Harper, M., & Cole, P. (2012). Member checking: can benefits be gained similar to group therapy? *The qualitative report, 17*(2), 510–517.

Hookway, C. (2012). *The pragmatic maxim: essays on Peirce and pragmatism*. Oxford: Oxford University Press.

Johnstone, L. (2012). Voice hearers are people with problems, not patients with illnesses. In M. A. J. Romme & S. Escher (Eds.), *Psychosis as a Personal Crisis* (pp. 27–36). Hove: Routledge.

Johnstone, L., with Boyle, M., Cromby, J., Dillon, J., Harper, D., Kinderman, P., Longden, E., Pilgrim, D., & Read, J. (2018). *The Power Threat Meaning Framework: Towards the identification of patterns in emotional distress, unusual experiences and troubled or troubling behaviour, as an alternative to functional psychiatric diagnosis*. Leicester: British Psychological Society.

Langley, E. (2020). 'In the Same Boat, Helping Each Other': a Grounded Theory of Growth and Emancipation in Peer-Led Hearing Voices Groups. (D.C.Psych.thesis, Middlesex University/ Metanoia Institute, London, UK.) Retrieved from https://eprints.mdx.ac.uk/

Longden, E., Corstens, D. & Dillon, J. (2013). Recovery, discovery and revolution: The work of inter-voice and the hearing voices movement. In S. Coles, S. Keenan & B. Diamond, (Eds.) *Madness contested: Power and practice* (pp. 161-180). Ross-on-Wye: PCCS Books.

Mead, G. H. (2015). *Mind, self, and society: The definitive edition*. Chicago: University of Chicago Press.

Mruck, K. & Mey, G. (2019). Grounded theory methodology and self-reflexivity in the qualitative research process. In A. Bryant, & K. Charmaz. (Eds.) *The SAGE Handbook of Current Developments in Grounded Theory* (pp. 470-496). London: SAGE Publications Ltd

Romme, M., & Escher, S. (1993). The new approach: A Dutch experiment. In M. Romme & S. Escher (Eds.), *Accepting voices* (pp. 11–27). London: MIND publications.

Romme, M., & Escher, S. (2000). *Making sense of voices: a guide for mental health professionals working with voice-hearers. (Includes interview supplement)*. London: Mind Publications.

Romme, M., Escher, S., Dillon, J., Corstens, D., & Morris, M. (2009). *Living with voices: Fifty stories of recovery*. PCCS: Ross-on-Wye.

Romme, M., & Morris, M. (2007). The harmful concept of schizophrenia. *Mental Health Nursing, 27*(2), 8–12.

Romme, M., & Morris, M. (2013). The recovery process with hearing voices: accepting as well as exploring their emotional background through a supported process. *Psychosis, 5*(3), 259–269.

Slade, M. (2009). *Personal recovery and mental illness: A guide for mental health professionals*. Cambridge: Cambridge University Press.

Strauss, A., & Corbin, J. (1994). Grounded theory methodology: An overview. In N. K. Denzin & Y. S. Lincoln (Eds.), *Handbook of qualitative research* (pp. 273–285). Thousand Oaks, CA: Sage Publications.

Strauss, A., & Corbin, J. (1998). *Basics of qualitative research: Procedures and techniques for developing grounded theory*. Thousand Oaks, CA: Sage Publications.

Strawbridge, S., & Woolfe, R. (2003). Counselling psychology in context. In R. Woolfe, W. Dryden, & S. Strawbridge (Eds.), *Handbook of counselling psychology* (pp. 3–32). Sage: London.

Strübing, J. (2007). Research as pragmatic problem-solving: the pragmatist roots of empirically-grounded theorizing. In A. Bryant., & K. Charmaz, *The SAGE handbook of grounded theory* (pp. 580-601). London: SAGE Publications.

Strübing, J. (2019). The pragmatism of Anselm L. Strauss: linking theory and method. In A. Bryant & K. Charmaz (Eds.), *The SAGE Handbook of Current Developments in Grounded Theory* (pp. 51–67). London: SAGE Publications Ltd.

Urquhart, C. (2019). Grounded theory's best kept secret: the ability to build theory. In A. Bryant, & K. Charmaz. (Eds.) *The SAGE Handbook of Current Developments in Grounded Theory* (pp. 89–106). London: SAGE Publications Ltd

Woods, A. (2013). The voice-hearer. *Journal of Mental Health, 22*(3), 263–270.

Woolfe, R. (2012). Risorgimento: A history of counselling psychology in Britain. *Counselling Psychology Review, 27*(4), 72–78.

Ethical Research? Examining Knotty, Moment-to-Moment Challenges Throughout the Research Process

Linda Finlay

Contents

© The Author(s) 2020
S. Bager-Charleson, A. McBeath (eds.),
Enjoying Research in Counselling and Psychotherapy,
https://doi.org/10.1007/978-3-030-55127-8_7

🔵 Learning Goals

After reading this chapter, you should be able to:

- Describe the ethical requirements arising in the planning and contracting phase of research, including managing confidentiality/anonymity and informed consent;
- Critically analyse the challenges posed by emotional intensity and power relations during data collection;
- Appreciate the need for researchers to attend to their own self-care;
- Discuss the ethical value of participant validation (or member checking) to 'prove' the validity of the research;
- List at least four potential risks of doing research on clients' experiences of therapy;
- Explain how researchers can take responsibility for their research and ensure the research has integrity.

Knotty Situations in Research

There are several kinds of knotty situations we regularly experience once we dig below the surface of ethics.

> ► Example
>
> » Peter has volunteered to be a participant in Vineeta's phenomenological study of the lived experience of being adopted. As the interview progresses he starts to sob as issues of feeling abandoned and not belonging surface. Vineeta feels torn. Their conversation has moved into an area which would add valuable dimensions to her data but she also recognises how Peter's welfare is paramount.

How should this researcher handle the dilemma confronting her: that the very act of collecting her research data makes Peter, her participant, dissolve into tears? At what point should the recorder be turned off or the interview ended? The researcher is caught in a balancing act in which the needs and integrity of the research become set against responding to Peter's needs. Was she aware that he might become distressed and does she have the right to use this situation for her own research ends? ◄

Professional guidelines on the ethical conduct of research are based on certain core principles: a concern to promote scientific integrity; an awareness of social responsibility; and respect for individuals' autonomy, privacy, values and dignity. To show a duty of care that maximises benefit and minimises risks or harm to individuals, researchers are asked to ensure confidentiality/anonymity and informed consent. Care is taken to brief and debrief participants, who are informed of their right to withdraw from the research if they so choose.

When we present our research, we lay claim to these guidelines and through them assert the ethical integrity of our work. In practice, however, every research encounter brings up context-specific ethical challenges. What may seem responsible, respectful and caring to one person may not to another. It depends. Negotiating an ethical path can often be tricky and compromises may need to be made (Finlay and Molano-

Fisher 2009). Ethics then can be understood as *ongoing reflexivity (critical self-awareness) of our research actions, thoughts and motivations* (Finlay 2019).

This chapter sketches some of the ethical tensions confronting us as researchers at each stage of a research project, drawing on different research examples. It starts by considering key ethical requirements of the pre-research planning stage. The next two sections explore the data collection and analysis phases. A final section looks at the challenges involved in writing up and disseminating the research. Most of the discussion relates especially to qualitative research given the unpredictable situations and complex dynamics usually involved. The aim is to get you thinking reflexively and ethically about the requirements of your own research....

Pre-research Phase

7

Research usually begins with a researcher's passionate concern to learn something more about a subject. Then comes the time-consuming planning process, where researchers work out how to operationalise the research. Often this involves a process of gaining 'official' ethics approval before any research can begin. There may even be the need to convince a formal independent Research Ethics Committee of the value and ethical rigour of the research.

But getting a proposal through an ethics approval process doesn't ensure that the research will be ethical. It's the ongoing *process* in which we engage that determines ethicality. Beyond procedures, it's about attending to the research context and relationship (Guillemin and Gillam 2004).

Perhaps the biggest challenge is drawing up the research agreement we use when meeting prospective participants. Often this takes the form of a written contract participants are asked to sign and date if they agree to participate in the research. As with contracting for counselling/psychotherapy, there are many issues to consider, including:

- Aims of the project
- Criteria for inclusion
- Informed consent (including 'process consent')
- Participant–*and researcher*–safety/risk
- Confidentiality and anonymity (including limits)
- How participants will be briefed, debriefed and/or given support if needed
- Division of labour and responsibilities of both researcher and participant (including involvement in subsequent research phases)
- Participant's right to withdraw from the study (including date beyond which they cannot withdraw)
- Storage and disposal of participant information and data (and General Data Protection Regulation [GDPR]).

A delicate balancing act is involved as we seek to set boundaries and establish mutual trust. What will work for one person or project may not be suitable in other situations. Two particularly knotty areas are *confidentiality/anonymity* and *informed consent*.

Confidentiality/Anonymity

As with confidentiality in therapy, a key ethical principle of research is that data will be treated respectfully, with attention paid to confidentiality, anonymity and data protection. Yet complications can arise, and there may be times when legal and safeguarding issues emerge.

More commonly, random details revealed in findings might mean participants can be identified. Below, two researchers discuss how they approached the ethical issues involved in conducting their study:

» Because of the highly sensitive nature of the information disclosed during the interviews special precautions were adopted. The possibility, however remote, that the therapists and the clients they discussed in their vignettes could be identified was a particular concern. All demographic and descriptive information about therapists was minimized and kept at a group level. In order to protect the participants' privacy, pseudonyms were used and any information that would make them susceptible to identification was omitted or deliberately made vague. (Thériault and Gazzola 2006, p.317)

In some situations, we might go beyond simply keeping details vague to changing participants' demographic details to further camouflage their identity. For example, I might say my participant lives in England when they live in Scotland; or I might change the sex or profession of the participant. While lying is unethical, concealing the truth may at times be necessary to preserve a participant's anonymity.

In legal terms, the removal of identifying information means that the data is no longer considered 'personal' and as such does not fall under the GDPR. However, it may not always be possible to fully de-identify data, and participants should be informed of how their data will be anonymised[1] so that they can make an informed decision about consent for its storage and sharing (for further information about the GDPR, see the document from the British Psychological Society (2018): *Data Protection Regulation: Guidance for researchers*).

The researchers above used pseudonyms, the most common way of de-identifying data. However, I've done some research where participants *wanted* their contribution acknowledged. Mindful of this, I now always ask participants to choose the name they wish to go by. Although participants can also be allocated numbers, I regard letting them choose a name more as humanising.

One final tip for data protection is 'data minimisation': keeping the details about personal data to a minimum. Not every survey or research study needs to collect data about participants' age, sexuality or ethnicity.

---

1 Legally speaking, data is only 'anonymised' when individuals can no longer be identified. A dataset that has identifying information removed but which is linked to a separate file (including consent forms) is not strictly anonymised (and hence it is often called 'pseudonymised').

Informed Consent

Informed consent in research means ensuring that participants know about their rights and understand what is expected of them. However, in qualitative research we rarely know in advance how the exploration will proceed and what will be 'unearthed'. In this situation, how can a participant give 'informed consent'?

This is where ethical, reflexive practice becomes imperative. We need to involve participants in an ongoing *consent process* in which we keep checking to see if they are okay with how the research is going and *negotiate* how best to proceed–relationally. Just as we do in therapy, we must regularly review the research agreement and check that the participant is prepared to continue.

Often researchers give participants the option of withdrawing from the research after they've had a chance to think about their contribution. It's good practice to make it clear to participants at the outset the date or stage after which they cannot withdraw. I know of a student whose participant asked to be withdrawn after she had handed in her project, creating considerable turmoil for all.

The examples below demonstrate the need to be careful when obtaining consent. The first is a reflexive dialogue between Kim Etherington (2007) and two co-researchers/participants who were her ex-clients.

► Example

Narrative inquiry and ethics

You will have read parts of this in-depth discussion in ► Chap. 5 where Etherington expands on this research. The following is a continuation from this relational negotiation of interest (Etherington 2007).

» Kim: The process of doing this may very well open up things again, and I wonder what that would be like for you…

– Stephen: I feel like I'm ready for that, I think I could cope with that now – at a distance. I could deal with that now.

Kim: How about you Mike?

Mike: [Pause] Mmm. Yes, I think so. I think I've demonstrated by recent events [his separation from his wife] that I can mobilize support if I need to.

Kim: But here we are now, moving into a different relationship, when I'm not your counselor. What would that mean if anything did come up? What might be your expectations of me if you got very distressed about something that was happening as part of the research process? I suppose my concern is – that if you needed counseling – I don't think it would be appropriate for me to offer that.

Stephen: That would be OK.

Kim [to Stephen]: But I am also aware that you have financial limitations that would make it hard for you to get counseling elsewhere. I just wondered if you had thought about that…There are other agencies where you can go for low-fee or reduced-fee counseling… That's not to say that I didn't expect this to be therapeutic, or, that I'm not going to be able to be supportive as a researcher. (pp. 606–607). ◄

The second example is from Morrow's (2006) feminist collaborative research with sexually abused women.

► **Example**

Morrow (2006) refers to how the process of gaining consent circumvented her control over data collection:

» I had originally planned to meet for a short time with each interviewee to explain the project, get acquainted, explain and have participants sign the informed consent form and schedule our longer interview. I had explained this expectation to the first participant, Paula, when we first made telephone contact. However, after we had finished the informed consent process and I pulled out my calendar to schedule our interview appointment, she objected, saying, 'I thought we were going to do the interview now. I'm ready to talk!' I consented and, feeling a little panicky, searched for my interview guide. Unable to find it, I finally responded,

'Well, uh, er, um. Tell me, as much as you are comfortable sharing with me right now, um, what happened to you when you were sexually abused.' This kind of question, both very personal and potentially disturbing for a participant, is not the kind of question with which I would normally begin an interview, but Paula's desire to tell her story and my own personal style (I've been described as an 'earth mother' who elicits trust very early in a relationship) converged to make the question both appropriate and effective (p.153).

Here, Morrow indicates that she placed her ethical concern for her co-researchers above her research strategy. The significant step demanded of the relationally minded researcher is to release control, or rather take "control in a new humanistic sense by being clearly conscious of the choice of letting the informant have a voice" and to lay the ground for an open, authentic, mutual interaction (Kruger 2007). ◄

Having gained ethical approval for a project, worked satisfactorily with official gatekeepers and then negotiated the appropriate consent, some researchers are content that they've gone through the required ethics hoops. However, ethics doesn't stop here. An ethical sensibility is needed at *every* stage of research.

Reflection

Reflect on the risks and benefits that collecting data online offers compared to face-to-face contact.

For relatively low-risk projects, such as an online survey, being able to collect data online could prove a highly efficient and effective route. Extra care, however, would need to be taken for higher-risk projects. Interviewing someone using a *video conferencing* platform about their experience of trauma could prove too challenging to conduct online.

In your reflection think about the difficulties of ensuring adequate care both during the interview and post-interview. Consider, too, the challenges of the possible *disinhibition effect* which is known to occur when working using online media. Unless well handled, it can lead to over-disclosure and much more emotionally intense material surfacing than had been intended. Much depends on the particular individuals involved and their circumstances and context.

Data Collection Phase

Professionally orientated research frequently uses data on sensitive areas of human experience: health, life experience and personal disclosure. With qualitative research, we might also aim to 'witness' and/or 'give voice' to our participants' experiences. We need to be mindful that research which encourages participants to reflect on themselves and the social world around them may evoke strong emotional responses. In such a context, risk assessment is complicated, and questions arise regarding *emotional intensity* and unequal *power* relationships.

Emotional Intensity

Emotional intensity in the data collection phase raises challenging issues. At what point should a participant be deemed 'at risk'? If a participant becomes irritated or offended, or feels uncomfortable while doing a survey, does that constitute 'harm'? If a person grows upset during an interview, is that a problem? Should researchers avoid tackling potentially emotive topics (something that goes against the very grain of our research curiosity)? And what if participants actually welcome the opportunity to talk at a deep, personal level and be 'seen'? For them, it's possible that getting upset may be a relief rather than a 'problem'; it may even be therapeutic. How we manage emotional intensity goes to the heart of negotiated ethics.

I collaborated with my friend/colleague Pat about her lived experience of receiving a cochlear implant (Finlay and Molano-Fisher 2008). I not only heard a story about new hearing and well-being, I also saw close-up her struggle with deafness and disability. Profoundly deaf for much of her life, after her implant Pat found herself in a surreal, alien world filled with hyper-noise. Over the course of the following year her life was turned upside down. She slowly learned new ways to connect with her world, but at a psychological and social level her relationships with others changed and part of her felt more disconnected than before. Loss of confidence, shame, alienation and isolation were some of the emotional themes which surfaced repeatedly. In the following extract from our interview, Pat expresses embarrassment about her disability:

» Pat: My sense of confidence is battered…How many mistakes have I made in my work and interactions? I cringe when I think about it.

The fact that our research tapped sensitive emotions made me worry whether our project of probing her lived world was forcing Pat to face her pain more than she would have otherwise. At times Pat seemed angry; her vulnerability was highlighted, and we had to work through that (Finlay and Molano-Fisher 2009).

In other words, there are no clear-cut answers about what level of disclosure or degree of restraint is desirable in relational research. Negotiations can only take place within the *relationship*, always with awareness of the power we wield as researchers.

The solution, says Krüger (2007), "lies within the relation itself". In a sense the researcher needs to be "aware of the obligation to stay in the impasse, and at the same time to situate the problem where it belongs: in the relationship". Here Kruger comes close to taking a therapeutic approach, highlighting the ethical value of working dialogically.

Activity
- Consider the ethical examples referred to so far with your own research in mind: What are the pros and cons about giving opportunities for participants to change their minds? How might this be negotiated from the start to fit in with your study? Is there a way you can leave your participants better off from taking part in your research?

The grappling with ethical questions does not only apply to qualitative research.
- Consider the following guidelines from the British Psychological Society: "Following an experiment in which negative mood was induced, it would be ethical to induce a happy mood state before the participant leaves the experimental setting" (p.26)
  ▶ https://www.bps.org.uk/sites/bps.org.uk/files/Policy/Policy%20-%20Files/ BPS%20Code%20of%20Human%20Research%20Ethics.pdf)
  Reflect on three things you could do to ensure that, following data collection, your participants are left feeling 'grounded and okay' if not exactly 'happy'.

Power

Research asks people "to take part in, or undergo, procedures that they have not actively sought out or requested, and that are not intended solely or even primarily for their direct benefit" (Guillemin and Gillam 2004, p. 271). More than this, research is inherently instrumental and uses participants for researcher benefit. Is there a way this unequal power relationship can be owned and managed with ethical sensibilities to the fore?

The examples above in this section all implicitly grapple with the power dimension inherent in data collection. We don't even need to think in extremes of manipulation and coercion. Researcher instrumentality is exposed at a simple level when (metaphorically speaking) we don the 'white coat' of the scientist and ask probing, intrusive, private questions while not disclosing ourselves. At a subtler level, the researcher is the one who uses 'expert' knowledge/techniques (such as using empathetic responses and reflecting back) to both open up participants and close them down again. Alert to opportunities to obtain data, we may push hungrily ahead instead of attending to participants' needs. A key question to ask of your research is: "Whose interests are being served?" (Finlay and Ballinger 2006).

However, as we know from our therapy work, power is not clear-cut or one-way, with researchers having power and participants being powerless. Instead, there's a complex interplay of structural dimensions: social position, race, gender and ethnicity. A young black female novice researcher-student may not feel any researcher power and authority when interviewing an older, white, male professor who is being dismissive of her research efforts. Power is layered, comes in different guises and is enacted between people in particular contexts. We need to be alert to how different types of power cross-cut each other and impact our research.

► Example

In the following example, Hunt (1989) discusses how her status as an unwanted female outsider studying police organisations raised some unexpected gender issues:

» Positive oedipal wishes...appeared mobilized in the fieldwork... The resultant anxieties were increased because of the proportion of men to women in the police organization and the way in which policemen sexualized so many encounters...The fact that I knew more about their work world than their wives also may have heightened anxiety because it implied closeness to subjects. By partly defeminizing myself...I avoided a conflictual oedipal victory. (p.40).

Here, Hunt 'defeminized' herself to circumvent being sexualised. This seems to be an attempt to minimise her impact on the participants' lives, but it may also have increased her authority. In other situations, we might want to do more to equalise our relationship. However, it is also not enough for researchers to relinquish some of their 'power' in favour of their participants. Efforts to 'empower' our participants may be misplaced, since we're still claiming power to control access to power. Instead, it's important to keep the communication channels open; be reflexive, acknowledge any emotional and political *tensions* arising from different social positions, and (where relevant) deconstruct the "researcher's authority" (Hertz 1997). ◄

Personally, I believe that Proctor's (2002) reasoning about our use of power as therapists can equally be applied to research:

» The ethical challenge in psychotherapy is to minimise the therapist's potential to violate the other through therapy...this is the potential violence of theory, authority, expertise and technology to override the client's contribution to their life narrative (p.60).

At its best, data collection can be both strategic *and* sensitively respectful. Here, the power within it emerges as an ongoing, mutual, interactive relationship where individuals exert degrees of agency, choice and control. As with therapy, we attempt a balancing act: we seek to enable and facilitate disclosure while at the same time intervening to protect our participants from too much exposure. Such "dialectical oppositions" (Ellis 2007, pp.20–21) involve moving back and forth between expression and protection, between disclosure and restraint (Bochner 1984). More than this, we need to be sensitive and recognise the importance of the relational context. Ellis (2007) sums this up well:

» Relational ethics requires [therapists]... to act from our hearts and minds, acknowledge our interpersonal bonds to others, and take responsibility for actions and their consequences. (p.3).

Data Analysis Phase

The analytical phase of research raises ethical issues relating to the *integrity* of the research. Another question which confronts (particularly qualitative) researchers is the extent to which participants can/should be involved in producing, or at least validating, the findings. The *respective roles* of researcher and participant may need to be carefully negotiated, and careful thought needs to be given to the degree of participant involvement in *validating* results. The researcher also needs to attend to their own *self-care*.

Research Integrity

Research integrity refers to the moral character of the research. Has it been done in a way that allows others to have trust and confidence in the methods and findings, and in subsequent publications? Is there a commitment to intellectual honesty and regard for the scientific record? Does the researcher take personal responsibility for their research actions? Such values are important for both qualitative and quantitative research, despite varying criteria for what makes a study 'trustworthy'. With *qualitative* research, trustworthiness is often displayed by methodological transparency and reflexivity (i.e. critical self-awareness). With *quantitative* research, trustworthiness is equated with scientific rigour and the use of both valid measurement tools and appropriate statistical tests. In all research there is a need for any interpretations to be set in context.

A key issue for quantitative researchers is the degree to which data might be falsified and/or subsequent analysis manipulated. (There is some truth to the phrase attributed to the British prime minister Benjamin Disraeli: "There are three kinds of lies: lies, damned lies, and statistics.") The trouble comes when researchers, keen to promote a position, 'massage their data' by taking out rogue or disconfirming bits so that the results fit their hypothesis or argument. They also might misrepresent their research by omitting key elements (e.g. an insufficiently representative sample). Or they might mislead by presenting results divorced from the larger context in which sense can be made of them.

Distortion can also occur at the very start of the research process, when researchers seeking an empirical rationale for their proposal assert that 'little or no research exists in the field' when a closer look says otherwise. Here, they are disrespectfully misrepresenting the work of others in order to shine a brighter light on their own.

Then there are those rarer cases of outright dishonesty and fraud where spurious results are fabricated. A colleague once told me about a student of hers who had produced some suspicious survey results. Initially, the student's sample contained only 25 participants, which did not offer statistically meaningful results. After just two days the number of participants had tripled. The tutor was concerned to see that all the new data seemed to say implausibly similar things, all supportive of the student's hypothesis, and that they all emanated from the same IP address.

A few high-profile historical cases of research fraud have been unearthed. In the field of educational psychology, Cyril Burt's case was particularly grave. He both manipulated and fabricated the research data in his study of twins to enable him to confirm his theory of the heritability of intelligence. It turns out that many of his twins did not exist; nor did some of the research collaborators he talked about.

Deception–at whatever level–within psychological research occurs with the pressure to publish, both to gain personal/professional status and to please stakeholders, putting grant money to good use (Lilienfeld 2017). Given these pressures, there is an ever-present need for care and critical awareness, alongside continued vigilance and monitoring of our research processes.

Negotiating Respective Roles

7

Professionally orientated researchers often confront the question of how transparent they should be with participants about research findings. To some extent this depends on the methodology involved. With qualitative discourse analysis, for instance, participants are unlikely to get involved given its highly technical nature. Discursive methods tend to "utilise counter-intuitive, and possibly impenetrable, understandings of subjectivity which participants may reject", not least because the participant's sense of lived experience can be undermined (Madill 2009, p.20). While these researchers usually carry out their analysis on their own, the process of identifying and naming discourses still involves ethical, moral and political choices on the part of the analyst (Parker 1992). For this reason, discursive researchers are encouraged to be reflexive about how they position themselves and their participants within the social world.

In contrast, collaborative and participatory action forms of qualitative research rely on the process of iteratively taking evolving understandings back to participants. Halling et al. (1999) suggest a kind of collaborative approach where the analysis is conducted through group members' dialogue. Their dialogical phenomenological study of forgiveness saw them collaborate with a group of Masters' students, with positive results:

» Working in dialogue and comparing personal experiences and the interviews with each other allowed us to come to a rich, collective understanding of the process of forgiving another… Freedom infused the process with a spirit of exploration and discovery, and is evident through the group members' ability to be playful and imaginative with their interpretations. Trust provides the capacity to be genuinely receptive to what is new and different in the others' experiences. (1999, pp. 253, 261).

While Halling et al. are committed to the fullest possible collaboration with co-researchers, others involve their participants only to the extent that the latter *wish* to be involved. With Pat and the cochlear implant research (Finlay and Molano-Fisher 2008), for example, we put effort into managing a division of labour. We decided we were both responsible for co-creating Pat's narrative. But I wanted to engage a more in-depth existential phenomenological analysis, not least because I was due to present these findings (with Pat's consent) at a conference. However, Pat was in a different place. She was finding her new implant difficult to cope with and was not ready to engage further analysis. We had to set the research aside for a few months, which later required a delicate process of re-contracting/process consent. I had to gauge when to gently nudge Pat to engage once more (or perhaps to disengage fully while giving me authorial control). I also had to be prepared to end the research.

► Example

Below is an extract from my reflexive diary (Finlay and Molano-Fisher 2008) indicating the questions I was asking:

» There's the issue of control and who has it. How ethical/acceptable is it for me to lead, reassure, persuade, convince, and in the process take more control? I don't want to take Pat's sense of control away. Yet are there dangers in my being too passive? Have I got the energy for this? (LF diary).

Later Pat contacted me, and we exchanged emails:

» Pat: Hi Linda. I am ready again, sorry about long time, thanks for the space... couldn't handle the analysis. Felt I wanted to move on, not to dwell in the past...
   Linda: It's understandable you want to move on – totally understandable. Rest assured that you don't need to do any more with the analysis if you don't want to... Let me know how you want to proceed... I want to understand more what is scaring you if you feel able to talk...
   Pat: What scares me is that I don't want to face deafness, disability, implants anymore. ..I don't like that I cannot follow things like others do even with the implant. It scares me that I really like my silence and miss it...Even if I have progressed, I feel I will never feel 'normal' as I felt before because my bubble has been burst!! ...I am scared about what else I don't know will come in the analysis and I rather hide it and don't face it!...

Pat eventually agreed to me doing the analysis, but she wanted to see and comment on everything (claiming some editorial control). Pat didn't want it to become *my* research. My (somewhat disingenuous) response was to emphasise she had been the 'expert' in the data collection; now I was taking on that mantle for the analysis (Finlay and Molano-Fisher 2009). ◄

Participant Validation?

Many qualitative researchers embrace the idea of participant validation or member checking to 'prove' the validity of their research. Here, researchers refer their evolving analysis back to their participants for confirmation: when the participant agrees with the researcher's assessment, it is seen as strengthening the researcher's argument. Time and again as you read reports you will see researchers claiming their research is trustworthy because participants have affirmed the results.

Such assurance and confidence, however, may be misplaced. It needs to be remembered that participants have their own motives, needs and interests. They also have varying degrees of insight. Moreover, what may have been true for them at the time of the interview may no longer be the case. Their ability to put themselves back into the specific research context may well be compromised. For all these reasons, processes of participant validation need to be conducted carefully and with awareness of the complex conscious, unconscious and contingent dimensions which may lead a participant to support or refute any one analysis. (Of course, the researcher, too, is subject to their own complex conscious, unconscious and contingent elements, and hence the need for researcher reflexivity.) It also comes down to the epistemological assumptions of the study and whether it can be validated in this way. Member checking might be appropriate in a post-positivist, realist study; it is less meaningful for interpretive, relativist studies where meanings are more fluid and there isn't one 'truth' to affirm.

When I did my PhD research, it was suggested that I take my interview transcripts back to participants to check them and share my findings to gain their approval. In practice, both processes proved sticky and backfired. I learned an uncomfortable lesson–namely to *avoid engaging procedures on autopilot*.

Do participants *want* to see interview transcripts? After all, they've already given their time to the researcher. Are we requiring they spend more time reading the transcript? Also, re-visiting the interview via the transcript can be emotionally taxing. If a distressing subject was talked about, do the participants want to be reminded of it yet again? More than this, if you've ever seen a transcript, you'll know words often come across as jumbled, rambling, full of 'ums' and 'errs'. People often feel embarrassed when they realise how inarticulate they have been.

Of course, there are situations where a participant would value seeing the transcript. It may give them an opportunity to pick out bits they'd prefer to be removed. In one study I participated in, I asked to see the transcript, following which I requested that a passage be removed: I felt too exposed especially as the passage compromised my anonymity. The point is to offer the participant a choice.

► Example

When it comes to participants 'validating' analyses, further critical questions arise. If it's an interpretive study, then who holds the authorial control? When carrying out some case study research on the lived experience of early stage multiple sclerosis (MS) (Finlay 2003), I did take my emerging analysis back to my participant, Ann, but this was more about collaborative sharing than validation (Finlay and Langdridge 2007):

» As Ann was a physiotherapist, she had a reasonable understanding of the aims, process and intended outcomes of my case study research. This was important as it meant that her consent to take part in the research was properly informed... While she wanted an opportunity for discussion, she seemed content to hand authorial control to me...

Ann was particularly active on hearing my preliminary analysis of the interviews with her. She affirmed certain themes, suggesting I had captured her experience 'nicely'. At other points she suggested my analysis (particularly my metaphorical flourishes) needed to be 'toned down' as she didn't feel they adequately represented her ordinary, everyday experience. One notable example here was my initial use of an analogy: that of Ann situation being akin to 'living with an alien monster'. I rather liked this metaphor, regarding it as both punchy and poetic, and was reluctant to let it go. However, it was not something Ann could relate to. I therefore deleted all references to the monster while retaining (I ruefully acknowledge) some sense of the notion of alien infiltration.

In retrospect, I can see that it was useful to get Ann's feedback. For one thing, it helped me to better appreciate how Ann had, in fact, managed to reconnect with her 'disconnected' arm… While Ann gave me some feedback, I retained control of my analysis and writing. In the end it is I who was choosing where, when, what and how to publish the findings. And, in the end, these are my findings, my interpretations. I could have involved Ann much more collaboratively but chose not to. (pp. 194–195).

Comments

It could be argued that Ann's involvement in co-producing the findings strengthens the trustworthiness and ethical basis of this research. This is not the same as saying that Ann has validated this study thus ensuring its veracity. It's about acknowledging that findings emerge in a specific context. Another researcher, or a study undertaken at another time, could unfold a different story.

In his critical exploration of participant validation, Ashworth (1993) supports it on political-moral grounds but warns against taking participants' evaluations too seriously: after all, it may be in their interest to protect their 'socially presented selves'. As he notes, "Participant validation is flawed…, since the 'atmosphere of safety' that would allow the individual to lower his or her defences, cease 'presentation', and act in open candour (if this is possible), is hardly likely to be achieved in the research encounter" (Ashworth 1993, p.15). ◄

Researcher Self-Care

The all-consuming nature of data analysis can be stressful, overwhelming, disorientating and painful. This was shown poignantly in a study looking at therapists' bodily engagement with research, by Bager-Charleson et al. (2018). One therapist owned: "It's been horrific, I've agonised so much, feeling like a fraud, so stupid … I've been feeling desperate, all the time thinking that I am doing this right with themes and codes and tables" (2018, p.14).

While formal ethical guidelines tend to focus on protecting the client, the researcher also needs protecting. Doing research can be stressful and lonely. "When support is present it can make the research process more bearable, less stressful, more manageable, more interesting and even quite an exciting process" (Sreenan et al. 2015, p.249).

When we engage relationally as researchers, we can be drawn into participants' own distress or trauma. There is an ethical imperative to be reflexive about our research processes; we need to make active use of supportive opportunities (such as continuing professional development and supervision). Without this reflexivity, we can be in danger of using the research to act out of awareness and simply reproduce prejudices and partialities, undermining the credibility of the researc. Also, as researchers we need to give ourselves time to think, build our confidence and trust our intuitions. We also need to make sure that we are kept safe as researchers. Supervision offers an opportunity to learn, be mentored and process ethical dilemmas where 'mistakes' can be viewed with curiosity, as a path to growth and learning (Finlay 2019).

Sometimes we need to prioritise our self-care. Indeed, this can be seen as an ethical-professional 'duty'. The analysis phase, especially, can be a taxing time for qualitative researchers, who can feel they are 'drowning' in data, including participants' emotions and vulnerability. A participant from the Bager-Charleson et al. (2018) study expressed this well: "There would be different sentences in each transcript, it was like a sword going through me, right there where my heart is, where my soul is, and then the tears would come and sometimes it's quite unexpected" (p.14).

> ► **Example**

Through my own research on trauma, I've experienced first-hand the challenge of managing my own emotions to minimise the danger of secondary traumatisation. The use of supervision (and an internal supervisor) becomes important. In the following example of reflexive journaling with my internal supervisor, I show how the process enabled me to better attune to my participant's experience while simultaneously protecting myself from getting lost in the trauma of my research topic (the experience of having a traumatic abortion–see Finlay and Payman 2013):

> »   The interview made a profound impact on me. I had anticipated finding Eve's experience intense and painful to hear. What I had not expected were certain disturbing images which haunt me still. Through these I caught the edge of a deep and abiding trauma. As I faced Eve in the interview and later dwelt with the data, I was aware of a continuing, lurking impulse to flee, cut off and deny… I forced myself to stay present with Eve's story and open to our relational space…

Transcription has been hard … I'm on my third day …I keep needing to stop. I recognize my sense of feeling disturbed, a fuzzy but tight spiralling anxious grip in my stomach. I want to stop. I tune into my felt-sense:

> »   I have that fuzzy feeling… I am finding it difficult to breathe – breathing shallowly. …There are some tears there; aloneness; an unspeakable horror. My tummy tightens some more… [and says] 'I need to hold on; I need to hold in; I need to not cry, not speak'.

> I reflect then on these words. I wonder to what extent they reflect Eve's experience and how she had to hold on to her emotions and push down her words (Finlay 2015). ◄

Concluding the Research and Dissemination

The end phase of research involves tying things up with participants, and then writing up and disseminating the research.

The process of tying up the research with participants usually involves some sort of debrief towards closure of the research relationship. When and how this is achieved varies enormously depending on the type of research involved. It may occur for a few minutes after the interview or survey, with researcher and participant perhaps sharing their observations and experience. In more collaborative types of research, the process is layered and ongoing. Whichever situation, participants should be offered an opportunity to reflect on their experience–and learn what will happen to their data.

Fresh ethical questions arise in the stages that follow relating to our sense of *discomfort when writing up* and when *presenting to the wider world*.

Discomfort When Writing Up

When settling down to write, researchers confront the ethical challenge of treating their participants as *objects* to 'talk about' rather than as persons to 'talk with'. Many will experience the discomfort that goes with writing about others in an objectifying way. Josselson (1996) expresses this discomfort well as she owns some guilt and shame:

> » My guilt, I think, comes from my knowing that I have taken myself out of relationship with my participants (with whom, during the interview, I was in intimate relationship) to be in relationship with my readers. I have, in a sense, been talking about them behind their backs and doing so publicly…for my own purposes…I am guilty about being an intruder and… betrayer… I suspect this shame is about my exhibitionism, shame that I am using these people's lives to exhibit myself, my analytic prowess, my cleverness. I am using them as extensions of my own narcissism and fear being caught, seen in this process. (Josselson 1996, p.70).

There are no easy ways to preclude such feelings of discomfort. However, being reflexively aware of both the nature of our research enterprise and our ethical responsibilities is a good place to start. Just as in life, we make choices in difficult, uncertain circumstances, and cope with competing demands and responsibilities.

It also helps if you believe your research has the potential to benefit, at some level, your participants even if your initial intention was to benefit a wider community. In the following extract, a co-researcher in Morrow's study of the experience of sexual abuse (mentioned above) shares her positive response to the experience of being a co-analyst:

> » The participant co-researcher analytic process was a shared voice…That creates the experience of being understood. The amount of, just, honor and respect – it's just not like anything I've ever experienced, Sue. The research is also…it rings true…You have done something really extraordinary. It's so much more than a dissertation… Honor and respect. That's what we all lost. Reading it was an experience of that. It's touching the place I've been protecting, I think – the place I'm afraid to open up, even to myself. It's the place that believes I'm honourable, worth knowing. (Morrow 2006, p.165).

Presenting to the Wider World

When researchers present their findings to wider professional and academic circles, the first ethical priority is to re-present the research honestly, accurately and with integrity. This means, for instance, not plagiarising another's work and owning any investments and competing interests. The Committee on Publication Ethics (2019) conducted a survey and focus group of 656 editors of humanities and social science journals. They found that the two most pressing ethical problems editors face were: i. writing quality barriers and English language while remaining inclusive (64%) and ii. plagiarism and poor attribution practices (58%). Participants noted that the likelihood of self-plagiarism and predatory publishing was likely to increase given our current output-orientated academic culture.

Beyond issues around getting published, further ethical discomfort can arise when disseminating research. It's important to factor in how others may react to experiences that participants have been willing to share. For example, in the Ellis et al. (1997) research on the experience of bulimia, the co-researchers needed to think carefully about how they would be seen by others after telling their stories— particularly as they were about to apply for academic jobs. The research article they collaboratively wrote was to become part of their job application packets and clearly identified them as women with eating disorders if not other emotional vulnerabilities (Ellis 2007).

We also carry the responsibility to respect and be sensitive to our audiences. When I've talked of my traumatic abortion study at conferences, I've been acutely aware of the need to avoid burdening the audience with excessive detail and painful imagery. Mindful that there will be people in the audience who themselves have had distressing abortion experiences, I try to offer warnings that give them some choice over whether they hear/read my work.

In my research with Ann about her experience of MS, Ann was keen for me to share her story. She wanted me to 'spread the word' to health care professionals about what it was 'really like to have MS'. Over the last 15 years, I have written about and presented our research many times. I have remained mindful of the ethics of protecting Ann's identity by changing random biographical details given the risk of her being identified by those reading the research. I have also sought to evoke and represent *her* experience while transparently owning my interpretive flourishes. I remain touched when I recognise how others have been impacted by hearing Ann's poignant story. People who themselves had had their lives affected by MS seemed grateful for the way the research voiced something of their experience. But it was the wider impact on health professionals which I particularly valued. The research helped them recognise the need to tune in more to their patients' inside experience. In this respect, I believe I have honoured Ann's experience.

Activity

Imagine you were proposing to do research on clients' experience of therapy. List four potential risks you would need to consider when planning this research. (Hint: consider all phases of research.) Explain how you will mimimise or manage each risk. Then reflect on the following questions: (1) Do you agree that having your own clients as participants would be problematic given the issue of dual relationships? (2) What would you tell the participant to do if they should experience any problems during or after the research?

Summary

In this chapter, I've highlighted some of the ethical dilemmas we face when conducting research. I've argued for the need to be ethically sensitive and reflexive *throughout* the research process, handling each situation as it arises in context. I've also shown how care of participants *and* researcher self-care go hand-in-hand. The trustworthiness and integrity of the research must be balanced by our respect and concern for our participants' well-being, ourselves and our wider communities.

As you engage in research, you'll need to apply the code of ethics relevant to your professional situation. That said, professional ethical guidelines, while useful, can never prepare us sufficiently for situations arising in the research which make our heads spin and hearts ache (Ellis 2007; Finlay and Molano-Fisher 2009). As Reid et al. (2018) note, "Troubling dilemmas are sometimes hard to anticipate and require response in the moment". At every stage of your study, you'll find yourself reflexively grappling with the minutiae and conundrums that surface in all worthwhile research. The challenge is to make our ethical judgements with care, humane intention, reflexivity and as much conscientiousness as we can summon.

Ethical tensions confront researchers at each stage of research. In the pre-research phase, particular attention needs to be paid to anonymity/confidentiality and informed consent. During data collection and analysis, care of participants and researcher self-care go together, and there is a need to manage emotional intensity and power relations. In the writing up and dissemination phases research integrity and care for wider communities are prioritised. There is a need to be ethically sensitive and reflexive throughout, handling each individual situation and the complex relational dynamics involved as they arise *in context*. What may seem responsible, respectful and caring to one person may not to another. It depends. Negotiating an ethical path can often be tricky and compromises may need to be made. The trustworthiness and integrity of the research must be balanced by respect of, and concern for, the well-being of participants, researchers, and wider communities. The challenge is to make ethical judgements with caring, humane intention, reflexivity, and as much conscientiousness as researchers can summon.

References

Ashworth, P. D. (1993). Participant agreement in the justification of qualitative findings. *Journal of Phenomenological Psychology, 24*, 3–16.

Bager-Charleson, S., Du Plock, S., & McBeath, A. (2018). Therapists have a lot to add to the field of research, but many don't make it there: A narrative thematic inquiry into counsellors' and psychotherapists' embodied engagement with research. *Language and Psychoanalysis, 7*(1), 4–22. Retrieved from https://doi.org/10.7565/landp.v7i1.1580.

Bochner, A. P. (1984). The functions of communication in interpersonal bonding. In C. Arnold & J. Bowers (Eds.), *The handbook of rhetoric and communication* (pp. 544–621). Thousand Oaks: Sage.

British Psychological Society. (2018). Data protection regulation: Guidance for researchers. Retrieved from https://www.bps.org.uk/sites/bps.org.uk/files/Policy/Policy%20-%20Files/Data%20Protection%20Regulation%20-%20Guidance%20for%20Researchers.pdf

Committee on Publication Ethics. (2019). Exploring publication ethics in the arts, humanities, and social sciences: COPE (Committee on Publication Ethics). *Initial Research Findings*. Retrieved from https://publicationethics.org/files/u7140/COPE%20AHSS_Survey_Key_Findings_SCREEN_AW.pdf

Ellis, C. (2007). Telling secrets, revealing lives: Relational ethics in research with intimate others. *Qualitative Inquiry, 3*, 13–29.

Ellis, C., Kiesinger, C. E., & Tillmann-Healy, L. M. (1997). Interactive interviewing: Talking about emotional experience. In R. Hertz (Ed.), *Reflexivity and voice* (pp. 119–149). Thousand Oaks: Sage.

Etherington, K. (2007). Ethical research in reflexive relationships. *Qualitative Inquiry, 13*(5), 599–616.

Finlay, L. (2003). The intertwining of body, self and world: A phenomenological study of living with recently diagnosed multiple sclerosis. *Journal of Phenomenological Psychology, 34*, 157–178.

Finlay, L. (2015). The experience of '*Entrapped Grief*' following traumatic abortion. *International Journal of Integrative Psychotherapy, 6*, 26–53.

Finlay, L. (2019). *Practical ethics in counselling and psychotherapy: A relational approach*. London: Sage.

Finlay, L., & Ballinger, C. (Eds.). (2006). *Qualitative research for allied health professionals: Challenging choices*. Chichester, West Sussex: Wiley.

Finlay, L., & Langdridge, D. (2007). Embodiment. In W. Hollway, H. Lucey, & A. Phoenix (Eds.), *Social psychology matters* (pp. 173–198). Maidenhead: Open University Press.

Finlay, L., & Molano-Fisher, P. (2008). Transforming' self and world: A phenomenological study of a changing lifeworld following a cochlear implant. *Medicine, Health Care and Philosophy, 11*, 255–267. (Online version available from 2007.).

Finlay, L., & Molano-Fisher, P. (2009). Reflexively probing relational ethical challenges. *Qualitative Methods in Psychology, 7*, 30–34.

Finlay, L., & Payman, B. (2013). This rifled and bleeding womb: A reflexive-relational phenomenological case study of traumatic abortion experience. *Janus Head,* In E. Simms (Ed.). *Special issue on 'feminist phenomenology', 13*(1), 144–175.

Guillemin, M., & Gillam, L. (2004). Ethics, reflexivity, and 'ethically important moments' in research. *Qualitative Inquiry, 10*(2), 261–280. Retrieved from https://doi.org/10.1177/1077800403262360.

Halling, S., Leifer, M., & Rowe, J. O. (1999). Emergence of the dialogal approach: Forgiving another. In C. T. Fischer (Ed.), *Qualitative research methods for psychology: Introduction through empirical studies* (pp. 247–278). San Diego: Elsevier Academic Press.

Hertz, R. (1997). Reflexivity and Voice. Thousand Oaks, CA: Sage.

Hunt, J. C. (1989). *Psychoanalytic aspects of fieldwork (Qualitative Research Methods, 18)*. Newbury Park: Sage.

Josselson, R. (1996). On writing other people's lives: Self analytic reflections of a narrative researcher. In R. Josselson (Ed.), *Ethical process in the narrative study of lives* (Vol. 4, pp. 60–71). Thousand Oaks: Sage.

Krüger, A. (2007). An introduction to the ethics of gestalt research with informants. *European Journal for Qualitative Research in Psychotherapy, 2*, 17–22.

7

Lilienfeld, S. O. (2017). Psychology's replication crisis and the grant culture: Righting the ship. *Perspectives on Psychological Science, 12*(4), 660–664.

Madill, A. (2009). Construction of anger in one successful case of psychodynamic interpersonal psychotherapy: Problem (re)formulation and the negotiation of moral context. *The European Journal for Qualitative Research in Psychotherapy, 4*, 20–29. Retrieved from https://ejqrp.org/index.php/ejqrp/article/view/23/20.

Morrow, S. L. (2006). Honor and respect: Feminist collaborative research with sexually abused women. In C. T. Fischer (Ed.), *Qualitative research methods for psychology: Introduction through empirical studies* (pp. 143–172). Amsterdam: Elsevier.

Parker, I. (1992). *Discourse dynamics: Critical analysis for social and individual psychology*. London: Routledge.

Proctor, G. (2002). *The dynamics of power in counselling and psychotherapy: Ethics, politics and practice*. Ross-on-Wye: PCCS Books.

Reid, A.-M., Brown, J. M., Smith, J. M., Cope, A. C., & Jamieson, S. (2018). Ethical dilemmas and reflexivity in qualitative research. *Perspectives on Medical Education, 7*(2), 69–75. https://doi.org/10.1007/s40037-018-0412-2.

Sreenan, B., Smith, H., & Frost, C. (2015). Student top tips. In A. Vossler & N. Moller (Eds.), *The counselling and psychotherapy research handbook* (pp. 245–256). Los Angeles: Sage.

Thériault, A., & Gazzola, N. (2006). What are the sources of feelings of incompetence in experienced therapists? *Counselling Psychology Quarterly, 19*(4), 313–330. https://doi.org/10.1080/09515070601090113.

Doing Qualitatively Driven Mixed Methods and Pluralistic Qualitative Research

Nollaig Frost and
Deborah Bailey-Rodriguez

Contents

© The Author(s) 2020
S. Bager-Charleson, A. McBeath (eds.),
Enjoying Research in Counselling and Psychotherapy,
https://doi.org/10.1007/978-3-030-55127-8_8

⊜ **Learning Goals**

After reading this chapter you should be able to:
- Describe the values, underlying philosophy and epistemological principles of qualitatively driven mixed methods;
- Know more about methodological pluralism;
- Understand the rationale for a qualitatively driven mixed methods study in the context of other mixed methods;
- Be aware of differences and overlaps between analytical, within-method* and across-method pluralistic research;
- Understand the implications of applying a 'both/and' position when exploring the elements that produce change;
- Know more about pluralism and pragmatism, including understanding more about the implications of paradigmatic flexibility, 'paradigmatic peace' and how methodolatry privileges certain research methods and underlying frameworks;
- Have considered how to ensure quality (including ethics) when conducting pluralistic research;
- Understand practical aspects of being a pluralistic researcher working alone, or working as part of a team, and conducting a pluralistic case study.

Introduction

Many researchers and clinicians take an 'either/or' position regarding factors responsible for change when conducting research (Cooper and McLeod 2007). Some methods emphasise lived experience, others focus on identity construction, and yet others focus on cognitive processes and so on. In this chapter, we will explore how these *together* can produce change and may be important to the reality of the individual. We will specifically look at the application of a *qualitatively driven mixed methods* approach to produce more holistic and multi-dimensional insight into phenomena by using a combination of methods.

A qualitatively driven mixed methods applies a *both/and* position when exploring the elements that produce change, or that are under investigation, which can be of particular value to counselling and psychotherapy research. There are various ways of engaging with qualitatively driven mixed methods, and pluralism in qualitative research (PQR) is one such method, and is the focus of this chapter.

Pluralistic Qualitative Research in Counselling and Psychotherapy Research

A pluralistic approach seeks to minimise reductionism and enhance more holistic understandings of experiences, changes and practices of behaviours in context by engaging with a plurality of meanings. Counsellors and psychotherapists recognise that all understanding is dependent on experience. In a complex world, humans will have a variety of experiences and likely a degree of disagreement and contradiction, in addition to some consensus (Rescher 1993).

Pluralism views peoples' experience as multi-dimensional and as something which requires the adoption of multiple theoretical and methodological frameworks (Chamberlain et al. 2011; Frost 2011). Further, it is worth highlighting the overlap between therapeutic practice and pluralistic qualitative research, of the multiplicity of meanings and multi-layered understandings of client experiences, illustrating the suitability, value and importance that this approach brings to counselling and psychotherapy research. Mono-method approaches cannot capture multi-layered understandings around behaviour. Therefore, the application of a pluralistic qualitative approach when inquiring into counselling or psychotherapy allows for a deeper engagement with the subjective meanings attached to multi-dimensional experiences and behaviours (Josselin and Willig 2014).

Mixed Methods and Qualitatively-Driven Mixed Methods

People's experiences and lived realities are, as suggested, multi-dimensional; and if phenomena have different layers, then choosing to view these phenomena from the perspective of a single dimension may mean that our understanding is inadequate and incomplete (Mason 2006). Mixed methods research refers to the use of two or more methodological strategies in a single research study with the purpose of gaining insight into another aspect of the phenomenon under investigation which cannot be accessed by use of one method alone. Therefore, mixed methods research is a systematic way of using at least two research methods in order to answer a single over-arching research question; these research methods can be either all quantitative or all qualitative, or can be both quantitative and qualitative (Morse and Niehaus 2009). The value of combining methods is that it provides a more enhanced understanding than using a single method (Creswell and Plano Clark 2007), which in turn offers a more balanced perspective of phenomena (Morse and Chung 2003). Furthermore, mixing methods goes beyond solely the mixing of type of data, such as whether it is quantitative or qualitative, and rather, it is also concerned with the mixing of worldviews and ways of understanding these as well (Moran-Ellis et al. 2006).

Activity
- What is your favoured research approach? Consider some of its key advantages.
- What might another method bring or add to your study?

Qualitatively driven mixed methods privilege the qualitative approach. It is a particularly suitable approach when there is a lack of clarity in a theoretical framework and when exploring areas which have not received much attention (Hesse-Biber et al. 2015). Drawing on qualitatively driven mixed methods offers the opportunity to generate multi-dimensional material (Gabb 2009) and permits a more holistic insight into experiences that can be understood from a combination of epistemological and ontological stances (Frost and Nolas 2011), suggesting that the ability to perceive these layers is rooted in paradigmatic flexibility. Qualitatively driven mixed methods offer the opportunity to explore and understand phenomena and their complexities in a manner that is not bound by methodological dogma and constraints (Elichaoff et al. 2014). This approach also pursues access to unique perspectives on experience and seeks to highlight the dynamism and complexity of phenomena by its use of multiple paradigms (Hesse-Biber et al. 2015).

The use of several paradigms may incur tension, but the dialogue between contrasting ideas can provide a space for new insights and understandings (Creswell 2009). Gabb (2009) puts forward the notion of 'messiness' of research in analysis and representations of phenomena, rather than the tidying away of experiential loose ends that illustrate lived lives. The retention of messiness in the representation of findings does not indicate that analytical rigour is at risk. Rather, it reflects the complexity of experiences that may otherwise be lost; loose ends do not mean frayed ends (Rodriguez and Frost 2015). This may go some way to further illustrate how the richness of multi-dimensionality can be understood through the use of qualitatively driven mixed methods. Therefore it is recognised that multi-dimensionality and multi-methodological perspectives offer some means to access these additional layers, conflicts, contradictions and messiness (Frost et al. 2011), where a co-operative relationship between question, epistemology, paradigm and researcher is part of an ongoing reflexive process (Chamberlain et al. 2011).

Another way of acknowledging and upholding the multi-dimensionality of experience is through a pluralistic qualitative approach. This recognises that different perspectives produce distinct pictures of meaning-making, and the layering of different approaches creates a tapestry of insights of the same phenomenon (Josselin 2013).

Pluralism in Qualitative Research (PQR)

A qualitative pluralistic approach recognises that there are multiple ways of viewing phenomena rather than there being a single 'truth', and it also understands that different methods set out to achieve different things, and thus provide diverse insights into the same phenomena. Reality and existence are seen to be multiple (Johnson 2015), and as previously alluded to, people's experiences are multi-dimensional as well as fragmentary and contradictory. Pluralism argues that a single method cannot convey everything there is to know about a phenomenon, and therefore a choice should not have to be made between which method to use, as employment of two (or more) can provide multi-perspectival and holistic understanding (Frost 2011; Willig 2013). Consequently, the presence of multi-ontological stances and the tensions they generate are strengths of a pluralistic approach, which involves moving away from an 'either/or' position to a 'both/and' position (Frost and Nolas 2011). Furthermore, analytical rigour is strengthened by making explicit the ontological and epistemological assumptions underlying the different methods, demonstrating the researcher's conceptual clarity of these (Barbour 1998), as well as by highlighting the gaps and divergences arising from the separate analyses (Frost and Nolas 2011). In addition, by analysing the data in this manner and acknowledging the 'experiential loose ends' without tidying it up to construct a coherent and neat story represents the messiness, uncertainties and contradictions of human experience (Gabb 2009), which may be particularly salient in counselling and psychotherapy research.

Pluralism in qualitative research mixes different qualitative approaches, where the use and status of each method is determined to combine with others in order to provide a more holistic insight into phenomena than can be gained using one method alone. Crucially, this approach recognises the plurality of epistemological and ontological paradigms underlying each of the qualitative approaches (Nolas 2011), and values the tensions and benefits of combining methods within paradigms as well as across them. It does not confine individuals to being understood from only one epistemological stance, and allows for flexibility by building up layers of insight which can provide multiple understandings of a person's reality. This can be particularly helpful in research that seeks to understand the complexity of perspectives of those for whom reality and meanings can change (Frost 2011), such as for clients in psychotherapy or counselling. Therefore, a qualitative pluralistic approach seeks to avoid reductionism and allows for a holistic view of phenomena which would not be possible with the use of a mono-method approach (Frost 2008).

How to do Pluralistic Qualitative Research

Doing qualitative research pluralistically means combining methods and analytical techniques to bring different perspectives to a research focus. This is not to say that an 'anything goes' approach is appropriate in pluralistic research. Methods are not selected at random, and careful thought must be given regarding why and how they are being combined, as well as to which methods are chosen and how they are employed.

Human experience or behaviour tends to be the research focus in pluralistic research, with the openness to different views that this approach allows. This enables researchers to gain a more rounded insight into how humans live their lives and make sense of the events and experiences within them. For pluralistic researchers, human experience is seen as fragmented, lived in different dimensions and as having meanings influenced by context and other factors. To best explore this requires a flexibility that may mean, for example, using different types of data, gathering views on a topic from different stakeholders or employing different methods of analysis to ask different questions of the same data. Whichever approach is taken, pluralistic research strives to keep the research focus central, and to resist falling into methodolatry where arguments over methods can become more important than the research focus itself (Chamberlain 2000; Chamberlain et al. 2011; Curt 1994).

This means there is no one way to engage in pluralistic research as it provides a way to conduct exploration in accordance with research questions and is not limited in what it can ask of data, such as might be the case if using only one method. In practice, this can mean that pluralistic studies are designed from the outset to include different methods or forms of data, or evolve in response to new research questions arising from findings and observations of the data. Regardless of the manner in which the pluralistic research process develops, there must be a clear rationale for including different methods in the study that demonstrates how these are selected and combined, and how they address the research question. There is a vast range of qualitative methods available to ask different questions of data in order to understand more about how meaning is made by humans of their experiences. It may seem to a novice pluralistic researcher that it is simply a matter of matching a method to a research question and carrying out the research according to steps or stages delineated by each method. In practice, however, it will soon become clear that almost all qualitative methods offer only guidelines as to how they should be employed – all recognise the subjective element of qualitative research and the reflexive engagement of the researcher with the data. This means that in addition to the systematic analysis the method offers, the findings that are constructed will also depend on how the method is used, the worldview of the researcher, the ways they have adapted the method, and the personal elements of its employment (deciding which aspects of the transcript to focus on, what is important and is not important to them, and so on).

In the next sections, we consider some of the ways in which this can be done.

Methodological Pluralism

Methodological pluralism refers to drawing on multiple methods of data collection to enable insight into different dimensions of human experience. Widely employed in sociology (although not without debate, e.g. Baker et al., 1998, who warn of a dilution of methods, and Payne et al. 2004, who do not regard all methods as equal), it offers a way of examining data drawn from different artefacts such as documents, photographs and interviews, and may include observation, asking questions and ethnography. Methodological pluralism takes the view that human experience is formed by a variety of dimensions (affect, vision, discourse and so on) and is thus best understood by exploring different forms of data.

This approach can be useful in counselling and psychotherapy research because accessing transcripts of sessions, or audio recording them for research purposes, is not always possible. With a methodological pluralistic approach, a researcher may, for example, gain access to institutional and training documents or ask participants to keep diaries about their experience of counselling, and can conduct interviews with them about the process. Although this process relies on participant recall rather than relating their here and now experience, bringing a pluralistic approach allows consideration of what is said about counselling sessions in official documents, how therapists are trained to deliver counselling sessions and what participants say about sessions, thus enabling a multi-perspective picture from which consensual and disensual insights can be gathered.

Analytical Pluralism

Analytical pluralism refers to the mixing of several methods of qualitative data analysis on a single dataset (Clarke et al. 2015).

> » Pluralistic qualitative research recognises that a data set can tell us about a number of different things, depending on the questions we ask of it. A pluralistic approach involves asking a series of questions of the same data; each new question that is asked of the data requires that the researcher returns to the data and interpret it in a new way (Willig 2013, p. 19).

Use of multiple methods of qualitative data analysis enables different things components of the data to be attended to, as diverse forms of knowledge are produced through different methods of analysis. Therefore, a pluralistic analysis produces multi-layered and multi-perspectival interpretations which allow for a richer understanding of phenomena. These various forms of knowledge do not attempt to achieve an ultimate 'truth' or consensus (Dewe and Coyle 2014) but are instead viewed as complementary rather than in competition with each other; each analysis reflects another dimension of the experience (Frost et al. 2011).

Therefore, analytical pluralism uses different methods of data analysis to understand, usually textual, data. Generally, accounts are gathered from participants using semi-structured interviews that aim to gather rich data about the experience or phenomenon that is the research focus. However, if it is possible to analyse a transcript of a counselling or psychotherapy session, then a pluralistic approach to analysing it can be very valuable in accessing more meaning than would be possible using one method alone. In this case, a researcher may choose to explore language use and function using discourse analysis, as well as conversation analysis to understand the dynamics of the interaction, for example. Combining narrative analysis to understand how stories are used by the counselling client, together with Interpretative Phenomenological Analysis to understand the lived experience being recounted in the counselling setting, may also be of interest.

Analytical pluralism can use either a within-method or across-method approach, which are explained in the sections below.

Within-Method Pluralistic Research

Within-method pluralistic research refers to using the same method to analyse data in different ways, but with an underpinning of the same philosophical assumptions. The aim remains to explore the data in a way which is as open as possible, whilst addressing an overarching research question. For example, this could mean using different methods within narrative analysis to construct different meanings from the content form and function of stories within the same data corpus from textual data, as described below, or to understand experiential meanings within data from different reflexive standpoints using a method such as Interpretative Phenomenological Analysis (IPA) (e.g. King et al. 2008).

Frost (2006, 2009) applied a within-method pluralistic approach to narrative analysis when exploring the transition to second-time motherhood. Labov's structural narrative analysis (1972) was applied to the data to explore how stories are constructed, followed by the application of Gee's poetic model of narrative analysis (1991), which is useful for identifying changes of topics within sections of text. Applied together, these models of narrative analysis helped identify what stories were told and what aspects of them were significant to women when they were asked to talk about their experiences of second-time motherhood. In turn, this allowed for more informed and considered interpretation of the meanings within the narratives (see Frost 2006, 2009).

Another example of a within-method pluralistic approach can be seen in King et al.'s (2008) study which applied a phenomenological analysis to an interview on the topic of mistrust. There were six members of the group, and each researcher analysed the text using different approaches to phenomenology. For example, one member was committed to a Heideggerian worldview and centrality of participants' experiences, which enabled features such as selfhood, sociality, temporality, spatiality, embodiment, project and discourse to be tended to. Another member drew on Kelly's analysis of self-characterisation sketches (Kelly 1955) which paid attention to the close interaction with the interviewer and how this impacted the shape the particular narrative took. Yet another member made use of the *epoché* by upholding an open and curious phenomenological standpoint as well as constant reflection, which allowed for a deeper understanding of her meanings as well as what was being revealed about the participant's experiences of mistrust (see King et al. 2008). ◄

Whatever the reason for employing the same method in different ways, it is always important for the researcher(s) to make as explicit as possible their reflexive engagement with the research so that their impact on it is as transparent as possible. In this way, the research is grounded in theoretical foundations appropriate to the research question, as well as being rigorous. The findings of each layer of analysis can be considered separately to address the question brought to the data by the use of individual methods, and together to build a fuller picture than possible with the use of one application of the method.

Across-Method Pluralistic Research

In contrast to within-method pluralism, across-method pluralistic research refers to using different methods to analyse data in different ways, and so this approach may be underpinned by differing philosophical viewpoints (e.g. social constructionism *and* interpretivism). All qualitative methods have assumptions about what they are looking for in data: stories, language, themes, lived experience and so on. Using different methods allows for distinct ways of exploring the data, so that by applying multiple methods of analysis to the same data, researchers can inquire into language used through a discourse analysis, *and* stories told through a narrative analysis, *and* themes generated through a thematic analysis, for example. By combining, the pluralistic researcher assumes that meanings can be accessed in different ways, and that meanings constructed from the analysis are not constrained by what one method is able to tell them. Sometimes meanings found using different methods can complement each other, but the pluralistic researcher is always open to new findings, or findings that contradict those of another method. This is not a problem in pluralistic research as its aim is not to triangulate, but instead to understand the many ways in which human experience can be understood in different contexts and with different audiences.

► **Example**

Bailey-Rodriguez (2017) applied an across-method pluralistic approach when exploring the attachment behaviours of a couple relationship during their transition to second-time parenthood. Narrative analysis was used to understand how identities were formed and reformed over the longitudinal period, and gave insight into how the participants made sense of their feelings and emotions. A psychosocial reading of the data enabled understanding of some of the internal and external conflicts that the participants negotiated during this period. The plurality of philosophical paradigms brought by the different methods highlighted the complex variation and intricate manners in which the couple's emotion regulation strategies affected the dynamics of their relationship (see Bailey-Rodriguez 2017).

Another example of an across-method pluralistic approach can be seen in Josselin's (2013) counselling psychology doctorate which explored the meanings attached to self-harming and experiences of this. IPA was applied to understand how the participant made sense of their repetitive self-injury behaviour. The application of narrative analysis allowed for the framing of the personal significance of the self-injury experiences in the context of the life story, as well as a focus on the linguistic properties of the data. Finally, a psychosocial approach drew out contradictions and underlying psychic structures around the meaning-making of the self-injury behaviours. Together, these different methods created a rich, complex and multi-layered understanding of the experiences of self-injury (see Josselin 2013). ◄

In both case study examples the reflexive awareness and stance of the researcher(s) is, again, paramount. It is only by making transparent what a researcher understands they have brought to the analysis and interpretation of the data that the process is credible and trustworthy. Pluralistic researchers see the use of each method as contributing to an overall understanding of the experience at the centre of the research, even if this means there is an apparent lack of coherence in the meanings that are derived. As previously discussed, the strength of pluralistic research is that it is seen as reflecting the complexity, and messiness, of human experience and emotion. Although this can present challenges in deciding how to present the research, pluralistic researchers maintain that this is true to the ways in which humans do make sense of their relationships, experiences and sense of self.

Carla Willig (2017) and others extend this thinking to 'dual focus' methodology–the combining of Foucauldian Discourse Analysis (FDA) and IPA to examine the phenomenological repercussions of being positioned within dominant discourses (Willig 2017). In other words, dual focus methodology explicitly looks to understand the role of language in shaping experience.

So far we have discussed some of the different ways in which pluralistic research can be undertaken and have emphasised the importance not only of choosing appropriate methods, but also of making clear how each method is being used. We have considered different approaches to combining methods with the aim of developing more holistic insight into the meaning of experiences. We have also discussed the importance of maintaining a theoretical foundation by clearly linking each choice of method and rationale for its use to the research question.

Activity

By using a method that examines the role of language with another method that seeks to understand experience, the interplay between language, culture and experience can be explored, and subjective experiences situated within their socio-cultural contexts. For example, Colahan (2014) explored relationship satisfaction in long-term heterosexual couples, and analysed the data using FDA and IPA in order to draw out the complexity of the relation between the private-subjective, the interpersonal and the social life worlds of 'satisfied' partners (p. i).

- *Return to ▶ Chaps. 2, 3, 4, 5, and 6 in this book about IPA, Narrative research and Grounded theory. Try to think of a problem in the fields of emotional wellbeing and mental health which might benefit from a combination of those approaches. Consider a problem which benefits from being researched from what we describe as a 'multi-dimensional, holistic' insight into experiences? Consider the options of drawing from either analytical, within-method and across-method pluralistic research.*

Whatever form of pluralistic research is used, access to and skill in a range of different methods is required. As a researcher you may know what it is you want to find out but are unsure or unskilled in the appropriate method that can aid you to achieve this. This is a fundamental consideration in pluralistic research, and in the next section we turn to more pragmatic aspects of working pluralistically.

Practicalities of Pluralistic Research

We have seen that in order to carry out pluralistic research there is the same need for rigour and accountability that is expected in all qualitative research.

Later on in this chapter we will discuss how to ensure quality when conducting pluralistic research, but first we will turn to the practical aspects of (a) being a pluralistic researcher working alone, (b) being a pluralistic researcher working as part of a team and (c) conducting a pluralistic case study.

Being Pluralistic Alone

Working as a lone pluralistic researcher requires skills in a number of qualitative methods so that you can choose the most appropriate methods to combine. This means knowing the assumptions and underpinnings of several methods, as well as what each method aims to find out, and the techniques of data collection and analysis with which they do this. Experienced researchers may have become familiar with a number of different methods in their research career, but new and trainee researchers may still be discovering methods they are interested in using. It can be frustrating to know that further expertise would be beneficial to the research as new questions emerge from it, or you may feel that there is more in the data than the methods being used allow access to. If enough time has been factored into the research design (an essential consideration for all qualitative research but, arguably, particularly for pluralistic qualitative research), then the lone researcher can either teach themselves or undertake training in another method if they know the type of knowledge they are seeking from the data and how a different method may help to access it. Working as a lone pluralistic researcher and its challenges will be particularly salient for counsellors and psychotherapists in training. However, the adoption of a pluralistic approach will inevitably enrichen the lone researcher's research experiences and toolkit.

Alternatively, if possible, the lone researcher can recruit other researchers to contribute their skills in another method, perhaps in return for their name on any publication. Sometimes, as a lone researcher, it is just not possible to bring other methods and this can sometimes lead to a sense of compromise, of having to 'settle' for a less than desirous approach. If this happens, it is often useful to highlight the new avenues of research or potential insights gleaned from the study, and to highlight methods that can be used in future research instead.

Working as Part of a Team

Working as one researcher in a team can be rewarding, challenging and productive. If the team is working well, more work can be carried out in a shorter space of time than can be achieved by a researcher working alone. A range of methods, carried out to the required standards, can be brought to the research, and choice and use of each method will be explicitly justified and accounted for. By providing a rationale to team members, listening to their rationale for using other methods, and addressing any questions that arise about methods and their use means that a parallel pluralistic process takes place in which the many perspectives brought by group members are carefully considered in relation to the research focus. This process highlights and enhances many of the quality criteria of qualitative research such as reflexivity, transparency and trustworthiness, ensuring that they are all brought to the study.

By contrast, though, frustrations regarding working as one of a team can emerge. Bryman (2007) found that in mixed methods research, individuals often have an unconscious bias towards their preferred method. This can mean that when it comes to considering the findings of a pluralistic study, the findings of one method may be prioritised over those of another. This can mean that one or more methods are treated as secondary, or that one or more may play less of a role in the development of the overall insight. This can be averted to some extent if the status of each method is determined and agreed by the team at the outset of the study (if it is pluralistically designed from the start), or with the introduction of new methods as the study progresses. If, for example, a method has been brought in response to findings in the data, then this decision should be made clear, and the choice of method explained in the write-up.

Another challenge of working pluralistically as a team can be that some methods of data analysis are regarded as needing less time to carry out than others. This can lead to a sense of unfairness or resentment amongst team members, either feeling that one method is holding up completion of the study or, conversely, that not enough time is being allowed by the rest of the team to ensure that the analysis is carried out rigorously. The value of the contribution of different methods may be questioned, and time pressures applied to try to chivvy analysts along at an unrealistic pace. A reminder that careful planning at the design stage of team-based pluralistic research projects should include agreement of the status of each method and its analysis, and sufficient time for all analyses to be carried out.

Case Studies

A case study allows for in-depth investigation by focussing on one participant, group or setting. Case study approaches which centre on one 'unit', whether that is an individual, a couple, a group or a setting, can be used to generate rich accounts by seeking depth rather than breadth in producing context-dependent knowledge (Flyvbjerg 2006). This may be of particular relevance to counsellors and psychotherapists and other clinicians who draw on research to inform practice (Radley and Chamberlain 2001).

The adoption of a single case study in pluralistic research not only provides the opportunity to show how the focus of the research unfolds in an insightful and detailed manner, but also enables the ability to work in a justified way that aims to access as much meaning as possible in the data. Furthermore, the single case study approach facilitates an extensive and multi-layered pluralistic analysis of one set of data, which would otherwise not be possible with a mono-method approach.

As with all pluralistic research there is no one way to conduct a case study. Once the unit of analysis is clear, the researcher must then decide what knowledge they wish to generate from its investigation and how best to access this knowledge. This is clearly related to the research questions and identifying the best methods to address them, but also requires the researcher to think about issues such as whether the case study is to be longitudinal or not.

The research examples provided earlier for both Josselin (2013) and Bailey-Rodriguez (2017) respectively adopted a single case study pluralistic approach. Josselin (2013) conducted three separate semi-structured interviews lasting between one hour and one hour and a half with the same participant at weekly intervals.

This allowed for the opportunity for an in-depth exploration which was built on a more trusting relationship between Josselin as the researcher, and the participant. Bailey-Rodriguez (2017) gathered interviews, photos and diary entries over a period starting at pregnancy and ending some four months after the second child was born. This allowed for a rich and prospective understanding of the changes over time for this couple across a significant life event.

Pluralistic case studies focus on one experience or the experiences of one participant (or couple). In the examples above, the researchers identify the pragmatic considerations as well as the conceptual ones when making their decisions to conduct their research as a single case study. They wanted to carry out an in-depth investigation in which they did not have to compromise on time or data, and the pluralistic case study approach enabled this. Undertaking research as part of a busy counsellor or psychotherapy training course may be of particular relevance and an asset for conducting a pluralistic single case study.

Pluralism and Pragmatism

8

Differing philosophical assumptions allow for differences in their beliefs about the nature of existence and reality (ontology–what is there to know?), and they also differ in their beliefs about the nature of valid and reliable knowledge (epistemology–how and what can we know?) (Willig 2013). Criticisms have been put forward regarding the incompatibility and mutual exclusivity of these underlying philosophical assumptions, which has served to further perpetuate the divide between positivist quantitative and constructivist qualitative research, resulting in a paradigm war when attempting to integrate these stances. There remain some concerns around the issue of incommensurability in mixing the sometimes discordant and conflicting methods of analysis undertaken in a qualitative pluralistic approach. Such concerns centre on the tensions and discord between the different beliefs of the underlying philosophical assumptions which are seen to be in conflict with each other.

Nevertheless, ensuing debates around the mixing of methods have led to the achievement of 'paradigm peace' (Bryman 2006) as alternative conceptual frameworks underpinning mixed methods have been put forward (e.g. Mertens 2012; Shannon-Baker 2016). One such framework which overthrows the dogma of the paradigm wars and supports the mixing of methods is pragmatism, which focuses on determining the meaning of phenomena (Johnson and Onwuegbuzie 2004). The pragmatic approach breaks down the hierarchies between positivist and constructivist paradigms by looking at what is meaningful from both, and understands that different knowledge claims arise from different ways of engaging with the world (Biesta 2010) (see ◘ Fig. 8.1). It achieves this by placing the research question in a central position in order to attain the richest possible response to it and by basing itself on the assumption that there is not a single set of methods that is correct (Mertens 2012). Choice of method(s) is subsequently driven by the aim of finding those that are best suited to addressing the research question rather than being hindered by debates of incommensurability (Elichaoff et al. 2014).

◘ **Fig. 8.1** Pragmatism as a
paradigm to overcome
incommensurability issues

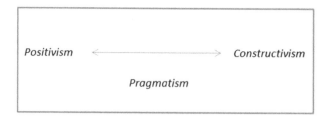

Positivism ←——————————————→ Constructivism

Pragmatism

Qualitative pluralistic approaches are interested in prioritising the research focus over the methods used, and achieve this by ensuring clear theoretical foundations that link the research question to the choice of methods employed. This enables a renewed focus on the need to understand and highlight the ways in which research questions are addressed. Such a focus allows for flexibility in research design that promotes the seeking of tailored insight into the complexities of human experience (Frost 2011). Furthermore, adopting a pragmatic approach helps to avoid the issue of methodolatry, where the privileging of certain research methods and their underlying frameworks, as opposed to the topic under investigation, discourages the adaptation of methods to suit said research topic (Chamberlain 2000; Chamberlain et al. 2011). A pluralistic approach addresses this concern of methodolatry by its consideration of several qualitative methods within the context of the same study.

Ensuring Quality in Pluralistic Qualitative Research

Evaluating the quality of qualitative research can be complex due to the heterogeneity of the many approaches. Pre-defined sets of quality criteria may not be applicable to all qualitative methods due to their differences (O'Reilly and Kiyimba 2015). Similar to issues arising from the application of quantitative quality criteria to qualitative research–such as validity, reliability and generalisability–it is also troublesome to judge qualitative research conducted within one paradigm using criteria developed from another one (Collingridge and Gantt 2008). Nevertheless, some researchers have recognised the heterogeneity within qualitative research and have attempted to develop universal criteria (e.g. Tracy 2010; Yardley 2008). However, others have voiced their concerns about the appropriateness of these universal checklists and emphasise the risk of accepting this 'one size fits all' as it may engender role reversal in qualitative research and quality criteria, resulting in 'the tail wagging the dog', where the quality standards become the main focus, and the actual qualitative research is rendered a subsidiary (Barbour 2001, p. 1115). Therefore, qualitative researchers are advised not to succumb to meeting the demands of a fully unequivocal set of universal quality standards as it is the characteristics of the specific qualitative approach that prescribe what the quality criteria should be. Therefore, undertaking a universal approach may not necessarily align with the particular requirements of the research (Hammersley 2007).

Table 8.1 Spencer et al.'s (2003) quality guiding principles

Principle	Description
Contributory	Contributes to advancing wider knowledge
Defensible in design	The design includes strategies which address the research question
Rigorous	Systematic and transparent data collection, analysis and interpretation
Credible	Claims should be credible, grounded and plausible in relation to the evidence generated

This is particularly pertinent in the case of a pluralistic qualitative approach as it is not possible to maintain the same quality measures across the different methods (Barker and Pistrang 2005), and the epistemological scope of this approach to research may be too broad for universal quality standards. Spencer et al. (2003) developed four overarching guiding principles based on a review of published quality frameworks devised in extensive consultation with qualitative experts. The review found that all frameworks have been recognised to have a primary concern with identifying good practice in qualitative research, and that it is up to the researcher to judge the overall value of the research based on choice of the most relevant principles.

As Spencer et al.'s (2003) guiding principles are at a sufficiently high level of abstraction to encompass a diversity of qualitative approaches, they meet the quality demands of a pluralistic qualitative approach; Table 8.1 shows the principles and their descriptions.

Reflexivity is also considered to be an essential quality standard as the researcher unavoidably influences the conduct of the inquiry. Therefore it is important that the researcher reflects on their role in the research process and considers the ways in which they may have had an impact (O'Reilly and Kiyimba 2015). Qualitative researchers are encouraged to disclose relevant personal background, as well as relevant personal characteristics, and describe any first-hand experience with the phenomenon under investigation that may have influenced how the data were collected and analysed (Barker and Pistrang 2005). This is also relevant to pluralistic approaches.

Ethical Considerations in Pluralistic Qualitative Research

The ethical considerations given to planning and conducting pluralistic qualitative research do not differ significantly to those required to carry out all qualitative research. However, the capacity to gather perspectives from different stakeholders and methods means there are additional issues to consider in ensuring ethical clarity for all those taking part. By considering 'ethics at every step' (Palmer 2017), practical realities can be addressed and potential challenges minimised whilst also attending to researcher positions and roles as the study unfolds. In addition, adopting a positive ethical stance (Knapp, VandeCreek and Fingerhut 2017) promotes the understanding and appreciation of traditionally marginalised groups, and strives to maximise participant involvement, and thus may be particularly relevant to studies undertaken by counsellors and psychotherapists.

> **Box 8.1 Kvale's (1996) Five Ethical Questions**
> - What are the benefits of carrying out this research?
> - How is informed consent ensured?
> - How are participants assured of confidentiality?
> - What are the consequences of conducting the study?
> - What is the researcher's role in the study?

In an ethical chain Palmer (2017) interlinks procedures and practice of ethics whilst acknowledging that the links in the chain can be lengthened or shortened in response to the unpredictable nature of qualitative research (▶ Box 8.1):

Practice and procedure are connected and always underscored by the researcher position. This is useful in pluralistic research when researcher positionality is likely to vary according to who data is being gathered from and the method being used to analyse it. The flexibility of the ethical chain, and its presence throughout the research process, allows for different worldviews to be accommodated and for changes in status of different methods as they are brought to the research simultaneously or sequentially (◼ Fig. 8.2).

Kvale (1996) suggests five ethical questions to be addressed when planning and carrying out research, and it is useful to consider these in relation to pluralistic research.

Kvale's (1996) five questions provide a useful framework to think about ethical considerations in pluralistic studies. The process can be further enhanced by adopting an explicit positive ethical stance. This approach aims to actively think about how psychologists can do better in helping those they conduct research with (Knapp, VandeCreek and Fingerhut 2017). This is done by seeking to place participants as central to the research, striving to form high-quality relationships with them, and regarding them as moral agents rather than as a 'means to an end'. For pluralistic researchers, this means equipping themselves with as much knowledge as necessary of the different fields that participants from different groups represent, and disseminating the research appropriately to a range of scholarly communities (Nolas 2011), so that the value of the research can be accessed by the diverse audience to whom it may have meaning. The relationships with participants can be

Procedural ethics --- Ethical positions --- Ethics in practice --- Writing about ethics

◼ **Fig. 8.2** The ethical chain. (Adapted from Palmer, 2017)

enhanced by developing trust in all aspects of the research process, from explaining decisions and changes in the research as it develops if necessary, to making transparent the steps taken to ensure confidentiality, and being open about the researcher role. Working alone as a pluralistic researcher requires ongoing review and reflection on these issues, whilst pluralistic researchers working as part of a team can be accountable to and question each other, to ensure an ongoing consideration of ethical concerns.

Pluralistic research often involves gathering and analysing data from different stakeholders, each with different perspectives on a topic. Benefits can be directly applicable to some or all of the stakeholders–for example, those developing services may understand more about the importance of accessibility to counselling for people who have been bereaved by considering accounts of clients gathered as part of the research–and it may also be of indirect benefit to a wider audience such as counsellors wishing to know more about the value of, say, individual counselling compared to group counselling. Ultimately, the findings can be of interest to policy-makers and other support providers who read about the study and take from it the aspects of most relevance to their perspective. The key thing to remember is that the pluralistic nature of the study allows for different expressions and understandings of human experience and this requires the researcher to think carefully about its impact on, and benefit to, all those taking part.

This thinking has to extend, of course, to ensuring that consent is fully informed. There may be a need in a pluralistic study to explain differently to different stakeholders what the study aims are, for example if data is to be collected from children as well as adults. Similarly, it should be made clear to all participants that the data will be analysed in different ways, and why this is.

If the study involves service users, providers and developers, there is a need to ensure that all those taking part understand and agree with what their involvement in the study means. There may be different consequences for participants from different groups who may be required to talk about their experience of counselling services, for example. It is ethically essential that all participants are fully apprised of what data is being sought from them, how it is to be collected and what will be done with it, before they consent to taking part.

Similarly, in a pluralistic study, it is important to ensure that all participants are clear about how confidentiality will be ensured. Data in different forms such as photographs, drawings, diaries and interview transcripts may be gathered and each may require different considerations of how best to disguise its author. Similarly, it may be very important that different stakeholders are not identifiable to each other. Participants should be assured that their data will be kept confidential from others taking part in the study, as well as from wider audiences, unless the researcher has reason for legal concerns about safeguarding or child protection. Pluralistic studies also need to consider all the researchers involved and make clear to participants that consent is given to, and confidentiality assured, by all members of the research team.

Thinking about the consequences for participants of taking part in a study is a key ethical underpinning of all research; steps must always be taken to ensure as far as possible that participants are not harmed or distressed as a result of taking part in a study. In pluralistic research there is a need to retain a heightened awareness of the different understandings of a topic or experience that may be held by different participants, or participants from different groups, or constructed using different methods of analysis. Without due care, researchers may become complacent that, because talking about a topic is not distressing to a participant from one group, it will also not be to another. This may be particularly pertinent when carrying out research with vulnerable adults, or children, and those who provide support and other services to them, for example. It is also important to retain an awareness of how the findings from different methods are published in order to minimise distress and confusion, so that particular attention is paid to contradictions, challenges and different interpretations of data.

Writing Up Pluralistic Qualitative Research

Writing up a pluralistic qualitative research study requires researchers to think about how best to present the distinct yet complementary layers of understanding of the phenomenon under investigation. In some cases they may want to present them separately, and in others in combination. The decision will often rest on the context of the study and how it was carried out (sequentially or simultaneously, designed as pluralistic from the outset or evolved as a pluralistic study, and so on). We have previously discussed the value of pluralistic research in acknowledging the 'messiness' of human experience, and how this 'mess' may be reflected in contradictions and tensions that the use of multiple qualitative methods allows for. A challenge therefore is to find a way to present the findings without tidying them up and risking obscuring or misrepresenting meanings.

As with many forms of research writing, this process in pluralistic research can also act as part of the inquiry, with new insights being gained and relationships between methods and findings recognised as the write-up is crafted. Pluralistic research write-ups, like all qualitative research write-ups, can be challenged by the need to adhere to journal article formats and word counts, often predicated on traditional scientific styles. It can be hard to find space to include the researcher voice, and even harder if the research has involved a team of researchers, each making different contributions to the study. Pluralistic research enables enhanced reflexive awareness by researchers as they engage both with different methods and with other researchers in a study, and presenting this can be a key consideration of writing up pluralistic research.

There are many ways in which pluralistic research can be written up, and finding what will be most appropriate for your study will depend in part on the target audience, the focus of the study and the agreement between the team of researchers about the status of each method employed. A range of styles have been adopted in dissertations, theses and published articles and some are discussed below.

One way of writing up the pluralistic research is to present the findings for each analytical method separately, enabling comparisons to be drawn between the interpretations (Clarke et al. 2015). This enables each finding to be treated with equal significance, and to be considered to reflect a different dimension of the same phenomenon. This allows for multiple possibilities to be constructed rather than limiting phenomena to an either/or ontological perspective, thus recognising the complexity of participants' lives (Frost et al. 2011). The different interpretations offered by each method of analysis stand alone, and taken together offer multilayered insights into phenomena (Clarke et al. 2015). Following the different analyses and interpretation write-ups, the pluralistic researcher can then draw out and highlight the overlap and differences in meanings between these. This would make explicit any tensions, contradictions and consensus, without the tidying away of loose ends, in the building of a holistic, complex and multi-layered understanding of the phenomenon being researched pluralistically.

It is important to find ways of providing evidence of the analyses in pluralistic studies, and this is often in the form of quotes and/or visual images. The pluralistic researcher is aware that any decisions they make about which to include and how to display them has an impact on the research and can inform the interpretation of its meanings. Therefore they aim to present as much data as possible in appropriate and accessible ways. From a pragmatic perspective, pen-drives or online videos offer ways to include the bulk of the data and the data contained within the main text of the paper or thesis is then selected to best illustrate how meanings were reached.

Many researcher and participant groups may be involved in pluralistic research, and it can be useful to present data in collage form. Using computer technology, boxes can show voices with differing descriptions of the same phenomenon, and foregrounding some of this can be part of the findings. Researcher voices can be included as text or pictures from reflexive journals, and data from different researchers can be displayed together to show how each experienced a common challenge in the research process. Disagreement or contradiction between stakeholders can be illustrated by arranging them around a central box.

Whilst most write-ups of pluralistic research are text based, this does not preclude the inclusion of drawings and diagrams to enhance, support or add new findings. As previously discussed, these can provide understanding from a different dimension about what is significant to participants. Note that when including photographs in write-ups, it is important to think carefully about anonymity and confidentiality as well as inclusion of children or others who have not consented to appear in them.

Even with only textual data, innovative ways of writing up can be found. An example of one that incorporates many 'pluralisms' is by Chamberlain et al. (2011). In order to embrace pluralisms of method, of occasion, of researchers and of disciplines, the paper includes email correspondence, and written responses to interview questions posed by two of the researchers to the other two members of the team about their own multi-method research. Readers are told that discussions and debates about these responses informed the writing and rewriting of the paper, as did further discussions and responses to challenges posed by the editors of the journal in which it was to be published. The outcome is a detailed and informative paper that retains multi-dimensionality and plurality in a style that draws the reader in to understand the context, conduct, theory and outcomes of the study of pluralisms.

It is also possible to present theoretical pluralisms, as has been done by Honan et al. (2000), who use distinctive theoretical approaches to present and compare three qualitative analyses and show how subjects and the character of the social world they inhabit can be constituted differently depending on the theoretical approach used. To show how theoretical approaches radically influence what can be found in data and how it can be found, their three readings of the same data are presented separately by different researchers, each writing in the first person. Different scenarios are presented by each researcher to illustrate and explain the 'subject' they construct. The paper raises questions within and across the readings so that when one has reached the Discussion, it is clear not only that there are a number of other possible readings but also how the title of the paper, *Producing Possible Hannahs*, can be understood. The write-up is subjective, theoretically informed and compelling in its level of detail and explanation.

The value of pluralistic research is in representing the non-linear, multi-dimensionality of human experience, whilst also acknowledging the role of the researcher, and to show this as far as is possible in writing up the research is challenging. However, with an increasing openness to the publication of qualitative research, and the growth in online journals, there is a growing acceptance of creative and non-conventional styles of research write-ups which enables pluralistic researchers to ensure that not only the innovation but also the rigour of their work is disseminated.

Summary

In this chapter we suggest that qualitatively driven mixed methods and qualitative pluralistic research offer opportunities to generate multi-dimensional material for holistic insight into experiences. We have explored different approaches regarding how to engage in qualitative pluralism. For instance, 'analytical pluralism' refers to the mixing of several methods of qualitative data analyses on a single dataset; 'within-method pluralism' involves using the same method to analyse data in different ways but with the same underpinning philosophical assumptions. In contrast to this, 'across-method' pluralistic research uses different methods to analyse data in different ways, and thus the approach may be underpinned by differing philosophical viewpoints. We have explored pluralism and pragmatism and considered them with the issue of 'paradigm peace' (Bryman 2006) and the issue of methodolatry: the privileging of certain research methods and underlying frameworks. We have referred to how to ensure quality, including ethics concerns, when conducting pluralistic research, and looked at ways in which you may practice as a pluralistic researcher alone or as part of a team.

References

Bailey-Rodriguez, D. (2017). *"We're in the trenches together": A pluralistic exploration of attachment behaviour dynamics in a heterosexual couple relationship across the transition to second-time parenthood* (Unpublished doctoral thesis). Middlesex University, London.

Baker, C., Norton, S., Young, P., & Ward, S. (1998). An exploration of methodological pluralism in nursing research. *Research in Nursing & Health, 21*(6), 545–555.

Barbour, R. S. (1998). Mixing qualitative methods: Quality assurance or qualitative quagmire? *Qualitative Health Research, 8*, 352–361.

Barbour, R. S. (2001). Checklists for improving rigour in qualitative research: A case of the tail wagging the dog? *British Medical Journal, 322*, 1115–1117.

Barker, C., & Pistrang, N. (2005). Quality criteria under methodological pluralism: Implications for conducting and evaluating research. *American Journal of Community Psychology, 35*(3-4), 201–212.

Biesta, G. (2010). Pragmatism and the philosophical foundations of mixed methods research. In A. Tashakkori & C. Teddlie (Eds.), *Sage handbook of mixed methods in social and behavioural research* (pp. 95–117). Thousand Oaks: Sage.

Bryman, A. (2006). Integrating quantitative and qualitative research: How is it done? *Qualitative Research, 6*, 97–113.

Bryman, A. (2007). Barriers to integrating quantitative and qualitative research. *Journal of Mixed Methods Research, 6*(1), 8–22.

Chamberlain, K. (2000). Methodolatry in qualitative health research. *Journal of Health Psychology, 5*, 289–296.

Chamberlain, K., Cain, T., Sheridan, J., & Dupuis, A. (2011). Pluralisms in qualitative research: From multiple methods to integrated methods. *Qualitative Research in Psychology, 8*(2), 151–169.

Clarke, N. J., Willis, M. E., Barnes, J. S., Caddick, N., Cromby, J., McDermott, H., & Wiltshire, G. (2015). Analytical pluralism in qualitative research: A meta-study. *Qualitative Research in Psychology, 12*(2), 182–201.

Colahan, M. (2014). *Satisfaction in long-term heterosexual relationships: An exploration of discourse and lived experience* (Unpublished doctoral thesis). University of East London, London.

Collingridge, D. S., & Gantt, E. E. (2008). The quality of qualitative research. *American Journal of Medical Quality, 23*(5), 389–395.

Cooper, M., & McLeod, J. (2007). A pluralistic framework for counselling and psychotherapy: Implications for research. *Counselling and Psychotherapy Research, 7*(3), 135–143.

Creswell, J. W. (2009). Editorial: Mapping the field of mixed methods research. *Journal of Mixed Methods Research, 3*, 95–108.

Creswell, J. W., & Plano Clark, V. L. (2007). *Designing and conducting mixed methods research*. Thousand Oaks: Sage.

Curt, B. C. (1994). *Textuality and tectonics: Troubling social and psychological science*. Buckingham: Open University Press.

Dewe, M., & Coyle, A. (2014). Reflections on a study of responses to research on smoking: A pragmatic, pluralist variation on a qualitative psychological theme. *Review of Social Studies, 1*(1), 21–36.

Elichaoff, F., Rodriguez, D., & Murphy, A. (2014). More than just a method: Doctoral students' perspectives on the place of qualitatively driven mixed methods. *Qualitative Methods in Psychology Bulletin. Special Issue: The Place of Qualitative Methods in Mixed Methods Research, 17*, 17–22.

Flyvbjerg, B. (2006). Five misunderstandings about case-study research. *Qualitative Inquiry, 12*(2), 219–245.

Frost, N. A. (2006). *Taking the other out of mother: The transition to second-time motherhood* (Unpublished doctoral thesis). Birkbeck University, London.

Frost, N. A. (2008). Pluralism in qualitative research: Some emerging findings. *Qualitative Methods in Psychology Bulletin, 6*, 16–21.

Frost, N. (2009). 'Do you know what I mean?': The use of a pluralistic narrative analysis approach in the interpretation of an interview. *Qualitative Research, 9*(1), 9–29.

Frost, N. A. (2011). Interpreting data pluralistically. In N. A. Frost (Ed.), *Qualitative research methods in psychology: Combining core approaches* (pp. 145–160). Maidenhead: Open University Press.

Frost, N. A., & Nolas, S. M. (2011). Exploring and expanding on pluralism in qualitative research in psychology. *Qualitative Research in Psychology, 8*, 115–119.

8

Frost, N. A., Holt, A., Shinebourne, P., Esin, C., Nolas, S.-M., Mehdizadeh, L., & Brooks-Gordon, B. (2011). Collective findings, individual interpretations: An illustration of a pluralistic approach to qualitative data analysis. *Qualitative Research in Psychology, 8*, 93–113.

Gabb, J. (2009). Researching family relationships: A qualitative mixed methods approach. *Methodological Innovations Online, 4*(2), 37–52.

Gee, J. P. (1991). A linguistic approach to narrative. *Journal of Narrative and Life History, 1*(1), 15–39.

Hammersley, M. (2007). The issue of quality in qualitative research. *International Journal of Research & Method in Education, 30*(3), 287–305.

Hesse-Biber, S., Rodriguez, D., & Frost, N. A. (2015). A qualitatively-driven approach to multimethod and mixed methods research. In B. Johnson & S. Hesse-Biber (Eds.), *The Oxford handbook of multimethod and mixed methods research inquiry* (pp. 3–20). New York: Oxford University Press.

Honan, E., Knobel, M., Baker, C., & Davies, B. (2000). Producing possible Hannahs: Theory and the subject of research. *Qualitative Inquiry, 6*(1), 9–32.

Johnson, R. B. (2015). Dialectical pluralism: A metaparadigm whose time has come. *Journal of Mixed Methods Research*, 1–8.

Johnson, R. B., & Onwuegbuzie, A. J. (2004). Mixed methods research: A research paradigm whose time has come. *Educational Researcher, 33*(7), 14–26.

Josselin, D. (2013). *Wording the pain: An exploration of meaning-makings around emotions and self-injury* (Unpublished doctoral thesis) City University, London.

Josselin, D., & Willig, C. (2014). Layering the wounded self: Using a pluralistic qualitative approach to explore meaning-making around self-injury. *QMiP Bulletin, 17*(Spring), 21–32.

Kelly, G. (1955). *Personal construct psychology*. Nueva York: Norton.

King, N., Finlay, L., Ashworth, P., Smith, J. A., Langdridge, D., & Butt, T. (2008). "Can't really trust that, so what can I trust?": A polyvocal, qualitative analysis of the psychology of mistrust. *Qualitative Research in Psychology, 5*(2), 80–102.

Knapp, S.J., VandeCreek, L.D. and Fingerhut, R. (2017). *Practical ethics for psychologists: A positive approach*. Washington, DC: American Psychological Association.

Kvale, S. (1996). *InterViews: An introduction to qualitative research interviewing*. London: Sage.

Labov, W. (1972). The transformation of experience in narrative syntax. In W. Labov (Ed.), *Language in the inner city: Studies in the black English vernacular* (pp. 354–395). Philadelphia: University of Pennsylvania Press.

Mason, J. (2006). Mixing methods in a qualitatively driven way. *Qualitative Research, 6*(1), 9–25.

Mertens, D. M. (2012). What comes first? The paradigm or the approach? *Journal of Mixed Methods Research, 6*, 255–257.

Moran-Ellis, J., Alexander, V. D., Cronin, A., Dickinson, M., Fielding, J., Sleney, J., & Thomas, H. (2006). Triangulation and integration: Processes, claims and implications. *Qualitative Research, 6*(1), 45–59.

Morse, J. M., & Chung, S. E. (2003). Toward holism: The significance of methodological pluralism. *International Journal of Qualitative Methods, 2*(3), 13–20.

Morse, J. M., & Niehaus, L. (2009). *Mixed method design: Principles and procedures*. Walnut Creek: Left Coast Press Inc.

Nolas, S. M. (2011). Pragmatics of pluralistic qualitative research. In N. Frost (Ed.), *Qualitative research methods in psychology: Combining core approaches* (pp. 121–144). Maidenhead: Open University Press.

O'Reilly, M., & Kiyimba, N. (2015). *Advanced qualitative research: A guide to using theory*. London: Sage.

Palmer, C. (2017). Ethics in sport and exercise research. In B. M. Smith & A. C. Sparkes (Eds.), *Routledge handbook of qualitative research in sport and exercise* (pp. 316–329). London: Routledge.

Payne, G., Williams, M., & Chamberlain, S. (2004). Methodological pluralism in British sociology. *Sociology, 38*(1), 153–163.

Radley, A., & Chamberlain, K. (2001). Health psychology and the study of the case: From method to analytic concern. *Social Science & Medicine, 53*(3), 321–332.

Rescher, N. (1993). *Pluralism: Against the demand for consensus*. Oxford: Oxford University.

Rodriguez, D., & Frost, N. A. (2015, May). A methodological reflection on the application of qualitative pluralistic research to couple relationships. Paper presented at the American Psychological Association's Society for Qualitative Inquiry in Psychology Second Annual Conference, City University New York, New York.

Shannon-Baker, P. (2016). Making paradigms meaningful in mixed methods research. *Journal of Mixed Methods Research, 10*(4), 319–334.

Spencer, L., Ritchie, J., Lewis, J., & Dillon, L. (2003). *Quality in qualitative evaluation: A framework for assessing research evidence.* Government Chief Social Researcher's Office. Accessed on 3rd January 2019 at http://dera.ioe.ac.uk/21069/2/a-quality-framework-tcm6-38740.pdf

Tracy, S. J. (2010). Qualitative quality: Eight "big-tent" criteria for excellent qualitative research. *Qualitative Inquiry, 16*(10), 837–851.

Willig, C. (2013). *Introducing qualitative research in psychology.* Maidenhead: Open University Press.

Willig, C. (2017, July). The case for combining FDA and IPA in a dual focus methodology. Paper presented at the British Psychological Society's Qualitative Methods in Psychology Section Conference, Aberystwyth.

Yardley, L. (2008). Demonstrating validity in qualitative psychology. In J. A. Smith (Ed.), *Qualitative psychology: A guide to research methods* (pp. 235–251). London: Sage.

8

Doing Quantitative Research with Statistics

Alistair McBeath

Contents

© The Author(s) 2020
S. Bager-Charleson, A. McBeath (eds.),
Enjoying Research in Counselling and Psychotherapy,
https://doi.org/10.1007/978-3-030-55127-8_9

Learning Goals

After reading this chapter, you should be able to:

- Recognise the different types of descriptive statistics;
- Understand the properties of the normal distribution;
- Understand the concept of statistical significance;
- Differentiate between different measurement scales;
- Choose appropriate statistical tests to analyse data.

Introduction

A Formula-Free Introduction to Statistics

Within the counselling and psychotherapy professions there are some very good reasons for having a working knowledge of statistics. First, from a research perspective a basic knowledge of statistics allows informed decisions to be taken about the choice of research design and methodology. Second, as the amount of published research in the fields of counselling and psychotherapy continues to grow there is a need for practitioners to be research-literate and this requires a basic knowledge of statistics. A closely related point is the fact that important policy and organisational decisions are often made about counselling and psychotherapy services on the basis of statistics and it is important to be able to assess the evidence.

Without a grounding in statistics practitioners run the risk of being unable to fully assess and absorb research-led knowledge and, consequently, will be limited in their ability to engage in professional debate. Statistics have delivered some truly important findings within counselling and psychotherapy. For example, it is now generally accepted that what is really important in therapeutic work is the relationship between practitioners and their clients rather than the efficacy of any particular theoretical orientation. This finding has been accepted through research where key arguments have been based on statistics (e.g. Barth et al. 2013).

This chapter is focused on introducing sufficient basic information to allow the reader to grasp the fundamental meaning of some key statistical concepts. It is not about how to do statistics but about how to understand statistics. Ultimately, the objective is to allow the reader to acquire what McLeod (2015) has termed a 'reading-level knowledge' of statistics, which itself is a key element of research-literacy. There are no formulae or calculations in this chapter.

The chapter is designed to introduce statistical concepts in a manner that promotes a cumulative acquisition of knowledge starting with some very basic ideas, which will underpin more advanced concepts. There will be a gentle introduction to some basic statistical terminology, different types of statistics, and different data types or measurement scales, and an explanation of statistical significance. Other topics will include hypothesis testing and an introduction to some commonly used statistical tests.

Introductory Concepts

A very broad definition of statistics is a set of procedures and rules that allow large amounts of data to be summarised and which also allow conclusions to be drawn from those data. More specifically, statistics allow data to be meaningfully described and they provide systematic ways to investigate relationships between different sets of data So, for example, is there a relationship between scores on a depression test and the number of weeks people have been absent from work?

There are two broad categories of statistics: *descriptive statistics* and *inferential statistics*. Descriptive statistics provide meaningful ways to summarise data and to identify patterns in data. A familiar descriptive statistic is the mean or average of a set of numbers. Inferential statistics allow researchers to investigate relationships between variables within a subset of data (i.e. *the sample*) and to make inferences from a sample to much larger data sets (i.e. *the population*). A *variable* is a characteristic or property that may take on different values. Height, blood pressure, ethnicity and gender are all examples of variables. Numbers that summarise populations are called *parameters* whilst numbers that summarise samples are called *statistics*.

An example of the power of inferential statistics comes from research by Poulsen et al. (2014),[1] who compared psychoanalytic psychotherapy and cognitive-behavioral therapy (CBT) in the treatment of bulimia nervosa. The authors reported that CBT was found to be the significantly more effective treatment modality. This study is an example of an inference being made about treatment efficacy from a sample (i.e. 70 patients) to a wider population (i.e. sufferers of bulimia nervosa in general). In this study the variable controlled by the researcher (i.e. treatment modality) is known as the *independent variable* and the measured response to it (i.e. frequency of binge eating) is known as the *dependent variable*.

Descriptive Statistics

There are several different types of descriptive statistics and they can be grouped as follows:

1. Measures of *frequency* – include count, percent and frequency (used to show how often an event has happened);
2. Measures of *central tendency* – include the mean, median and mode (used to show the most common response);
3. Measures of *dispersion* – include range, variance and standard deviation (used to show how spread out values in our data might be);
4. Measures of *association* – include correlation (used to show the extent that variables might be related).

---

1   This research is a rare example of one treatment modality being shown to be more effective than another and is very illness-specific.

◘ Table 9.1   Examples of mean, median and mode

Type	Description	Example	Result
Mean	Total sum divided by number of values	(4+4+4+4+5+5+6+8+10)/9	5.5
Median	Middle value in a data set. Same number of values above and below	4, 4, 4, 4, 5, 5, 6, 8, 10	5
Mode	Most frequently occurring number in a data set	4, 4, 4, 4, 5, 5, 6, 8, 10	4

Descriptive statistics can be very useful and can be illustrated by looking at the mean, median and mode. The mean is what we know as the average; we add up a set of numbers and divide this number by how many individual numbers contribute to that total. In statistics the mean is represented by the symbol $\bar{x}$.

The median is the middle number in a data set and the mode is the most frequently occurring number in a data set. The definitions and examples of the mean, median and mode are shown in ◘ Table 9.1.

Although the mean is a very commonly used statistic, it is not always the best measure because it is sensitive to extreme scores, also called *outliers*. Imagine that there has been a request to identify the average length of stay in a secure psychiatric unit. In this context it is likely that a few exceptional very long and very short stays would distort the mean and hence the median would provide a more reliable and accurate 'typical length of stay'. Extreme scores do not affect the median.

At this point it is appropriate to introduce a very important concept in statistics, namely, the *Normal Distribution* (also called the bell-shaped curve). An example of a normal distribution is shown in ◘ Fig. 9.1. A normal distribution is an arrangement of a data set in which most values cluster in the middle of the range and the rest taper off symmetrically towards either extreme. The mean is in the middle and divides the distribution into two symmetrical halves. In a normal distribution the mean, median and mode occupy the same central value.

A variable that classically falls near to normal distribution is height. Thus, the most common heights will cluster in the middle, with less common heights (either very tall or very short) showing up at either end or tail of the distribution. But what are the numbers shown at the base of ◘ Fig. 9.1? They represent a very important statistic called the *standard deviation*, which is a measure of the spread or variability within data sets.

Let us illustrate how the standard deviation is valuable. Imagine that there are two counselling clinics which offer short-term support to young mothers. Over the course of a year each clinic takes on six trainee counsellors for their clinical placement. In seeking to review the training experience the question is asked: What is the average number of sessions conducted by trainee counsellors during their first two months? ◘ Table 9.2 shows the data concerned with each tick mark representing a single trainee counsellor. For both clinics the total number of sessions con-

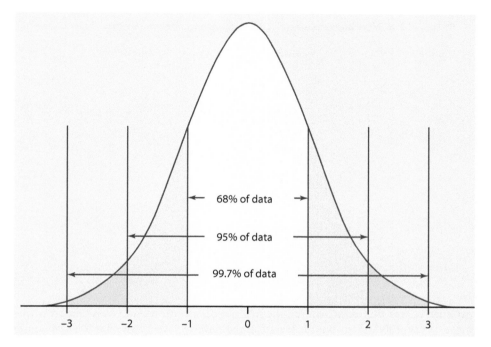

□ Fig. 9.1   Example of a normal distribution

ducted is the same (i.e. 24), as is the mean (i.e. 4). However, we can see from
□ Table 9.2 that the data are much more spread out in Clinic A than in Clinic
B. Hence simply comparing the means between the clinics may be misleading as it
overlooks the issue of the variability or dispersion of data between the clinics.

What we need in order to make the data more intelligible is a measure of data
spread, and that is exactly what the standard deviation delivers. The standard
deviation gives us a quality rating of the mean of a set of numbers. In effect the
standard deviation indicates the extent to which the numbers that go into an average deviate from that average. The larger the standard deviation the more the data
are spread out. In □ Table 9.2 the standard deviation for clinic A is 2.9 and for
clinic B it is 0.9. The standard deviation is often shown as SD or the lower case of
the Greek letter alpha – σ. The standard deviation is one of the most commonly
reported statistics in published research.

The standard deviation is an important statistic in understanding some of the
properties of the Normal Distribution. If a data distribution is 'Normal' then 68%
of the data will lie within one standard deviation of the mean (plus and minus).
□ Figure 9.1 shows this, and also that 95% of data will lie within two standard
deviations of the mean and 99.7% will lie between three standard deviations of the
mean. So how might this information be useful?

The standard deviation statistic and its relationship to the normal distribution
can provide an intuitive understanding of extreme conditions and recovery.
Consider a psychometric test designed to measure depression, which is known to

◘ Table 9.2 Number of sessions conducted by trainee counsellors in two separate clinics

Clinic A	No of sessions	Clinic B
✓	1	
✓	2	
✓✓	3	✓✓
	4	✓✓
	5	✓✓
	6	
✓	7	
✓	8	
	9	
Mean = 4		Mean = 4

produce scores that approximate the normal distribution and is associated with a mean ($\bar{x}$) of 100 and standard deviation (SD) of 15. We know that 95% of scores will fall within 2 SDs of the mean, which is 100 plus or minus 30. After translating this into test scores the range will be from 70 up to 130. We might judge that scores lying outside this range would indicate a severe clinical condition.

Staying with this example allows us to see how we could discern the impact of a treatment programme for depression from the normal distribution and standard deviation. If we have individuals with assessment test scores that lie beyond 2 SDs (i.e. 70–130) we might decide that post-treatment scores that lie within 1 SD of the mean (i.e. 85–115) would indicate successful treatment as test scores would have moved back closer to the mean (i.e. normal functioning).

It is important to note that the properties of the normal distribution and the standard deviation that have been described apply to continuous variables that approximate a normal distribution. A *continuous variable* is one that can take almost any value; examples are height, weight and money.

Measurement Scales

In considering any manipulation or presentation of data it is important to be aware that there are different types of data or what is termed *measurement scales*. Measurement scales refer to the ways in which data and variables can be defined and categorised. There are four different measurement scales in statistics and each has differing properties, which determine how their data may be presented and analysed. The four scales of measurement are *Nominal, Ordinal, Interval and Ratio*. The four scales are ordered so that all later scales have all the properties of earlier scales plus additional properties. How do they differ?

Nominal

Nominal scales describe variables using labels and without any quantitative value. The key point in nominal scales is that they uniquely identify response categories with no overlap. ◘ Figure 9.2 shows an example of a question that generates nominal scale measurement. In terms of measures of central tendency only the mode is appropriate as the mean and median cannot be defined. The most common statistics associated with nominal scales are frequencies and percentages.

Within nominal scales there is no order. There is no positional meaning or numerical distance between Yes and No responses. Nominal scale data are non-numeric.

Ordinal

In ordinal scales response categories have order and can be ranked. Likert-scale questions, as shown in ◘ Fig. 9.3, are a classic example of ordinal scale measurement. The response categories in ◘ Fig. 9.3 have an order that is meaningful.

Therefore, we know that the response *Very likely* is more positive than *Not likely*. Ordinal data are labelled data but in a specific order and often numbers are assigned to place response categories in order.

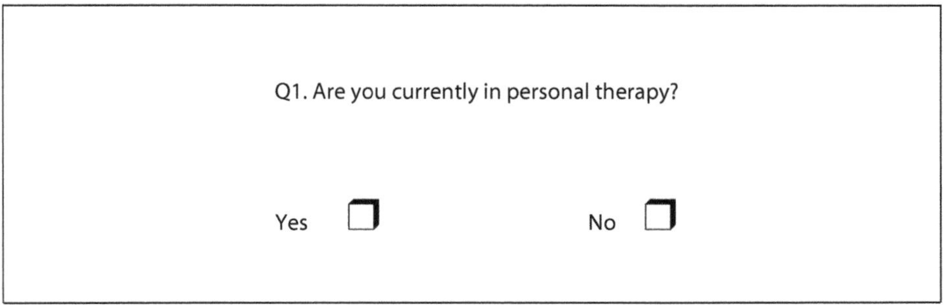

Q1. Are you currently in personal therapy?

Yes ☐   No ☐

◘ **Fig. 9.2**   Example of a nominal scale data question

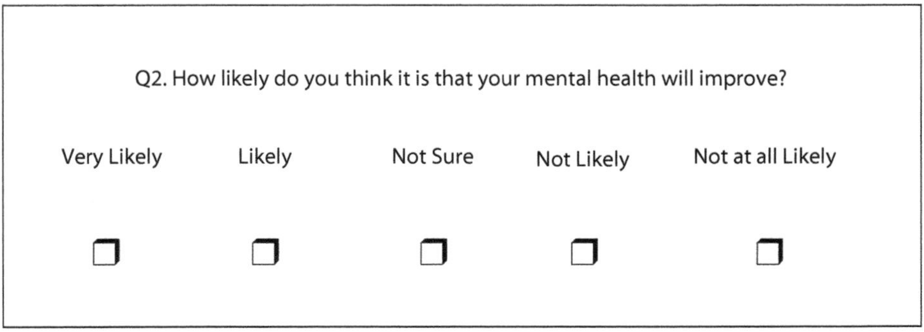

Q2. How likely do you think it is that your mental health will improve?

Very Likely   Likely   Not Sure   Not Likely   Not at all Likely

☐   ☐   ☐   ☐   ☐

◘ **Fig. 9.3**   Example of Likert scale question

It is important to be aware that with ordinal data we don't know the distance between response categories. Thus, it makes no sense to say that the difference between *Very likely* and *Likely* is the same as the distance between *Not likely* and *Not at all likely*. This factor limits the range of statistical tests that can be used with ordinal data. The median is an appropriate measure of central tendency with ordinal data. Ordinal scale data are quantitative.

Interval

The data in interval scales come in the form of a numerical value where the difference between points is standardised and meaningful. The most common example of interval data is temperature; the difference in temperature between 10° and 20° is the same as the difference in temperature between 20° and 30°. The data from IQ tests are another example of an interval scale.

Interval scales allow various forms of statistical analysis. For example, central tendency can be measured by mode, median or mean; the standard deviation can also be calculated. An important point about interval scales is that they lack a true zero point, which means that one can add or subtract values but cannot meaningfully divide or multiply them. Hence, while the difference between 10° and 20° is the same as the difference in temperature between 20° and 30° it cannot be said that 40° is twice as hot as 20°. Temperature has no meaningful zero point–there is no 'zero temperature'.

Ratio

Ratio scales are the highest level of measurement scale because they tell us about the order of data, they tell us the exact value between intervals, and they also have a true zero point which allows a wide variety of descriptive and inferential statistics to be applied. Ratio scale data are rich in possibilities where variables can be meaningfully added, subtracted, multiplied and divided (ratios). With ratio scales central tendency can be measured by mode, median or mean, and measures of dispersion such as the standard deviation can be calculated. Good examples of ratio scales are height and weight.

It is important to know the properties of different measurement scales because this largely determines the choice of the most appropriate statistical analysis. For example, there is no meaning in describing the mean value of nominal or ordinal data because they can't be quantified. Novice researchers often want to know what statistical test they can use to analyse their data. Ideally this question should be answered before any data are collected. If the data type and scale is known, in advance of data collection, then the choice of appropriate statistical analysis options should be relatively straightforward. Think about the data first and then the analysis.

9

Statistical Significance

One of the most important concepts in research and statistics is the concept of *statistical significance*; it is important to know what it means when doing research and it is important when reading research. Earlier in the chapter reference was made to a study that reported that CBT was significantly more effective in treating bulimia than psychoanalytic therapy (Poulsen et al. 2014). This finding was reported as a statistically significant result. So, what does it mean?

Statistical significance is derived from a few related ideas; these include *hypothesis testing* and a probability statement known as a *p value*. In researching the efficacy of CBT and psychoanalytic psychotherapy in the treatment of bulimia the researchers were in fact engaged in hypothesis testing.

There are two classic and competing hypotheses in statistics: the *null hypothesis* and the *alternate hypothesis*. The null hypothesis is a statement that says there is no systematic relationship between different data sets or variables. Thus, in the bulimia research study this would translate to saying that there will be no expected difference in the effectiveness of CBT and psychoanalytic psychotherapy in the treatment of bulimia in the population. What researchers seek to do is to reject this hypothesis–to conclude that it is false; they can then assert the alternate hypothesis, namely, that there will be a systematic difference between CBT and psychoanalytic psychotherapy in the treatment of bulimia. Hence, in effect, researchers are really exploring which of the two hypotheses is better supported by the data.

In the bulimia research study the researchers rejected the null hypothesis, but on what basis was this done? It was based on the probability (i.e. the *p* value) being so low of getting the results reported if the null hypothesis is true (i.e. there will be no difference between CBT and psychoanalytic therapy in treating bulima) that the null hypothesis could be rejected. Thus, this was a case where the odds of the data reported being due to chance were so low that the researchers concluded that the variables must be systematically related in some way. Hence, the rejection of the null hypothesis is really a probability argument.

Statistical convention has formalised this type of probability argument using two specific levels of probability (i.e. *p* values)–set at 0.05 (1 in 20) and 0.01 (1 in 100). These *p* values are often referred to as *significance levels*. Across a large range of statistical tests the results of testing are accompanied by a *p* value. If the *p* value is either less than 0.05 ($p < 0.05$) or less than 0.01 ($p < 0.01$) the result of the test is judged to be statistically significant. This is the key meaning behind the reporting of statistically significant results.

A statistically significant finding is one that is taken to reflect a systematic relationship within a data set or between variables that is not accountable by chance or other extraneous factors.

Correlation

Correlation is one of the most common and most useful concepts in statistics. Correlation is a statistical technique that can show whether pairs of variables are related, and if so, how strongly. More specifically, a correlation coefficient is a statistical measure of the degree to which differences to the value of one variable are associated with differences to the value of another.

Variables may have a positive or negative correlation (as well as no correlation). With positively correlated variables values increase or decrease in tandem. One example is the reported positive correlation between depression and alcohol dependency where higher scores on the Beck Depression Inventory were associated with higher scores on an alcohol dependence scale (Choi and Jeong 2015).

With a negative correlation there is an inverse relationship between variables, and thus when one increases the other decreases and vice versa. A good example is a study that investigated the relationship between self-esteem and suicidal ideation (Manani and Sharma 2013). A significant negative correlation was reported between ratings on the Rosenberg Self-Esteem Scale (Rosenberg 1965) and a suicidal ideation questionnaire (Reynolds 1987). Thus, extrapolating from this study the expectation is that higher self-esteem is associated with lower suicidal ideation and vice versa. The researchers summarised their findings as follows: '

» The result of the present research leads to the rejection of the hypothesis that there is no significant relationship between suicidal ideation and self-esteem' (p 81).

Hence, as we now know, this means a rejection of the null hypothesis.

A correlation has both magnitude and direction and can take a value from -1 through zero to $+1$. A correlation of -1 would indicate a perfect negative relationship between variables and likewise a correlation of $+1$ would indicate a perfect positive relationship between variables. A value of 0 indicates no relationship between variables. In reality values will lie between -1 and $+1$. The *Pearson product-moment correlation* is a common measure of correlation and is usually represented by the letter r.

In the study noted above which reported a positive correlation between depression and alcohol dependency the authors reported their correlation as follows: '$r = .283$, $p = .031$'. Thus here we see that r is positive and the p value of 0.031 is less than the 5% significance level (i.e. $p < 0.05$) and hence the result is a statistically significant positive correlation.

Statistical Tests

Within inferential statistics there are two categories of statistical tests, *parametric tests* and *non-parametric tests*, and they are based on some important differing assumptions. Parametric tests assume that the data being tested approximate the normal distribution. Non-parametric tests are sometimes called 'distribution-free' tests because they do not rely on data approximating a particular distribution.

If the assumptions of parametric tests cannot be met there are some useful non-parametric alternatives. For example, when comparing data from discrete groups the main parametric choices are *the independent samples t-test* and *analysis of variance* (ANOVA). The non-parametric alternatives are the *Mann-Whitney U test* and the *Kruskal-Wallis test* respectively. There are also correlation options. The *Pearson correlation (r)* measures the association between two continuous variables; if the data are ordinal then *Spearman's rank correlation (ρ)* is appropriate.

Certain tests are particularly suited for certain types of research design and data. For example, comparing mental health literacy test scores from trainee nurses before and after a training course in basic mental health problems would be suitable for analysis by a *paired groups t-test*. In contrast, we might want to explore the impact of a variable between different groups of people. An example might be to compare post-treatment scores on a depression inventory (*dependent variable*) for those who received different types of therapy (*the independent variable*); for example, this could be CBT compared to psychodynamic therapy. The null hypothesis would assume no difference between these two groups. In this research design the *independent t-test* would be appropriate.

The *Chi-square test* is a useful non-parametric test. Imagine two groups of therapists: (a) those with up to two years post-training experience and (b) those with up to 10 years post-training experience. Both groups have answered the question: 'To what extent would you agree that the concept of transference is important in clinical work?' The answers fall on a typical Likert scale: 'strongly agree', 'agree', 'unsure', 'disagree', 'strongly disagree'. The Chi-square test (for independence) can determine whether the distribution of responses across the Likert scale systematically varies between the two groups of therapists; the null hypothesis would assume they do not.

There is a truly extensive range of statistical tests available to the researcher, and this may seem somewhat daunting. The best approach in choosing appropriate tests is to consider the assumptions on which they are based; these will sensibly narrow down the choice of statistical testing options. There are numerous analysis platforms such as JASP, SPSS and PSPP that offer easy access to a wide range of statistical tests. Such ease of access offers considerable opportunities to the researcher but only as much as the choice of statistical test is an informed choice.

Activity

In the context of a reduced budget a therapy clinic wishes to explore whether online therapy is as effective as face-to-face therapy in the treatment of clients with severe anxiety. A placement student at the clinic is assigned this piece of research as part of their MA studies. The following research approach was used:

A sample of 140 individuals diagnosed with severe anxiety (using the GAD-7 assessment test) was identified and 70 were randomly assigned to treatment with online therapy and 70 were assigned to treatment with face-to-face therapy. At the end of six sessions all individuals were re-assessed with respect to whether their anxiety had been reduced or not. The data could be presented in a simple 2 × 2 table as shown below.

	Anxiety reduction	No change
Online therapy	30	40
Face to face	50	20

- What possible statistical approaches might be used to analyse these data?
- What would the null hypothesis be?
- Are there any missing data (e.g. increased anxiety)?
- Is the sample random?
- Are there any ethical issues (e.g. assignment to treatment condition)
- Would a parametric or non-parametric test be most suitable?
- Would statistical significance be of importance in this research?
- Would a Chi-square test be appropriate?

9

Summary

Having a basic understanding of statistics is important for counsellors and therapists. The emphasis on evidence-based practice and studies of therapeutic efficacy is underpinned by statistical information. For many practitioners unfamiliar with statistical concepts and statistical tests this subject area can seem daunting. In part, this situation reflects a relative lack of basic and easy to assimilate information about rudimentary statistical concepts and examples which show the relevance and application of statistics to counselling and psychotherapy. This chapter has sought to show how some basic statistical concepts can be understood and applied by therapeutic practitioners with a view to promoting their own working knowledge of statistics.

References

Barth, J., Munder, T., Gerger, H., Nüesch, E., Trelle, S., Znoj, H., Jüni, P., & Cuijpers, P. (2013). Comparative efficacy of seven psychotherapeutic interventions for patients with depression: A network meta-analysis. *PLoS Medicine, 10*(5), e1001454. https://doi.org/10.1371/journal.pmed.1001454.

Choi, B.-Y., & Jeong, H.-C. (2015). Relationship between alcohol dependence and depression of alcohol dependent inpatients. *International Journal of Bio-Science and Bio-Technology, 7*(5), 375–382. https://doi.org/10.14257/ijbsbt.2015.7.5.37.

Manani, P., & Sharma, S. (2013). Self-esteem and suicidal ideation: A correlational study. *MIER Journal of Educational Studies, Trends and Practices, 3*(1), 175–183.

McLeod, J. (2015). *Doing research in counselling and psychotherapy*. London, UK: Sage Publications Ltd.

Poulsen, S., Lunn, S., Daniel, S. I., Folke, S., Mathiesen, B. B., Katznelson, H., & Fairburn, C. G. (2014). A randomized controlled trial of psychoanalytic psychotherapy or cognitive-behavioral therapy for bulimia nervosa. *American Journal of Psychiatry, 171*(1), 109–106. https://doi.org/10.1176/appi.ajp.2013.12121511.

Reynolds, W. M. (1987). *Suicidal ideation questionnaire*. Odessa: Psychological Assessment Resources.

Rosenberg, M. (1965). *Society and the adolescent self-image*. Princeton: Princeton University Press.

Doing Quantitative Research with a Survey

Alistair McBeath

Contents

© The Author(s) 2020
S. Bager-Charleson, A. McBeath (eds.),
Enjoying Research in Counselling and Psychotherapy,
https://doi.org/10.1007/978-3-030-55127-8_10

🔄 Learning Goals

After reading this chapter, you should be able to:

- Understand the different types of survey questions;
- Comprehend different approaches to survey sampling;
- Decide what would be a reasonable survey sample size;
- Differentiate between different data types;
- Understand how surveys might be analysed and reported

Introduction. Why Use Surveys?

Surveys are one of the most commonly used approaches in research activity and they can deliver important new knowledge for a wide array of research questions. Surveys can cost-effectively reach large numbers of people as well as specifically targeted groups, and can generate findings that are representative of much larger groups of people. For example, if we survey an appropriate sample of therapists about their views on the value of anti-depressants we should have confidence that our findings will be reasonably representative of the views of all therapists. Thus, surveys can be powerful in creating new findings that can be used for wider generalisation.

There's never been a better time to utilise the power and flexibility of survey techniques. Ready access to the Internet and the growth in social media platforms allow surveys to be designed with ease and there are countless numbers of people, groups and professions that are almost immediately accessible through technology. Historically, surveys have been seen as an exclusively quantitative research method but this is really an outmoded view. A carefully designed survey can generate significant amounts of qualitative data that can enhance and illuminate the quantitative product of surveys (e.g. McBeath 2019; McBeath et al. 2019).

In this chapter some of the key issues around designing an effective survey will be discussed with some examples from a recent survey conducted by the author that explored the motivations of psychotherapists (McBeath 2019). Topics will include question types, data types, sampling, statistical significance, analysis techniques, graphical presentation and survey design.

Surveys in Counselling and Psychotherapy

The use of surveys in counselling and psychotherapy research has become commonplace and they have been used to address a wide range of issues. The following surveys serve to illustrate just how diverse survey-based research activity can be within the therapeutic domain.

- What do psychotherapists really do in practice? An Internet study of over 2000 practitioners (Cook et al. 2010)
- The protection we deserve: Findings from a service user survey on the regulation of counsellors and psychotherapists (Mind 2010)

- Becoming a psychotherapist or counsellor: A survey of psychotherapy and counselling trainers (Richardson et al. 2009)
- Dance movement therapy with the elderly: An international Internet-based survey undertaken with practitioners (Bräuninger 2014)
- Psychotherapy clients' attitudes to personal psychotherapy for psychotherapists (Ivey and Phillips 2016)
- Honesty in psychotherapy: Results of an online survey comparing high vs. low self-concealers (Love and Farber 2018)
- Psychotherapists' motivations: an in-depth survey (McBeath 2019).

The main professional regulatory bodies (e.g. British Association for Counselling and Psychotherapy [BACP], British Psychological Society [BPS], United Kingdom Council for Psychotherapy [UKCP]) run regular surveys both within the public domain and within their own membership. Some of the surveys have generated quite politically sensitive headlines such as "Older people are not getting the mental health support they deserve" (BACP 2017) and "NHS psychotherapy services under threat shows UKCP/BPC survey" (UKCP/BPC 2012). Thus, surveys are being used for diverse purposes within the counselling and psychotherapy worlds and it seems likely that their popularity and usage will continue to increase as the survey process itself continues to become even more accessible and user-friendly. In addition, conducting surveys can be a very enjoyable and stimulating research activity.

Online Survey Platforms

Before the advent of the digital age creating surveys could be rather a tedious and prolonged process where questionnaires were typically posted to individuals. But now there are a number of powerful online survey platforms available which allow a survey to be designed, tested and distributed in a very short period of time. Currently, one of the better-known platforms is SurveyMonkey which, in 2017, claimed to have delivered a total of 100 million surveys worldwide. Online surveying is big business.

The majority of online survey platforms offer a number of common features. These include survey design options, which allow the use of differing question types and formats and the potential to brand surveys with logos and other artwork so that a survey has the look and feel of a particular research or educational organisation. Online survey platforms typically offer some quite powerful functionality around data analysis and description. A number of descriptive statistics are usually offered such as frequency counts, as well as statistical tests such as Chi-square where the statistical significance of differences in data can be tested. Some of the survey platforms allow data to be directly exported into such powerful analysis tools as Excel and SPSS, which opens up even more analysis options. In cases where a survey allows free-text comments some survey platforms offer the ability to conduct text analysis, which can contribute to a meaningful thematic analysis. Online survey platforms also offer useful graphics options where data can be easily presented in a variety of formats such as pie charts and bar charts.

Designing a Survey

When designing a survey it is important to do some thorough pre-design thinking which should subsequently help the survey process to run smoothly. Here are some key issues:
- What is the issue that we are going to research?
- What would we like to know?
- What do we intend to do with the survey findings?
- Who is our target audience?
- Can we access an appropriate sample?
- How big a sample do we need?
- How long will the survey take to complete?
- What analysis do we plan to do?
- How will we present the survey findings?
- Are there any ethical issues?

It is well worth investing time in rehearsing our thoughts on these issues. The ready accessibility of online survey platforms can sometimes tempt us to start surveying without a thorough planning phase, and this can cause problems. For example, what if we find out that our survey doesn't actually give us the information that we wanted? Or perhaps our survey sample is too small to look at the influence of potentially important variables such as length of training, gender or age. Finally, do we actually know what analysis is possible or appropriate to obtain a desired piece of information? If surveys are conducted without appropriate planning it's more likely that they will fail in some respect, and this may present difficulties in reporting and disseminating survey findings.

Types of Survey Questions

Surveys are all about asking questions, and there are several different types of questions that can be used. Perhaps the most basic is the *dichotomous question* where there can only be two answers; an example is shown in ◘ Fig. 10.1.

Dichotomous questions give survey respondents a straight choice between two answers; they are typically easy to comprehend and quick to complete. Although dichotomous questions may seem quite limited in the information that they provide they can be very useful in further survey analysis. For example, in the example

Q1. Have you completed your counselling training?

Yes ☐   No ☐

◘ **Fig. 10.1**   Example of a dichotomous question

above an analysis could examine whether survey answers differed systematically between those who have completed their counselling training and those who have not.

One area where the dichotomous question format has been challenged concerns gender. Traditionally it has been commonplace to ask survey respondents to identify their gender and only two choices were offered: male or female. This binary approach to gender is now recognised as outmoded and ethically wrong as it excludes the reality of gender diversity. There has been some recognition that gender goes beyond a binary formulation and additional responses such as 'transgender' and 'other' are now used in surveys. However, this approach can still be seen as limiting. One way to sensitively record gender is simply to ask: What is your gender?

One of the most common question types in surveys is the *Likert scale* format where survey respondents are typically offered either a 5- or 7-point scale from which survey respondents choose the option that most agrees with their opinion. A Likert scale offers a range of answer options going from one extreme to another such as *Very Likely* to *Not at all likely;* Likert scales usually have a moderate or neutral mid-point such as *Not sure.* ◘ Figure 10.2 shows a typical Likert scale question.

There are several advantages to using Likert scales. They are undoubtedly the most common way to collect survey data and are typically easy to understand. Unlike a dichotomous question, a Likert scale doesn't force a survey respondent into making a choice but allows a degree of agreement, which makes questions easier to answer. Likert scales also allow for neutral or undecided responses from survey respondents.

Likert scales are very easy to analyse but one must be aware of two important issues. First, one cannot assume that the intervals between responses are equal. Therefore, the difference between 'Very likely' and 'Likely' cannot be assumed to be the same as the difference between 'Not likely' and 'Not at all likely'; this is why Likert scales are described as an *ordinal measure* of attitudes. The order of responses on a Likert scale is something we can analyse but we cannot analyse the differences between responses.

Q2. How likely do you think it is that you are not fully aware of the motivations that made you want to become a psychotherapist?

Very likely	Likely	Not sure	Not likely	Not at all likely
❒	❒	❒	❒	❒

◘ **Fig. 10.2** Example of a Likert scale question. (From McBeath 2019)

Likert scales are prone to two particular types of bias. The first is a tendency to avoid extreme responses, which is known as the *central tendency bias*. A second potential source of bias is termed *sequential anchoring*, which is when the rating given for one question influences the rating given to a following question in favour of providing similar ratings. Overall, however, Likert scales are a powerful and flexible survey tool when the objective is to dig deeper into a research question. Moreover, Likert scales are generally what people would expect to be included in a survey, and this will make completing a survey a more user-friendly experience.

Another common question format in surveys is the *multiple-choice question* as shown in ◘ Fig. 10.3. Here the respondent can choose more than one response from a selection of answer responses. The multiple-choice question allows respondents the opportunity to think more deeply about a research question as they have the freedom to choose more than one answer. For some research questions there may well be several significant factors to consider and multiple-choice questions offer the opportunity to capture this diversity.

When creating multiple-choice questions it's important to use precise wording and to keep answer choices to approximately the same length. It's also important in multiple-choice questions to offer the answer response 'other' because some survey respondents will not identify with the list of answer choices. Without the 'other' response there is a risk that respondents will either make no choice or will choose an answer response that isn't an accurate reflection of their thoughts.

The three question types that have been described are all examples of a *closed-ended question* where survey respondents choose from a predefined set of answer responses. In contrast, *open-ended questions* are those that allow respondents the freedom to answer in their own words. The answers could come in the form of a few sentences or something longer such as a paragraph. Both question types have their advantages. Closed-ended questions are quantifiable and usually easy to analyse. The significant advantage of open-ended questions is that no restrictions are being placed on respondents and they are free to say what they like. Open-ended

10

Q3. What do you think are the key attributes needed to be an effective therapist? (You can tick more than one)

❏ Good at listening.   ❏ Being non-judgemental.

❏ Good at problem solving.   ❏ Use of theoretical knowledge.

❏ Empathy.   ❏ Feeling able to challenge client.

❏ Accepting uncertainty.   ❏ Respect for the client.

❏ Other (please specify)

◘ **Fig. 10.3**   Example of a multiple-choice question. (From McBeath 2019) questions offer the opportunity to collect data that expands and clarifies responses to closed-ended questions; they tell you more about how your respondents think and are therefore a potentially rich source of information.

Offering respondents the opportunity to say what they want can be as simple as including this statement at the end of a survey questionnaire:

Q 9. Please add any comments you may wish to make in the space below.

Open-ended questions can provide a lot of valuable qualitative data within a survey. The author's survey exploring the motivations of psychotherapists recorded 109 individual free-text answers, which was 20% of the sample (McBeath 2019).

Analysis and Presentation of Survey Findings

Data Types

In considering the analysis and presentation of survey data it is important to have an understanding of the different *data types* or *measurement scales* that can occur in a survey. How surveys are analysed and how findings may be presented varies significantly with different data types.

The most basic type of data is *nominal data*. We've already come across nominal data in ◘ Fig. 10.1 where survey responses could fall into only two categories, namely, Yes or No; because there were only two possible values the term dichotomous data is used, which is a sub-type of nominal data.

Nominal data consists of discrete units or labels such as Male, Female, Transgender, Other. Nominal data has no intrinsic quantitative value, and thus you could move the labels about without altering their meaning. Nominal data are sometimes referred to as 'non-numerical'.

The next significant type of data is *ordinal data*, which was mentioned in connection with the Likert scale shown in ◘ Fig. 10.2. With ordinal data it is the order or scale of values that is important. Thus, we know that the response 'Very likely' means something quite different from 'Very unlikely'. Ordinal scales are typically used to measure non-numerical concepts such as satisfaction.

The next type of data is *interval data* where, unlike ordinal data, both the order and difference between values is known. A good example of interval data is temperature where the numerical difference between 10° and 20° is the same as the difference between 30° and 40°. However, interval scales don't have a true zero point and this means that you cannot calculate ratios. Hence, for example, it cannot be concluded that 20° is twice as hot as 10°.

The final type of data and the most powerful is *ratio data* where the order of value labels is known, as is the exact value between value labels; in addition, ratio scales have what's termed a 'true zero' value. Good examples of ratio data are height and weight where values can be accurately added, subtracted, multiplied and divided (i.e. ratio calculation). Ratio data scales open up many possibilities when it comes to statistical analysis.

Sampling

Surveys almost always focus on a group or sub-set of people (i.e. *the sample*) with similar characteristics (e.g. occupation, health status) with the intention of generalising to all people with those same shared characteristics (i.e. *the population*). The way the sample is selected is very important and has implications for how confident we might be in our survey data. The overriding goal of sampling is to obtain reliable and unbiased values that can serve as accurate estimates of population values. There are several different types of sampling and they all have some advantages and disadvantages.

All of the various sampling techniques fall within two overarching approaches, namely, *probability* and *non-probability sampling*. Probability sampling refers to sampling techniques where some form of random selection process allows individuals or groups to have an equal chance of being selected for a sample. This principle is viewed as a safeguard against bias and one that should provide representative samples, as no individual is favoured over another. Examples of probability sampling techniques include *systematic random sampling* where a population exists in some order (e.g. the telephone book) and a random starting point is then selected and every *n*th individual is added to the sample.

The significant feature of non-probability sampling techniques is that the samples selected for study are based on the subjective judgement of the researcher rather than random selection. There are a variety of non-probability sampling techniques including what is called *purposive sampling* or *judgemental or subjective sampling*. This particular sampling approach was used in the author's survey exploring the motivations of psychotherapists, and illustrates how the views of large numbers of practitioners can be successfully surveyed.

The overriding aim of the study was to secure a large sample of experienced psychotherapists. To achieve this goal a sampling technique known as *homogeneous sampling* was used. Homogeneous sampling is a purposive sampling technique that aims to achieve a homogeneous sample of people who share the same or very similar characteristics (e.g. age, occupation, specific illness).

So, how do you achieve a large sample of experienced psychotherapists? The first point to make is that it can't really be done by a probability sampling technique because there is no access to databases such as those held by UKCP and BACP that would hold the details of thousands of practitioners from which a sample could be randomly selected. This means that the researcher has to proactively target an appropriate sample of practitioners, contact them and ask if they would participate in research activity.

To secure a large homogenous sample of experienced therapists the most obvious source from which to construct the sample was the social networking platform LinkedIn. The profiles of hundreds of practitioners are accessible on LinkedIn and

10

with a level of detail that shows the achieved level of training and also some indication of clinical experience. The author successfully used this source to achieve a sample size of 540 psychotherapists.

To construct the sample certain key selection criteria were adopted. Potential survey participants had to be demonstrably post-training and show experience of having done or actively doing clinical work. Over several weeks suitable potential participants were identified, their profiles were read and, if judged suitable, they were then invited to participate in an online survey. All participants received the same structured invitation to participate. A few therapists declined to participate but the vast majority indicated their willingness to be involved and subsequently completed the online survey.

Within the literature one can find an emphasis that non-probability sampling techniques are inferior to probability techniques because the sample chosen relies on the researcher's judgement and therefore the risk of bias is high. However, a legitimate alternative view is that there are practical reasons why some research questions can only be investigated by non-probability techniques, and furthermore that the researcher's judgement can be an asset and not a weakness. Hence, for some research questions there needs to be a realistic pragmatism in choosing methodologies rather than being hamstrung by adherence to the purity of theory. In reflecting upon the business of achieving survey samples it's worth noting a key point made by Smith and Osborn (2008), who state that "it should be remembered that one always has to be pragmatic when doing research; one's sample will in part be defined by who is prepared to be included in it" (p 56).

Statistical Significance

Before considering different ways of analysing survey data and discussing the issue of sample size it's timely to briefly introduce the concept of *statistical significance*. A *statistically significant difference* means that one set of data is substantially and meaningfully different from another set of data. Statistical significance comes from statistical tests, which, in a variety of ways, can determine if differences between data are due to chance or reflect something systematic and reliable. Statistical convention has two *levels of confidence* that differences between data are real; these are the 95% and 99% levels of confidence–often written as $p > 0.05$ and $p > 0.01$ respectively. These confidence levels are equivalent to saying that the difference between groups of data has a probability of less than 5% ($p < 0.05$) or a probability of less than 1% ($p < 0.01$) of occurring by chance.

Sample Size

The issue of sample size is crucial to conducting surveys and one where there are a number of factors to consider. Determining what would be an appropriate sample size for a survey is usually a key focus. Although larger samples tend to be better than smaller samples this will not be the case if the sample is either unrepresentative of the target population or is subject to systematic bias. Thus, bigger isn't always better. In some ways focusing on the quality of a sample is more important than the size of a sample.

The most important feature of a survey is that the sample is representative of the target population. There are a number of factors to be considered here. A significant issue is managing the risk of systematic bias, which will contaminate and degrade our survey data. There are two important sources of bias, *selection bias* and *non-response bias*. Selection bias usually occurs if a sample is not representative of the population; the bias may be systematic in excluding certain sub-groups because the survey can't reach those groups. Non-response bias occurs when those respondents included in a sample do not respond and are somehow systematically different from those who do respond. Non-response bias can be minimised by good survey design and effective communications with survey respondents. Thus, we want to ensure that as many people as possible participate in a survey.

Most online survey platforms offer sample-size calculators. These allow an optimum sample size to be calculated using three different parameters. These are the *population*, which is the total number of people that a sample will represent; *confidence level*, which is the probability that attitudes shown by a sample accurately reflect the attitudes of the population; and *margin of error*, which is the percentage range that population values will differ from sample values; margins of error are commonly reported as plus or minus a certain percentage. The major caveat about using sample-size calculators is that they assume a normal distribution of data, which will not be true of all populations.

Here is an example of a sample-size computation from SurveyMonkey. First, the population of interest is all psychotherapists in the UK; let's go for 20,000.[1] Next, the level of confidence will be set at 95%, which is the survey industry standard. Lastly, let's set the percentage deviation range at + or –5%. If we plug these figures into SurveyMonkey's sample-size calculator it tells us that we would need a survey size of 377. Therefore, with this sample size we could be 95% certain that any main survey finding reported would be within plus or minus 5% of the figure that would be the true population value; this is the margin of error. Sample-size calculators are useful in providing some sense of just how big a sample might be needed for a given population.

Data Analysis and Presentation

Before reporting the results of a survey it's important to offer some sense of how representative the sample might be of the wider population. One way to do this is to look at a demographic breakdown within a survey and compare it to similar surveys. An example comes from the author's survey that focused on the motivations of psychotherapists (McBeath 2019). For the survey sample, the gender

---

1   Estimate based on BACP-accredited membership of approximately 11,000 plus UKCP membership of approximately 9000 (Source BACP and UKCP).

breakdown was 77.1% female, 22.8% male and 0.6% 'other'. These figures are very similar to those reported in the 2016 UKCP membership survey, where the comparable figures were 74% female, 24% male and 2% 'preferred not to say'. Hence, in terms of gender breakdown, the survey data do appear to match that of the wider profession.

When reporting survey data it is customary to report some basic demographic data, which shows the composition of the survey sample broken down by certain key variables. Examples shown in ◘ Tables 10.1 and 10.2 show a survey sample

◘ **Table 10.1** Survey sample broken down by the number of years respondents have been practising – $N = 540$

Years as a therapist	% of responses
1–4	28.0%
5–8	20.0%
9–12	17.0%
12 +	35.0%
	Total 100%

From McBeath (2019)

◘ **Table 10.2** Survey sample broken down by respondents' self-reported theoretical modality – $N = 540$

Theoretical modality	Percentage of sample
Integrative	42%
Person-centred	12%
Psychodynamic	12%
Existential	7%
Transactional analysis	4%
CBT	3%
Gestalt	2%
Pluralist	2%
Cross-cultural	0.4%
Other	15%
	Total 100%

From McBeath (2019)

broken down by the number of years respondents have been practising as therapists and also their self-reported theoretical modality. The total number of respondents is shown in both figures (i.e. $N = 540$).

The data shown in ◨ Table 10.1 are important in relation to our sampling target where purposive sampling was used to secure a homogeneous sample of experienced psychotherapists. The data show that (a) the sample does contain experienced therapists but also (b) with significantly varying years of post-training experience. Therefore, at least with respect to these data the survey sample looks quite healthy.

Most of the online survey platforms have a useful set of analysis tools. Likert scale responses can be easily computed and converted to a graphical presentation as shown in ◨ Fig. 10.4. It's important to note that ◨ Fig. 10.4 is a bar chart and not a histogram and this reflects the type of data being analysed. Bar charts are ideally suited for survey presentation as each bar represents a group defined by a categorical label. In contrast, in histograms each column represents a group defined by a continuous, quantitative variable.

Although pie charts are often used to present survey findings they can become very 'busy' if too many categories are shown and may make interesting data patterns harder to display. A case in point is shown in ◨ Fig. 10.5, which shows a striking finding around how likely it is that therapists are not fully aware of their motivations.

From ◨ Fig. 10.5 it can be seen that on either side of 'not sure' responses survey respondents were almost evenly split in holding opposing views about whether

10

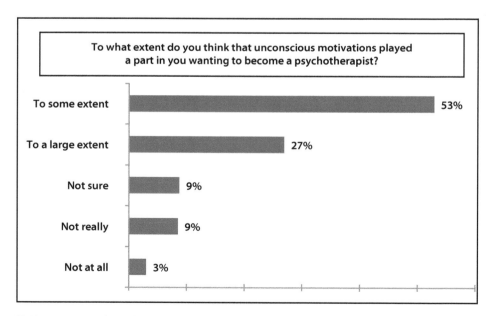

◨ **Fig. 10.4** Bar chart of Likert scale responses – The role of unconscious motivations in choosing to become a psychotherapist. (From McBeath 2019)

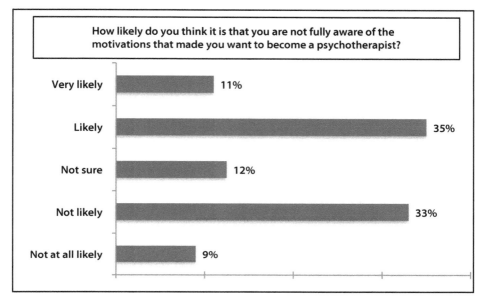

☐ Fig. 10.5 Bar chart – How likely is it that therapists are not fully aware of their motivations? (From McBeath 2019)

they might not be fully aware of their motivations for becoming a psychotherapist. This data pattern would not be so obvious if shown in a pie chart.

Drilling down into the data is also comparably easy by the use of certain analysis options provided by online survey platforms. One is *filtering* where selecting one specific filtering variable can identify a sub-group of survey data. An example would be to identify only those survey responses from therapists who reported their theoretical modality as psychodynamic. There is also a facility called *crosstabulation* that allows a comparison to be made between two or more categories, which can help to understand how they may be related to each other.

An example of a typical crosstabulation is shown in ☐ Table 10.3. Although it might look rather complex the data shown are quite straightforward and contain some very interesting findings. The bottom right cell contains the total achieved sample for the question being considered (i.e. 536). Rows show the frequency and percentage for each Likert scale response broken down by the number of years survey respondents have been practising, which is organised into four different intervals (e.g. 1–4 years).

How likely do you think it is that you are not fully aware of the motivations that made you want to become a psychotherapist? Crosstabulation of Likert scale responses by number of years practising (From McBeath 2019)

Two particularly interesting findings came from an analysis of the data in ☐ Table 10.3.

— Significantly more survey respondents with 12+ years clinical experience thought it 'very likely' (14.9%) that they are not fully aware of their motivations

Table 10.3 Crosstabulation of Likert scale responses by number of years practising From McBeath (2019)

	Very likely	Likely	Not sure	Not likely	Not at all likely	Total
1–4 years	10 (6.8%)	53 (36.1%)	23 (15.7%)	51 (34.7%)	10 (6.8%)	147 (27.4%)
5–8 years	5 (4.5%)	51 (46.4%)	9 (8.2%)	33 (30.0%)	12 (10.9%)	110 (20.5%)
9–12 years	11 (12.1%)	24 (26.4%)	10 (11.0%)	37 (40.7%)	9 (9.9%)	91 (17.0%)
12 + years	28 (14.9%)	66 (35.1%)	16 (8.5%)	55 (29.3%)	23 (12.2%)	188 (35.1%)
Total respondents	54	194	58	176	54	**536**

to become a psychotherapist when compared to less experienced therapists with 1–4 years (6.8%) and 5–8 years (4.5%) clinical experience.

- Significantly more therapists with 1–4 years clinical experience chose the 'not sure' (15.7%) response when compared to the most experienced therapists with 12+ years clinical experience (8.5%).

These two findings prompted further analysis to try to tease out differences between experienced and less experienced therapists on a variety of topics and illustrate just how stimulating survey data analysis can be. From a statistical perspective cross-tabulations can be analysed using the Chi-square test, which tests how likely it is that a distribution of data is due to chance.

With respect to ◻ Table 10.3 one hypothesis would be that there is no systematic relationship between the length of time therapists have been in practice and their responses on the Likert scale; in statistical terms this is called the *null hypothesis*. If we conduct a Chi-square test on the frequency data in ◻ Table 10.3 we find that the probability of the data occurring by chance is $p = 0.0159$, which is less than the 95% significance level (i.e. $p < 0.05$), and hence we reject the null hypothesis. In other words there is indeed some sort of relationship between the lengths of time therapists have been in practice and their Likert scale responses. The Chi-square result is expressed as follows: ($\chi^2 = 24.783$, $p < 0.05$).

As noted earlier, multiple response questions are treated somewhat differently than questions that allow only a single answer response. The issue is really to do with what's termed *the percentages base*. If you add up response percentages for multiple response questions the total will exceed 100%. This happens because survey respondents can give multiple response answers. One way to compute percentages with multiple response questions is to focus on the *raw counts* of responses.

Personal attributes	Percentage	Proportions
Empathy	16%	
Good at listening	15%	
Respect for client	15%	
Being non-judgemental	14%	
Accepting uncertainty	14%	
Feeling able to challenge client	10%	
Use of theoretical knowledge	9%	
Good at problem solving	3%	
Other	4%	
	Total = 100%	

◘ **Fig. 10.6** Most important personal attributes of therapists (multiple choice, $N = 540$). (From McBeath 2019)

This means that you look at the number of individual times a particular response answer was chosen; the totals for all different response answers are then totalled and this is the percentage base. The total number of times a particular response was chosen is then expressed as a percentage of this raw count percentage base. With this approach percentages will sum to 100% as shown in ◘ Fig. 10.6.

Text Analysis

There are several options for analysing the free-text material that comes from open-ended questions. Most of the online survey platforms have a word count facility, which will give the frequency occurrence of key words. This basic count is one route into drilling down into the data to find more meaning. There is also the possibility to generate *word clouds* as shown in ◘ Fig. 10.7, which portray the most important words and phrases used by respondents.; the larger the font size, the more important or significant the word. Word clouds are fun and a contrast to working with numbers.

More sophisticated textual analysis can be done with qualitative analysis software such as NVivo where one can identify, for example, the views of certain sub-groups (e.g. therapeutic modality) and examine how their views might differ from other sub-group members across a range of issues.

The potential richness of free-text data is almost limitless and can facilitate the growth of other research questions. Textual analysis can also reveal the impact of completing a survey on respondents; it can show how the survey experience impacted upon their thinking. In the author's survey on therapists' motivations a basic text analysis identified the word 'research' as one of the most frequently occurring words in free-text material. This finding facilitated further immersion in the data and allowed a group of related free-text comments to be identified. On the

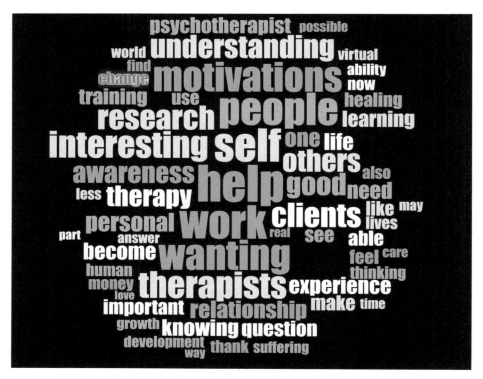

◨ **Fig. 10.7**   Word cloud. (From McBeath 2019)

theme of research the following comments serve as an example of the richness of the qualitative data that can be generated by a survey (from McBeath 2019)

- A very worthwhile piece of research to undertake; the questions have led me to reflect on various aspects of being a counsellor.
- Interesting research. I am more than 35 years in practice. I wonder if I knew then what I know now would I have still chosen to train as a psychotherapist.
- This is an interesting piece of research. I would expect that practitioners whose models are more instrumental, e.g. CBT, are likely to be less curious about their motivation and less willing to embrace the idea of the therapist as 'wounded healer'.
- Sounds [an] interesting piece of research; I am surprised no one has thought about it before. I wonder how honest people will be.

Comments such as these are notable in their own right but they also serve to sow the seeds of new research activity and the formulation of new research questions. This process is invigorating for our research activity and, in the author's opinion, makes it possible to actually enjoy doing research. Research is a friend not a foe.

10

Survey Design

It is essential that a survey has a good look and feel to make it more likely that potential respondents will want to complete it. Questions should be focused, written clearly and easy to understand; acronyms and jargon are to be avoided. The majority of questions should be closed and rating scales should be consistent in having the same number of response answers (i.e. 5 or 7). Survey questions should be arranged in a logical order with open-ended questions towards the end of the survey questionnaire. If appropriate, a survey can ask respondents for their contact information should they wish to contribute further to the research issue–perhaps by agreeing to be interviewed at a later date.

Well-designed surveys usually have a good introduction that will motivate potential respondents to complete the survey. The survey introduction is a form of research participant information sheet that explains the purpose of the survey. Survey introductions should also contain the contact information of a researcher and, most importantly, some statement or link that sets out a relevant data protection and privacy policy. It is good practice for a survey to state, at the beginning, that it is part of a research project that has received formal ethical approval.

One of the most important pieces of information contained in a survey introduction sheet is just how long the survey will take to complete. SurveyMonkey recommends 5 minutes or less; longer than this and potential survey respondents may decide not to take part.

It's important to make a survey stand out in some way, to catch the eye of a potential survey respondent. One easy way is a little bit of design at the top of a survey introduction sheet. ◘ Figure 10.8 shows an example.

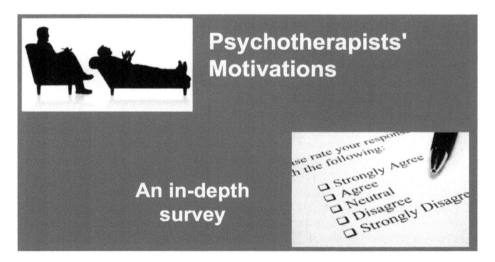

◘ **Fig. 10.8** Example of survey introduction sheet header

Finally, a good survey will have been pre-tested before going live. Being immersed in research can sometimes make us unaware of simple errors or assumptions that could jeopardise the success of a survey. Thus, it's important to do some trial runs and review any feedback.

Activity

Across the professional bodies that regulate psychotherapy and counselling there are currently differing requirements for students to undertake personal therapy. In the context of further standardising the training requirements of formal trainings it has been decided to undertake a consultative exercise which will involve surveying psychotherapy and counselling students about their own views on the value of personal therapy.

In thinking about planning and conducting the survey there are some key points to consider:

- Is the sample likely to be probability based (random)?
- What sort of sample size would seem appropriate and how would that be determined?
- How will potential survey participants be invited to complete the survey?
- Is there a risk that the sample might be biased?
- How could one get a sense that the sample was fairly representative of all counselling and psychotherapy students?
- What sensible demographic data might be collected?
- Approximately how long should the survey take to complete?
- How can qualitative data (e.g. free text) be sensibly analysed?

10

Summary

The use of surveys within counselling and psychotherapy is a rapidly expanding research tool used both by professional bodies canvassing their members' opinions and by researchers studying treatment efficacy and client outcomes. Surveys are often crucial in driving organisational change within the therapy world and also in giving clients a voice about their experience of treatment and therapy. An understanding of how surveys work and how to construct them allows practitioners to be able to assess the relevance and validity of survey-based information and also how to design surveys for their own research activity. In this chapter some of the key ingredients of a successful survey have been identified and discussed. These include different question types, different analysis options and some information about sampling, statistical significance, presentation options for survey data and survey design. If these factors are successfully managed then there is an opportunity to conduct new and invigorating research within counselling and psychotherapy. With smart technology ever more accessible there's never been a better time to conduct meaningful, exciting and enjoyable survey-based research.

References

BACP. (2017). Press release. Older people are not getting the mental health support they deserve. Retrieved from https://www.bacp.co.uk/news/news-from-bacp/2017/1-october-2017-older-people-are-not-getting-the/7

British Psychoanalytic Council. (2012). Quality psychotherapy services in the NHS. Summary findings from the UK Council for Psychotherapy and British Psychoanalytic Council members' survey. Retrieved from https://www.bpc.org.uk/sites/psychoanalytic-council.org/files/Summary%20findings%20from%20NHS%20survey.pd

Bräuninger, I. (2014). Dance movement therapy with the elderly: An international Internet-based survey under-taken with practitioners. *An International Journal for Theory, Research and Practice, 9*, 138–153. https://doi.org/10.1080/17432979.2014.914977.

Cook, J. M., Tatyana, B., Elhai, J., Schnurr, P. P., & Coyne, J. C. (2010). What do psychotherapists really do in practice? An Internet study of over 2,000 practitioners. *Psychotherapy (Chicago, Ill.), 47*(2), 260–267. https://doi.org/10.1037/a0019788.

Ivey, G., & Phillips, L. (2016). Psychotherapy clients' attitudes to personal psychotherapy for psychotherapists. *Asia Pacific Journal of Counselling and Psychotherapy, 7*(1-2), 101–117. https://doi.org/10.1080/21507686.2016.1157087.

Love, M., & Farber, B. A. (2018). Honesty in psychotherapy: Results of an online survey comparing high vs. low self-concealers. *Psychotherapy Research, 25*(9), 1–14. https://doi.org/10.1080/10503307.2017.1417652.

McBeath, A. G. (2019). The motivations of psychotherapists: An in-depth survey. *Counselling and Psychotherapy Research, 19*(4), 377–387. https://doi.org/10.1002/capr.12225.

McBeath, A. G., Bager-Charleson, S., & Abarbanel, A. (2019). Therapists and Academic Writing: 'Once upon a time psychotherapy practitioners and researchers were the same people. *European Journal for Qualitative Research in Psychotherapy, 19*, 103–116.

Mind. (2010). The protection we deserve: Findings from a service user survey on the regulation of counsellors and psychotherapists. Retrieved from http://www.cpcab.co.uk/Content/Publicdocs/The%20Protection%20We%20Deserve%20-%20survey%20report.pdf

Richardson, J., Sheean, L., & Bambling, M. (2009). Becoming a psychotherapist or counsellor: A survey of psychotherapy and counselling trainers. *Psychotherapy in Australia, 16*(1), 70–80.

Smith, J. A., & Osborn, S. (2008). Interpretative phenomenological analysis. In J. A. Smith (Ed.), *Qualitative psychology* (pp. 53–80). London: Sage.

Doing Quantitative Research with Outcome Measures

Charlie Duncan and Barry McInnes

Contents

© The Author(s) 2020
S. Bager-Charleson, A. McBeath (eds.),
Enjoying Research in Counselling and Psychotherapy,
https://doi.org/10.1007/978-3-030-55127-8_11

Learning Goals

After reading this chapter you should be able to:

- Outline the wider research and social policy contexts within which therapy outcome measurement sits;
- Describe the key incentives for implementing outcome measurement and how they shape its implementation;
- Appreciate the phenomenon of outcome variance across service and practitioners;
- Define the positive contribution that conscious application of feedback from sessional measures makes to improved outcomes for clients;
- Apply a range of key principles to the process of choosing an appropriate outcome measure;
- Describe how outcome measures are used in a range of research and routine practice settings.

Introduction

The use of outcome measures (OMs) in therapy, and arguments for and against their use, sits within a wider context of research evidence. Attitudes to the use of outcome measures range along a continuum. At one end of that continuum sit those who believe and argue passionately that measures have no place in the therapy room. At the other end are those who believe, equally passionately, that the use of measures provides valuable additional client feedback that can help us to deliver therapy more effectively and efficiently.

As practitioners, our attitudes may be shaped by a range of factors; research approaches will vary depending on our training and our philosophical stances. They might also sometimes depend on anxieties about having our impact or 'performance' measured.

In this chapter, we will explore a wider psychotherapy research context with an interest in a range of 'evidence' to support you through the process of making an informed choice about outcome measures in terms of questions such as the following:

1. What are outcome measures and why are they used?
2. To what extent may OMs have a place in routine practice settings, and why?
3. How can you choose an OM that is suitable for your purposes and setting?
4. How can you use OMs optimally to achieve your aims?
5. How are OMs used in a range of research and routine practice settings?

What Are Outcome Measures and why Are they Used?

Outcome research is often characterised by the use of outcome *measures*, designed to identify the *changes* that take place during therapy. These contrast with **process** measures, which aim to identify the variables that *cause* these changes. One example of an outcome measure is the PHQ-9, which is a self-report measure of depressive symptoms. This can be completed at various intervals throughout the therapeutic journey and allows for the 'tracking' of clients' symptoms. In contrast, the Working Alliance Inventory is a process measure which aims to quantify the 'strength' of the therapeutic alliance between practitioner and client. In an ideal world, outcome research would encompass both types of measure to allow us to say not only *what* changes as a result of therapy, but also *how* these changes come about.

One of the main assumptions of outcome and process measures is that the constructs they are attempting to measure (e.g. depression or the therapeutic alliance) are phenomena which can be *measured*. Inherently, this relies on there being a shared understanding of what practitioners, clients and society collectively mean by these concepts. Clinically, this can be challenging when working across disciplines where understandings of the nature and meaning of such concepts can vary (see Marsella 2003 for a more in-depth discussion of cultural differences in depression).

Two Incentives for Outcome Measurement

In our experience there tend to be two main incentives, or drivers, for implementing outcome measurement. Each has a different focus. The first focuses on demonstrating the impact of a service to external stakeholders, for example to funders or a board of governors. The second sees the use of measurement as a form of feedback to inform service and practitioner development. While both are perfectly valid incentives, the practical implementation of each is likely to take a very different form. Consider the two following scenarios.

11

▶ Example

Scenario 1.

Service A uses pre- and post-therapy outcome measures to determine the proportion of clients that show improvement in their levels of distress. Paper measures are administered by reception staff prior to their first appointment, and in the last session by the therapist. Therapists are not provided with training in the use and interpretation of measures and they are not routinely reflected on with clients in sessions. Data is collected and collated for quarterly and annual reports to funders. Feedback on individual improvement rates is not given to the therapist team.

Scenario 2.

Service B provides training for its practitioner team in the use of sessional measures of outcome with clients. Clients complete a brief measure at the start of each session and their responses form part of a discussion about the client's progress and their experience of the helpfulness of therapy. Clients also complete a brief measure of the working alliance at the conclusion of each session. The feedback from these measures is used collaboratively between therapist and client to monitor progress and adjust focus as necessary. Data about clients' progress also forms part of clinical supervision and practitioner development.

These two examples illustrate two very different sets of intentions. Service A's use of measurement is primarily to satisfy the requirements of funders and other stakeholders. Service B's approach is predicated (based on research evidence) on the assumption that the service and its practitioners can use the feedback generated from measures to reduce the likelihood of premature termination, enhance outcomes and create the best experience of therapy for every client. We will return to these themes later in this chapter. ◄

Activity

With which of these two drivers for outcome evaluations do you feel the greatest affinity? What, in your experience to date, has informed this view? To what extent, other than demonstrating the effectiveness of therapy to lay people, do you feel measures have a valid place in the therapy room? How familiar are you with the body of research showing that when used collaboratively with clients, feedback from measures can improve the outcomes of therapy?

To What Extent Do OMs Have a Place in Routine Practice Settings, and Why?

What is, first, known about the overall efficacy of therapy? Summarising the findings from a range of meta-analyses of the efficacy of psychotherapy, Wampold and Imel (2015) conclude that a reasonable estimate of the effect size of therapy would be $d=0.8$ (ref adjacent panel).

What Is Effect Size?

Effect size is an expression of the strength of the relationship between two variables. For example, we want to know the effect of using a particular therapy (**variable A**) for treating anxiety (**variable B).** The effect size value will show whether that therapy had a small, medium or large effect (or indeed no effect). Cohen's d is commonly used to express the strength (or size) of that effect. Cohen suggested that d=0.2 be considered a 'small' effect size, 0.5 a 'medium' effect size and 0.8 a 'large' effect size.

If we were to compare the effects of treatment with therapy to no treatment, a small effect size of d=0.2 would mean clients receiving therapy would be better off, in outcome terms, than 58% of people who did not receive therapy. A large effect size (d=0.8 or above) would mean clients receiving therapy would be better off than 79% of people not receiving therapy. In social sciences research, this is a large effect size. From the various meta-analyses conducted over the years, the aggregate effect size related to absolute efficacy is remarkably consistent and appears to fall within the range 0.75 to 0.85.

What Does Research Tell us about Variations in Outcomes across Therapists, Services and Settings?

The fact that therapy 'works', as suggested by Wampold and Imel (2015), and that there is broad equivalence among different models, does not mean that all services, or the practitioners within them, are equally effective. Research which considers the therapist as a variable which may impact the outcomes of therapy has found that therapist effects, as they are known, make a vastly greater contribution to therapy outcome than therapy models and techniques. There are different ways of seeking to understand the factors that lie behind these variations and their impact on outcomes. Chow et al. (2015) write, for instance, that 'Evidence has consistently shown that therapist effects dwarf the contribution made by the perennially popular treatment models and techniques, accounting for 5–9 times more variance in outcome'.

Given that variations in outcome exist between practitioners, and between services, where do we imagine we fit on this range of effectiveness? Equally importantly, what informs our view? A study of mental health professionals that included psychiatrists, psychologists and psychotherapists, published in 2012 (Lambert, 2013), refers to 'self-assessment bias' in noting that we are highly likely to rate our level of skill and performance as above average for our profession, and also to overestimate the actual impact of our work with clients. You'll be able to test your own level of self-assessment bias in the reflective questions that follow.

It may help both ourselves and our clients, then, if we can find some 'objective' measure of the true impact of our work with clients, and using percentage can help to discuss this in 'measurable' terms.

11

Activity
These are the same questions that were put to the subjects in the study of self-assessment bias highlighted above. Answers from those respondents are provided later in this chapter against which you may compare your own responses.

Compared to other mental health professionals within your field (with similar qualifications), how would you rate your overall clinical skills and performance in terms of a percentile (out of 0–100%: e.g. 25% = below average, 50% = average, 75% = above average)?
1. What is percentile?

A percentile is a number, between 1 and 100, where a certain percentage of scores fall below that number. Imagine that you are the fourth tallest person in a group of 20. This means that 80% of people in the group are shorter than you; you are in the 80th percentile. If you imagine that you imagine that you are more proficient in a particular skill than 75% of similarly qualified peers, that would put you in the 75th percentile.

2. What percentage (0–100%) of your clients get better (i.e. experience significant symptom reduction during treatment)? What percentage stay the same? What percentage get worse?

From the study above, in answer to question 1, respondents rated themselves on average in the 80th percentile–in other words, more highly than 79% of their peers. Just 8.4% rated themselves below the 75th percentile. None rated themselves below the 50th percentile, that is, below average.

In response to question 2 respondents believed, on average, that 77% of their clients improved significantly as a result of therapy. Fifty-eight percent believed that 80% or more of their clients improved, and just over one in five (21%) that 90% or more of their clients showed improvement. Almost half of practitioners (47.7%) believed that none of their clients deteriorated. In essence, they believed that their outcomes were far in excess of the rates of improvement shown by the evidence from both controlled and naturalistic settings.

Evidence of outcome *variability* has been demonstrated across several studies. Okiishi et al. (2003) compared the outcome data of 56 therapists in a university counselling service in the US. They found that those whose clients showed the fastest rate of improvement had a rate of change 10 times greater than the average among their colleagues in the same service. The clients of the therapists evidencing the slowest rates of improvement, on average, deteriorated. A more recent UK-based study (Firth, Saxon, Stiles & Barkham, 2019) included data for nearly 27,000 clients, seen by 462 therapists in 30 services. There was a wide range of recovery rates across therapists and services, with an 'average' recovery rate of 58% for therapists and 55.7% for services. However, significant variations in average recovery rates existed, ranging from 48.5% to 69.7% between services and 41.4% to 77.2% between therapists.

Our outcomes also don't appear to improve with experience. A longitudinal study which examined the outcomes of 6591 patients seen by 170 therapists (Goldberg et al. 2016) found that, on average–with some exceptions–therapists tended to obtain slightly poorer outcomes as their experience increased. It also appears that we may be poor at predicting which clients will reach a positive conclusion to therapy and which will not. Hannan et al. (2005) used session-by-session tracking of progress for over 11,000 clients and devised a test to make early predictions about which clients might be at risk of 'treatment failure'. They then compared its reliability with the prediction (based on clinical judgement) by the centre's therapists. Of 550 clients that attended at least one session, three were predicted by the therapists to deteriorate. Outcome data, however, showed that 40 clients had deteriorated by the end of therapy, though only one of these scenarios had been predicted by the therapists. The test tended to over-predict treatment failure, but overall it was far more accurate than therapists' predictions.

Can we Use Outcome Measures to Determine our Effectiveness?

Two key factors that have been shown to be strong and early indicators of a successful outcome are signs of improvement early in therapy and the client's rating of the therapeutic alliance. Numerous studies have shown that, in general, progress in therapy follows a relatively predictable trajectory, with most improvement occurring in the early stages. A study by Howard et al. (1986) found, for example, that up to 40% of clients show significant improvement in the first three sessions, 65% within 7 sessions, 75% within 6 months and 85% within 12 months. They also found that clients who don't display this pattern of early improvement are significantly less likely to improve later on. In another study, Brown et al. (1999) found that clients who showed no improvement by the third session did not, on average, improve over the entire course of therapy. Furthermore, those that showed deterioration by the third session were twice as likely to drop out as they were to progress. From these and other studies, we can conclude that if improvement is going to happen, there are likely to be early signs of it, and that early deterioration or lack of early progress is a potential predictor of drop-out.

Revisiting our earlier points about clarifying the basic 'why' of using measures of outcome, two questions emerge. The first of these is 'Can we use outcome measures to determine our effectiveness?' Whether we're using measures at the first or last sessions of therapy, or in the case of sessional use of measures the first and most recent, we are able to measure the degree of difference between the two.

The second question is 'Can we use outcome measures to track the progress of clients in a way that helps us to identify early those clients who are not "on track" and are therefore at risk of a poor outcome, including premature drop-out?' If we can identify these clients can we then intervene in such a way as to improve their chances of a beneficial outcome? A considerable and growing body of research evidence suggests that the answer to this question is also 'yes'. Lambert et al. (2005) studied the effects of four feedback conditions on clients at risk of treatment failure. The active feedback conditions improved the proportion of clients who clinically and reliably improved; no feedback or treatment as usual (21%); feedback to therapists about 'not on track' clients (35%); feedback to therapists with additional clinical support tools, for example measures of the working alliance (49%); and feedback to both therapist and client about the client's not on track status (56%).

They concluded that "It seems likely that therapists become more attentive to a patient when they receive a signal that the patient is not progressing. Evidence across studies suggests that therapists tend to keep 'not on track' cases in treatment for more sessions when they receive feedback, further reinforcing the notion that feedback increases interest and investment in a patient" (p.168).

Whipple et al. (2003) found that clients at risk of a negative outcome were less likely to deteriorate, more likely to stay in treatment longer and twice as likely to achieve clinically significant change when their therapists had access to information on outcome and alliance. Another study (Miller, Duncan, Brown, Sorrell & Chalk, 2006) examined the impact of introducing short measures of outcome and working alliance into an international employee assistance programme. In the early phase of the study, 20% of clients at intake had outcome measure but not alliance data. These clients were three times less likely to return for a second session and had significantly poorer outcomes. Improving a poorly rated alliance early in therapy was correlated with significantly better outcomes by the end of therapy.

Using outcome measures in a way that supports practitioners to improve the outcomes of clients at risk of a poor outcome requires something of a conceptual shift. It involves moving from using measures simply to determine outcome, to seeing them as a further way in which we can elicit feedback about client progress and build that feedback into our shared discussion. It needs to be part of a conscious and deliberate process.

Cycle of Excellence

Miller and colleagues (Miller, Hubble & Duncan, undated) propose a framework for the development of professional competence they call the "cycle of excellence". This comprises three principal components:
1. Determining a baseline level of effectiveness;
2. Obtaining systematic, ongoing, formal feedback and
3. Engaging in deliberate practice.

They argue that the establishment of our individual levels of effectiveness is a first basic step in identifying our learning and development needs. We will argue later in this chapter that the use of routine measures of outcome is a cornerstone in the process of gaining some objective measure of just how effective we are.

Activity
Anecdotally at least, much of the resistance towards using outcome measures is a result of practitioners believing that their clients won't like them or won't benefit from them–but is this really true? To our knowledge, there's been little research undertaken in this area from the client perspective. However, a public perceptions survey that was commissioned by the British Association for Counselling and Psychotherapy (BACP) in 2019–which surveyed over 5000 UK adults–found that just over half that clients who had had counselling or psychotherapy had completed outcome measures, and of these 80% said that they were happy to do so. Not only this but two-thirds felt that outcome measures helped both them and their therapist to track their progress and only 21% felt that they got in the way of the therapy. Another recent study which used a much smaller sample (Börjesson and Boström 2019) found that it's particularly important to make sure that clients are aware of the purpose and use of their outcome data and that it's used as part of therapy to increase awareness of inner states. Hence, whilst this shows that outcome measures might not be well-received by *all* clients, it appears that they're not quite so averse to them as people think.

How Can I Choose an OM that Is Suitable for my Purposes and Setting?

On Outcomes and OMs: an Overview

We have mentioned outcomes research and people often use the term. But what does this really mean? Jefford, Stockler and Tattersall (2003) describes it as

a broad umbrella term without a consistent definition. However, it tends to describe research that is concerned with the effectiveness of public-health interventions and health services; that is, the outcomes of these services. Attention is frequently focused on the affected individual – with measures such as quality of life and preferences – but outcomes research may also refer to effectiveness of healthcare delivery, with measures such as cost-effectiveness, health status and disease burden (p. 110).

Whilst this is a somewhat medicalised definition, essentially outcome research is asking: *What changes for a client or service as a result of therapy?*

This might be individual changes in terms of psychological distress, self-esteem, depressive symptoms and so on, or it might be changes in a service, for example 'How has the number of clients ending therapy prematurely changed as a result of this alteration I've made to my practice?'

> **Activity**
> Stop and consider the term 'outcome research'. What does it mean to you? What thoughts, feelings and emotions does it stir up in you? Just sit with that for a moment and think about why you feel like this. What, from your experience, has led to you feeling like this?

11

What Are the Key Features and Qualities that a Robust Measure Should Possess, and where Can I Find out More?

Choosing an outcome measure can, in turn, be a minefield as there are just *so* many different measures available. GAD-7, PHQ-9, CORE, WEMWEBS, GHQ, IES, HADS, BDI, SRS, OQ-45, Goal Based Outcomes (GBOs)—there's a measure for every condition and every setting. So how can you choose one that's right for you, your client and your service? Broadly speaking, there are two main types of outcome measure: nomothetic and idiographic.

Nomothetic Measures

The term 'nomothetic' has been referred to in earlier chapters. Nomothetic measures are, as mentioned, designed to establish general principles or assumptions by asking large groups of people a set of pre-determined questions and then making generalisations about them based on their answers. They are often quantitative in nature, that is, relating to 'numbers' or 'amounts' that can be measured. An example of a nomothetic measure is the PHQ-9 which asks questions like 'over the last two weeks, how often have you been bothered by any of the following problems: little interest or pleasure in doing things' and clients can choose 'not at all', 'several days', 'more than half the days' or 'nearly every day'. As you can see, there's no option for clients to change any of the items or response options, which can make these measures restrictive if you want to incorporate the client voice more. However, one of the benefits of using nomothetic measures is that their results can be compared with other services who are using the same measure as a 'benchmark'.

Idiographic Measures

Idiographic measures, on the other hand, are, as also described in earlier chapters, more able to focus on individual feelings and experiences, by collecting some qualitative data (typically text or words) about the individual. In the field of outcome measures, an example of an idiographic measure is the Goal Based Outcomes (GBOs) tool (Law 2018). This asks clients to state a goal for therapy in their own words–so no predefined question–and then rate their progress on that goal from 0 (not met at all) to 10 (fully met). Nomothetic measures can appeal to therapists because they allow clients the opportunity to set their own definition of what an 'effective' or 'desirable' outcome might be, rather than having it set for them. On the other hand, these types of measures can be criticised for not being generalisable across all clients because of their individualised nature.

Activity
Return to your ideas about outcome research, asking yourself, or someone else:
- What type of measure better fits my beliefs? Am I more interested in being able to provide a general overview of all my clients or do I want to tailor my therapy (and therefore what I measure) to my clients?
- What type of measures do my clients prefer? Would they struggle to come up with a goal because they don't know what they want from therapy yet? Do they want more direction from me as a therapist?
- Does my service need me to collect a particular measure for the funder or commissioner?
- Do I want to be able to benchmark client outcomes from my practice with a similar service so that I can make comparisons?
- Do I want to collect more than one measure with clients and use a mix of nomothetic and idiographic measures so that I'm able to capture the client voice but also make generalisations?

Ultimately, the decision around which type of outcome measure you use should be based on what works for you, your clients and your service. You even have the option to create your own bespoke measure if you don't think there's one out there which meets your or your clients' needs. If you're interested in creating your own measure, you might find the paper by Boynton and Greenhalgh (2004) helpful. However, the next section on reliability and validity may also help you decide what's right for you.

Reliability and Validity

The terms 'reliability' and 'validity' are often conflated, but there is a slight difference between them. We have looked at this in earlier chapters too, for instance in ▶ Chap. 2 in the context of qualitative research. Reliability refers to the consistency of a measure–its ability to return similar results from the same respondent (when used in the same circumstances) each time it is completed, while validity refers to the ability of a measure. A simple example of quantitative research given by Heale and Twycross (2015) is of an alarm clock that should ring at 7 am each morning but is set for 6:30 am. It is reliable in that it consistently rings at the same time every morning, but it isn't valid because it's not ringing at the time you want it to.

Understandably, there's a great deal to be said for choosing a reliable and valid outcome measure for your practice, not least because you can be fairly confident that there's some robust evidence underpinning its use. From the perspective of quantitative research, it is easier to determine the reliability and validity of *nomothetic* measures than for *idiographic* measures because of the former's focus on generalisations and standardisations. As explored elsewhere in this book, idiographic studies have other criteria for their reliability and validity.

Applicability, Acceptability, Practicality and Ethical Considerations

Whatever measures you choose to use, it is important that they are applicable, acceptable to those using them, practical and used ethically. You can have all the reliable and valid measures you want but if they don't meet these objectives then they probably aren't going to be appropriate for your work. Starting with **applicability**: the measure needs to be appropriate and relevant to the client group and setting where you work. If you see a variety of clients with a range of presenting issues then you might be more inclined to collect a global measure of distress such as the CORE-OM or CORE-10, which measure psychological distress more broadly, rather than the PHQ-9, which measures depression specifically. Or, you might pick from a selection of tools depending on the issues your client brings to therapy and choose to take a more tailored approach to outcome monitoring.

In addition, is it acceptable to both you and your clients, and do you both get something out of using it? If the answer to either of these questions is no, then the measure might not be acceptable. Best practice, and common sense, would tell us that both practitioners and clients should be clear on why a measure is being collected and what it will be used for. It's your responsibility as a practitioner to be clear on this yourself and to explain it to your client. If one or both of you don't know why you're collecting it then how ethical is it to be asking them to complete it?

Practicality

Sometimes practicality can trump other factors. If you are looking for a session-by-session measure, it will not be practical to use a measure which has 200 items and takes half an hour to score–there will be no time left for any therapeutic work. Another thing to consider in terms of practicality is whether there are any copyright factors you need to be aware of. Not all measures are free to use, and some can only be used in a certain format at the discretion of the author–so make sure you check! A good place to start is the Child Outcomes Research Consortium website ► https://www.corc.uk.net/outcome-experience-measures/ as they list this information for numerous measures, including those that are appropriate for adult and younger clients.

Finally, there are always going to be ethical issues to consider in your work with clients and using outcome measures is no different. This might include obtaining informed consent from your clients to use the measures in the first instance, which you might choose to include as part of your contracting. There's also the issue of data storage. Secure storage of the data, such as a locked filing cabinet or a secure online system, is paramount. Can you realistically collect it without compromising your data protection responsibilities? For more guidance on practice and research ethics, see BACP's Ethical Framework for the Counselling Professions (BACP 2018a) and its Ethical Guidelines for Research in the Counselling Professions (BACP 2018b).

It's important to consider these issues prior to the collection of measures, so we've put together the following checklist to help you:

- *Does the measure have good evidence of reliability and validity, consistent with the nomothetic research approach?*
- *Do you and your client understand why you are collecting this measure?*
- *Do you, as a practitioner, get something out of using this measure with your clients?*
- *Do your clients get something out of using this measure?*
- *Is it feasible to collect this measure at the timepoints that you have determined?*
- *Do you know how to interpret the measure which you have chosen to use?*
- *Are you collecting and using the data ethically?*
- *Do you have somewhere safe and secure to store the data you're collecting?*

Our suggested further reading materials may also help you with some of the practicalities of using outcome measures in your practice.

Creating your Own Measure

If you are interested in creating your own measure, you might find the paper by Boynton and Greenhalgh (2004) helpful. For any measure that you're considering we would recommend that you first test it on yourself, and other colleagues if possible, and are familiar with the measure's construction, scoring and clinical cut-offs. There is a rationale behind the construction of every properly validated measure. The CORE-OM, for example, is a 34-item measure that spans four key domains (Wellbeing, Problems/symptoms, Functioning and Risk) and contains high- and low-intensity items that relate to problems such as anxiety, depression, trauma, and aspects of life and social functioning. It is important that your choice of measure is based on a clear rationale and that it suits your purposes.

How Are OMs Used in a Range of Research and Routine Practice Settings?

Outcome measures can be used across many different research methods, from randomised controlled trials to case studies. Here, we'll provide some examples of how outcome measures have been used in some real-life research projects, with feedback from some of the practitioners involved.

> ► **Example**

Randomised controlled trial (RCT)

11

An RCT is a study where people are randomly assigned to two or more conditions to test a specific intervention or treatment, without any similarities or differences between the people in the groups being taken into account. This is often described as the 'gold standard' for research.

RCT will be explored in more depth in ► Chap. 13, by Megan Stafford. But let's look at an example from Stafford's research with Judith, a school counsellor who has taken part in a real-life RCT (Stafford et al. 2018):

>> Judith says: 'As a school counsellor, I was excited to take part in an RCT both to participate in gathering evidence and to extend my own experience. I quickly realised that being part of a research study - of course - involves measurement; far more measurement than I was accustomed to. As a counsellor in the study, I used the Outcome Rating Scale (ORS) with clients in each session, whilst also being measured myself (for adherence to the research protocol). As an assessor I met with young people who were interested in participating and administered a battery of measures to screen them for the study.

  I was apprehensive; would using the measures feel clunky or like minimising or marginalising client's experience? Sometimes this felt true, but often I found the opposite. In counselling, the ORS helped focus our joint attention on what was going on inside and outside sessions and often empowered clients to be able to quickly communicate more of this. As an assessor I only met the young person once but even in these paperwork intense meetings, it was possible to have a human and helpful interaction. The richness of the resulting information and the ease with which most of the young people communicated it via the measures surprised me. [One disclosed serious risk that he hadn't been able to voice before, and I was able to help him get the immediate support he needed.]

Since the study, I have incorporated measures into all my work. Now that I have become practised and familiar with using them collaboratively, I see them as an additional resource; more to do with input than outcome, another way of hearing clients, and often helpful for young people'. ◄

Naturalistic Study

A naturalistic study is one where the researcher observes or records a behaviour or phenomenon in its natural setting, whilst interfering as little as possible.

► **Example**

In counselling and psychotherapy research this might be similar to a service evaluation where the intervention and measures being collected don't change, but the researcher analyses the data collected to say something about the clients using the service.

Let's take a look at this example of a naturalistic study:

» Alicia is a counsellor working in a community counselling service for children and young people up to the age of 25. At every session, she asks her clients to complete either the YP-CORE or the CORE-10, depending on their age, and she also collects the Strengths and Difficulties Questionnaire (SDQ) at the first and last session with those aged 16 and under. Alicia uses the measures as a talking point during each session but does not score them and passes them on to her service manager. This is also how other counsellors in the service work.

Over the last few years, she's noticed that the clients coming to see her are increasingly distressed and many are on the waiting list for, or have been rejected from, a Child and Adolescent Mental Health Service (CAMHS). When Alicia raises this with her manager, her manager says that she has also become aware of this and has been having conversations about this with the commissioners in their local area. However, the commissioners believe that the interventions being provided in the community setting are for 'less distressed' clients and ask them what evidence they have that what they are providing 'works'.

Alicia and her manager decide that with the YP-CORE, CORE-10 and SDQ data that they collect as a service, they may be able to provide some evidence to back up what they're saying. When they analyse the data, they notice that 80% of the clients coming into the service are moderately to severely distressed, similar to those accessing CAMHS. They also find that 60% of the clients coming to their service 'recover', which again is similar to the recovery rate in CAMHS. They take this evidence back to the commissioners, who agree that they're providing a vital service which can operate alongside CAMHS. They agree to provide the service with some funding, allowing them to employ two additional full-time counsellors each week.

This is a very basic example and it might not be as easy as this in 'real life', but it's one way in which data can be used to evidence what it is that you're already seeing in your service and how that evidence might then be able to make a case for increased funding. ◄

Get Involved!

The British Association for Counselling and Psychotherapy (BACP) is a registered charity and membership organisation for counsellors and psychotherapists. They support practitioners and services to collect routine outcome data and can provide guidance and support in data analysis and interpretation. If this is something that you, or your service, would be interested in, please email research@bacp.co.uk.

If you would like to develop your knowledge about outcome research, we are hoping that you will find the following list of links helpful:

- How to choose a therapy outcome measure: ► http://therapymeetsnumbers. com/how-to-choose-a-therapy-outcome-measure/
- Introducing measures into working with clients: ► http://therapymeetsnumbers. com/introducing-measures-into-working-with-clients/
- How do I use the feedback from measures to reflect on work with clients? ► http://therapymeetsnumbers.com/every-picture-tells-a-story/
- Using sessional measures to deliver effective and efficient therapy–an example:► http://therapymeetsnumbers.com/deliver-effective-therapy-efficiently-at-reduced-cost/
- For an accessible and in-depth exploration into the development of methods to use for evaluating our own practice, please also see Biljana Van Rijn (2020).

11

Summary

Measurement of outcome in therapy settings, while not new, has until recently been an activity restricted mainly to research and selected practice settings. More recently, demands for evidence of effective use of public funds, and the accumulation of very large datasets in settings such as the UK's Improving Access to Psychological Therapies Programme, have moved the issue of routine measurement of outcomes centre stage. This chapter explores some of those contextual factors and the key drivers shaping this movement. We looked at the underlying philosophies behind two key drivers and how they differentially shape the way in which outcome measurement may be implemented. Moving on, we explored the body of research which demonstrates that while different therapeutic approaches are broadly similar in their outcomes, at a service and practitioner level there is considerable variance. Finally, we provide examples of outcome measurement from research and practice settings, and guidance for practitioners in the selection and implementation of measures appropriate to their practice.

References

BACP. (2018a). *Ethical Framework for the Counselling Professions*. Available at: https://www.bacp. co.uk/events-and-resources/ethics-and-standards/ethical-framework-for-the-counselling-professions/.

BACP. (2018b). *Ethical Guidelines for Research in the Counselling Professions*. Available at: https://www.bacp.co.uk/events-and-resources/research/publications/ethical-guidelines-for-research-in-the-counselling-professions/.

Börjesson, S., & Boström, P. K. (2019). "I want to know what it is used for": Clients' perspectives on completing a routine outcome measure (ROM) while undergoing psychotherapy. *Psychotherapy Research*. https://doi.org/10.1080/10503307.2019.1630780.

Boynton, P. M., & Greenhalgh, T. (2004). Selecting, designing, and developing your questionnaire. *BMJ, 328*(7451), 1312–1315. https://doi.org/10.1136/bmj.328.7451.1312.

Brown, J., Dreis, S., & Nace, D. K. (1999). What really makes a difference in psychotherapy outcome? Why does managed care want to know? In M. A. Hubble, B. L. Duncan, & S. D. Miller (Eds.), *The heart and soul of change: What works in therapy* (pp. 389–406). Washington, DC, US: American Psychological Association.

Chow, D., Miller, S. D., Seidel, J. A., Kane, R. T., Thornton, J., & Andrews, W. P. (2015). The role of deliberate practice in the development of highly effective psychotherapists. *Psychotherapy, 52*(3), 337–345. http://dx.doi.org/10.1037/pst0000015

Firth, N., Saxon, D., Stiles, W. B., & Barkham, M. (2019) Therapist and clinic effects in psychotherapy: a three-level model of outcome variability. *Journal of Consulting and Clinical Psychology*, 87(4), 345–356.

Goldberg, S. B., Rousmaniere, T., Miller, S. D., Whipple, J., Nielsen, S. L., et al. (2016). Do psychotherapists improve with time and experience? A longitudinal analysis of outcomes in a clinical setting. *Journal of Counseling Psychology, 63*(1), 1–11.

Hannan, C., Lambert, M. J., Harmon, C., Nielsen, S. L., Smart, D. W., et al. (2005). A lab test and algorithms for identifying clients at risk for treatment failure. *Journal of Clinical Psychology, 61*(2), 155–163.

Heale, R., & Twycross, A. (2015). Validity and reliability in quantitative studies. *Evidence-Based Nursing, 18*, 66–67.

Howard, K. I., Kopta, S. M., Krause, M. S., & Orlinsky, D. E. (1986). The dose-effect relationship in psychotherapy. *American Psychologist, 41*(2), 159–164.

Jefford, M., Stockler, M.R., Tattersa, M. (2003) Outcomes research: what is it and why does it matter? *Internal Medicine Journal*. 33(3):110–8. doi: 10.1046/j.1445-5994.2003.00302.x.

Lambert, M. J., Harmon, C., Slade, K., Whipple, J. L., & Hawkins, E. J. (2005). Providing feedback to psychotherapists on their patients' progress: Clinical results and practice suggestions. *Journal of Clinical Psychology, 61*(2), 165–174.

Lambert, M. J. (2013). Outcome in psychotherapy: The past and important advances. *Psychotherapy, 50*(1), 42–51. https://doi.org/10.1037/a0030682

Law, D. (2018). Goals and goal-based outcomes (GBOs): Goal progress chart. Available at: https://goalsintherapycom.files.wordpress.com/2018/03/gbo-version-2-march-2018-final.pdf

Marsella, A. J. (2003). Cultural Aspects of Depressive Experience and Disorders. *Online Readings in Psychology and Culture, 10*(2). https://doi.org/10.9707/2307-0919.1081.

Miller, S. D., Duncan, B. L., Sorrell, R., Brown, G. S., & Chalk, M. B. (2006). Using outcome to inform therapy practice. *Journal of Brief Therapy*, 5(1), 5–22.

Okiishi, J., Lambert, M., Nielsen, S. L., & Ogles, B. M. (2003). Waiting for supershrink: An empirical analysis of therapist effects. *Clinical Psychology and Psychotherapy, 10*(6), 361–373.

Stafford, M. R., Cooper, M., Barkham, M., Beecham, J., Bower, P., Cromarty, K., et al. (2018). Effectiveness and cost-effectiveness of humanistic counselling in schools for young people with emotional distress (ETHOS): study protocol for a randomised controlled trial. *Trials, 19*, 175. https://doi.org/10.1186/s13063-018-2538-2.

Van Rijn, B. (2020). Evaluating Our Practice. In S. Bager-Charleson (Ed.), *Reflective Practice and Personal Development in the field of Therapy*. London: Sage.

Wampold, B. E., & Imel, Z. E. (2015). *The great psychotherapy debate: The evidence for what makes psychotherapy work (Second Edition)*. New York, New York: Routledge. https://doi.org/10.4324/9780203582015.

Whipple, J. L., Lambert, M. J., Vermeersch, D. A., Smart, D. W., Nielsen, S. L., & Hawkins, E. J. (2003). Improving the effects of psychotherapy: The use of early identification of treatment and problem-solving strategies in routine practice. *Journal of Counseling Psychology, 50*(1), 59–68.

11

Doing Mixed Methods Research. Combining Outcome Measures with Interviews

Alan Priest

Contents

© The Author(s) 2020
S. Bager-Charleson, A. McBeath (eds.),
Enjoying Research in Counselling and Psychotherapy,
https://doi.org/10.1007/978-3-030-55127-8_12

🔊 Learning Goals

After reading this chapter, you should be able to:

- Gain confidence in bridging qualitative and quantitative research through mixed methods research;
- Develop more knowledge about pragmatism, constructivism and social constructionism;
- Consider options of combining quantitative outcome research with qualitative research;
- Know more about client-based research;
- Feel encouraged to combine clinical and research-based interests and concerns;
- Hopefully consider the significance of language use more;
- Continue to develop your own sense as a practitioner researcher.

Introduction

Mixed methods research is arguably an under-utilised approach which attracts debate. In this chapter, I will refer to my mixed methods study of clients' use of pronouns. I will describe some reasons for choosing mixed methods and provide definitions of some terms.

Mixed Methods: My Motivation

12

I have, first, always been interested in the individual 'reality' and sense of self. I have grown to see this as something that arises from the interaction between an individual and information, tempered by the context in which that information is presented, combined with pre-existing knowledge and experience, viewed through a cultural and sociological lens. Language plays, I believe, a central part here. I agree with Gadamer (2004) who suggests that the world is presented to us in and through language. Language is, in turn, learned and acquired, and its development is inevitably bound to the society and the culture in which it occurs (Ingarden, 1925).

This socially constructed aspect of meaning forms a part of my position. I also carry my own personal experiences, for instance from self-dialogue and from being a client in therapy. Throughout my career I have attempted to learn whatever I can about internal dialogues, the representation of experience in language, the role of communication in relationships and—crucially as far as this project is concerned—how words and in particular pronoun usage, work in the therapeutic relationship. Changing words can mean changing realities. Therefore, it is arguably important to focus on words and usage in order to be optimally effective for the client. This study is part of my need to understand as much as I can about how words work in a helping relationship.

Selecting Methods

In selecting a mixed methods approach my intention was, as some suggest (Silverman, 2010), to approach the qualitative and quantitative elements as complementary parts. Combining them provided an element of triangulation and complementarity, to clarify, explain or enhance my understanding of the findings (Greene, Caracelli & Graham, 1989).

I will begin with the qualitative part of my study. This was an analysis of interview transcripts representing a co-created conversation, positioned in time and culture. In conducting this study, I first and foremost wanted to understand my clients' *experience* of my interventions around pronoun usage.

My Clients' Experiences of Pronoun Usage in Therapy

A regular aspect of my practice is my interventions concerns pronoun usage. I invite clients to reflect on their feelings using the first person 'I' (FP), rather than using the second person (2P) (e.g. 'you') or 3P (e.g. 'there is'). At the time of this study I did not know what might be important for clients within their experience of such interventions, so I believed it necessary to use an exploratory and open-ended approach in which I adopted an attitude of curiosity, bounded by the limits of my research question. I wanted to understand what it felt like for them, how they were impacted, how their perception of their problem or presenting issue was affected and in what circumstances they regarded my interventions as helpful or unhelpful. How did my interventions—which ultimately comprised only a small part of a larger whole—relate to that larger whole?

A **qualitative approach** was, I felt, essential in order to understand my clients' experiences of differing pronoun usage. I wanted to understand the client's experience in situations where I intervened, inviting them to use the first person pronoun ('I') following them using 2P or 3P ('you', 'there is', etc.) in situations where I felt they might potentially be distancing themselves from the situation they described and their feelings about it, as in the case study below.

► Example

Ownership and Self-responsibility in Therapeutic Language

Harvey Sacks (Sacks & Schegloff, 1979) highlighted the different tactical functions associated with different pronominal forms. He suggested that there is a flexibility about 'you' that allows it to function tactically as "a way of talking about 'everybody' – and incidentally, of 'me'" (Sacks and Jefferson, 1995, p. 166; both cited on p. 536 in Yates & Hiles, 2010). One example of this type of usage was observed in a study of people diagnosed with myalgic encephalitis (ME), also known as chronic fatigue syndrome (CFS) (Guise, Widdicombe, & McKinlay, 2007). In eight of the ten extracts from the group discussions conducted, participants used 2P when describing what it was like to have ME. For example, "you can be sitting [...] and it's like somebody switches you off or you fall asleep" (ibid p. 98).

Placing responsibility for the experience on the experiencer and reflecting this in the use of appropriate language, Rogers (1976) emphasised increasing ownership of self-feelings along with acceptance of self-responsibility for the problems being faced by the client. "Owning the problem is a crucial step in the client's progress towards healing" (Stewart, 2005, p. 322).

In gestalt psychotherapy there is an emphasis on responsibility and ownership and on the importance of pronouns, in particular the first person singular pronoun 'I'. Fritz Perls believed that avoidance of responsibility via language was a way of avoiding contact with experience (Polster & Polster, 1973).

CBT also invites clients to take responsibility for themselves, to own responsibility for solving their problems (Mueller, Kennerley, McManus & Westbrook, 2010) and to be unafraid to own their needs and opinions, even when they conflict with those of others. ◄

To me, this called for a qualitative research approach. Despite the ethical challenges, the level of relationship and familiarity provided in the sessions became an important source of research. The meaning we each took out of it at the time was, in turn, inevitably influenced by the nature of our relationship and the social and therapeutic context of our meeting–which qualitative research can help to illuminate.

Looking at Symptoms

However, I also wanted to investigate what, if anything, *changed* in the use of pronouns between beginning and end of therapy. I wondered also if this might possibly be related in some way to reduction in symptoms. One way to do this was to analyse clients' language, counting the occurrences of different types of pronoun use. There is a rich tradition of this type of investigation in psycholinguistics; the means to do this exist and were available to me, and indeed I knew I could compare my findings against existing data, collected in the same way. I wanted my understanding to be illuminated from several perspectives, the focus on change being part of this.

My understanding and use of mixed methods was inspired by Creswell et al. (2003), who define it as:

» the collection or analysis of both quantitative and qualitative data in a single study in which the data are collected concurrently or sequentially, are given a priority, and involve the integration of the data at one or more stages in the process of research. (p. 224)

In my case, I combined a qualitative study of clients' experiences of my interventions around pronoun usage with a **quantitative comparison** of their language use in the first and last sessions. Language usage was explored in the context of outcome, as determined by CORE-OM (Evans et al., 2002). Whilst the client's experience when using or trying different personal pronouns in therapy is clearly individual, relational and wholly subjective, and thus is well-suited to qualitative study, the extent to which different categories of pronouns and were used was, I realised, amenable to quantification.

Mixed Methods — More or Mess?

You will already have become familiar with some valuable pluralistic and mixed methods approaches from my co-authors in this book. ► Chapter 8 explores aims, overlaps and bridges across research approaches both in general and with a special interest in qualitative pluralism and mixed methods.

Like the pragmatist philosopher Charles Sanders Pierce, I trained and worked originally as a chemist. Here, the combination of qualitative and quantitative approaches to analysis was entirely normal and natural. I've always been slightly bemused by the debate in the literature about the merits and demerits of mixed methods research. Admittedly, in the laboratory environment, both methods are utilised within the same overall scientific paradigm, but even so, I remain convinced that combining different approaches in finding solutions to research problems is entirely appropriate. The development of mixed methods is characterised by controversy (for a review see Creswell, 2011). Much of the criticism of a mixed methods approach falls into one or other of two categories: practical difficulties and paradigm conflict.

Some writers emphasise the practical and technical difficulties of combining approaches which may require different skills in the researcher and the resources available to them (see, e.g., Bryman, 1984). I believe that the strength of such arguments has receded as researchers begin to recognise, as I do, that the benefits of complementarity outweigh some of the practical challenges which are arguably fewer given the development of technology. Consider the role of software programs like NVivo or artificial intelligence in analysing qualitative data, and the use of so-called big data (e.g. from mobile phones) in providing insights into culture and society–areas traditionally the province of qualitative methods.

Paradigm Conflict?

Many arguments surrounding mixed methods fall into the category of what has been called *paradigm conflict*. Essentially, what authors say is that there are basic incompatibilities between qualitative and quantitative research because they are based on fundamentally different epistemologies. In other words, because different research methods are linked to different ways of knowing about the world, these ways may be non-complementary, even contradictory.

Paradigms frame the nature of the inquiry and hence the questions asked and knowledge gained (Sandelowski, 2000). In this perspective, mixing methods means mixing paradigms and this leads to confusion and conflict (Creswell, 2011, p. 275). Different paradigms, these authors argue, are based on fundamentally differing assumptions about the nature of the world and what can be known about it; an example would be realist versus relativist ontologies. Because qualitative research is interpretive and quantitative methods are usually based on postpositivist assumptions, it is not possible to combine them and produce meaningful results (see, e.g., J. K. Smith, 1983). In such a view, the perspectives and values held by proponents of qualitative and quantitative methods as being appropriate ways to look at the world are irreconcilable and even conflictual (Onwuegbuzie & Leech, 2005).

A less extreme version of this purist approach is held by so-called situationalists (ibid) who recognise the single method (paradigmatic) stance held by purists but accept that both methods have value. They believe, however, that certain research questions lend themselves to qualitative approaches, whereas other research questions are more suitable for quantitative methods. John Creswell has tended to adopt this position in his writing (Creswell, 2011; Hanson, Creswell, Clark & Petska, 2005). This seems to me to be entirely sensible and is consistent with my own experience as a social and health researcher. Morgan, for example, takes the view that mixing paradigms is indeed fraught with difficulty but states that this is quite different to "combining methods within a clear-headed understanding of paradigms" (D. L. Morgan, 1998, p. 363). McLeod, a leading proponent of creative approaches to research design, included a section on mixed methods as one of eight new chapters in the second edition of his book *Qualitative research in counselling and psychotherapy* (McLeod, 2011). He asserts that "research knowledge needs to be viewed as similar to a mosaic or jigsaw, with each individual piece adding to an overall picture or pattern" (ibid p. 286). Goss goes further, and whilst arguing for pluralism, his comments in a 2012 seminar are, I believe, relevant here:

Some research models are very good at recording outcomes; some are very good at dealing with stories of the journey; none are good at both. No study should be considered unflawed if it does not explicitly address both quantitative and qualitative kinds of enquiry (even where only one is actively pursued – we must live within resources). (Goss, 2012, p.111)

Pragmatism

At the other end of the spectrum to the purists are the views of the so-called pragmatists. They follow the tradition of Charles Sanders Peirce, who worked within the tradition of pragmatism associated with William James and John Dewey (McLeod, 2001). Pragmatists regard distinctions between quantitative and qualitative methodologies as representing a false dichotomy (Onwuegbuzie & Leech, 2004). In their view the optimal programme involves utilising the strengths of different approaches, avoiding overlapping weaknesses, and facilitating complementarity. This is known as the "fundamental principle of mixed methods research" (Johnson & Turner, 2003 cited on p. 771 of Onwuegbuzie & Leech, 2004).

Thus, whilst it would be inaccurate to say that for pragmatists 'anything goes' when it comes to mixing methods, they believe that "the research question should drive the method(s) used, believing that 'epistemological purity doesn't get research done'" (Miles & Huberman, 1984, p. 21 cited on p. 377 in Onwuegbuzie & Leech, 2005).

Moreover, pragmatists point out that even within a positivistic perspective, subjective judgements and assumptions are made, for example in deciding which questions to ask. Similarly, qualitative researchers need to provide a logically constructed rationale for interpretations of their data (ibid, p. 777), based on rigorous analytical methods which are transparent and available for inspection (Constas, 1992, p. 254).

What might be called a stronger version of paradigmatic pragmatism also exists; rather than seeing pragmatism as a means of reconciling differences and combining strengths in what some might consider to be conflicting methodologies, some assert that pragmatism is the best way to combine different approaches to answer research questions (Tashakkori & Teddlie, 2003). In this view, quantitative or qualitative methods in isolation are less effective than when combined. They complement each other and provide for a more complete understanding.

A logical extension of this view goes to the heart of what we mean when we talk about a paradigm; in his paper in the inaugural issue of the *Journal of Mixed Methods Research*, D. L. Morgan (2007, pp. 50, 53 citing Kuhn, 1970, 1974) argued for a paradigm to be defined not merely as the basis for thinking about research design, but as representing the "shared beliefs of a 'community of scholars' in a research field" (for a more detailed account, see Priest, 2013).

You and I

In my interpretation, Kuhn's idea means that if you and I (or indeed any specialist group within an endeavour) share the same view about what is important, about what questions are most meaningful, then we can also agree upon which procedures are most appropriate for answering those questions, without ever engaging in paradigm wars. Kuhn himself was said to favour this definition of a paradigm: our work based on our agreed-upon paradigm, within what he called a specific research community, comprising practitioners of a particular specialty (ibid p. 53).

I therefore invite you the reader to share in my paradigm; I believe the strength of my approach lies in its ability to illuminate 'what happened (for the client) when ...' and 'how often this happened', linking both of these categories of knowing, respectively, to subjective perception and quantification of effect.

Ethical Challenge

The focus in this chapter is mixed methods; however, I will briefly mention some of the ethical considerations involved in working with clients in research (for a more detailed account, see Priest, 2013).

My approach—researching my own clients—inevitably presented ethical challenges (Bond, 2004). The process is explained in full in Priest (2013). I took personal, theoretical, social and traditional pre-understandings of counselling and psychotherapy with me into research where I interacted with my clients as research participants, to approach a consensus of meaning in a dialogue with them. In this perspective I was a participant, not an observer; I am part of a client: therapist system. In my analysis, I focus on how this interaction (with specific interventions by me in the area of pronoun usage) contributes to the client's experiencing within this system.

Although it met the standards required by the Metanoia Institute and Middlesex University ethics bodies, this challenge nevertheless required me to confront personal and methodological difficulties. Involving my own clients in the research required my evidencing, first, that the client's need for therapy, the quality of that therapy and the outcome of that therapy were in no way compromised by my own need to conduct the research. This included evidencing throughout how the therapy process was overriding and prioritised over the research. It is not enough to say that clients will benefit in the long run; the ethical guidelines are clear in that the therapy helps and works in the way it is supposed to–with research forming a part of this work. This involved ensuring that the client's experience of therapy with me was as similar as possible to the experience they would have had had they not participated in the research. Before, during and after the research it was also important to evidence how the clients were made fully aware throughout of what was involved in participation, that their participation was entirely voluntary and that they realised they could withdraw at any stage without prejudice. In Priest (2013) I expand on post-therapy interviews, where several clients commented on their lack of awareness of participating in a research project: "it was all part of the counselling", said one client. Furthermore, I learned later that the differences which existed for a research client were often experienced as beneficial; many clients felt that writing in their notebooks aided their progress or was useful in and of itself. Similarly, the post-therapy interview was said to be a chance to reflect helpfully on their therapy, to identify what had helped and how. It was a chance for further learning and in many cases a pleasant and helpful way to end their journey.

Clients frequently commented in the interview that they had found the process interesting, had enjoyed the work and had found it useful. Some commented that, as I had done with them, they had intervened with family or friends regarding their pronoun usage.

Ultimately, the thing which reassures me most is the outcomes achieved by the clients in this study. The mean average reduction in CORE score (i.e. improvement) between beginning and end of therapy was 34.8, ranging from a maximum of 79 in one case (A659) to a minimum of 8 in the case of a client who discovered her husband's infidelity near the end of therapy (K666). This compares to 35.3 for clients seen over the last 12 months who did not participate in the study.

Recruitment Procedure and Sample

As mentioned and for ethical reasons, I designed the research method to mirror closely my usual way of working with clients in order to minimise the impact of the research on clients' progress through therapy.

At the time, I had worked for 17 years with a group of GPs who regularly invited patients to consider therapy with me as an alternative to NHS provision and a long wait for assessment. The arrangement I had with these GPs was that such patients were offered an initial meeting and assessment at no cost. I used this same system to identify potential research participants.

I briefed GPs on the nature and objectives of my research and provided them with literature that explained what participation involved for potential clients. They were able to give this to potential participants.

When GPs encountered patients who they felt might benefit from short- to medium-term counselling, as was their general practice, they explained to the patient that they could be referred through the regular NHS process or outside the NHS to a private provider. Some GPs made it their policy to offer a list of several private providers locally, including myself.

When such patients contacted me, I invited them to an introductory meeting explaining that this would be an opportunity for me to find out more about what had brought them to therapy and for them to find out more about my approach. I know that clients are often nervous as they make this call and it is usually fairly brief. Unless the potential client specifically mentioned the research to me at that point, I left all explanations of the research until the initial meeting.

This initial meeting proceeded as a standard assessment session during which I determined the suitability of the client's presentation for the type of counselling and psychotherapy I offer based on my experience.

Assessment, in my view, is never a precise process; initial and relatively straight-forward presentations sometimes grow into complex ones. As well as assessing the client's suitability for therapy, I was also assessing whether they might represent a potential research participant. Again, this is explained in full in Priest (2013).

Participants

Participants comprised nine women and two men aged between 24 and 55. The mean average age was 38 (SD = 8.81). Three participants withdrew from counselling, leaving a sample of eight. Of these, six participated in a qualitative interview and all eight contributed transcripts to the quantitative research.

Returning to Research Methods

Having explained my general and philosophical approach to this study, I now return to giving an overview of the data collection methods and sample. Methodological precedents for this study were unfortunately rare; few had combined qualitative and quantitative approaches with linguistic analysis. Among those that had, most had applied qualitative and quantitative content analysis techniques to writing rather than spoken content, as is the case here (see, e.g., Johnston, Startup, Lavender, Godfrey, & Schmidt, 2010). In designing my study there was little I could use as a pre-existing template. However, although the totality of the study reported here may not have had direct precedent, it was nevertheless based on integrating well-established elements of previous studies and I reference these where appropriate.

My aim was to conduct the research as unobtrusively as possible from the client's perspective. Clients completed a CORE-OM in the first session and again in the final session. Data from these responses was used in a quantitative analysis in which I looked for correlations between outcome as measured by CORE and pronoun usage. This is discussed in the next section on quantitative method. Save for the fact that all sessions were audio recorded, therapy sessions then proceeded as usual, during which I made interventions around pronoun usage, where appropriate, as is my general practice. Clients were provided with a notebook in which they could record their responses to such interventions, or anything else they felt was relevant. Following completion of therapy, clients attended a post-therapy interview in which I discussed with them their experiences of my interventions. This process was assisted by the client referring to their notebook and me to my case notes, in which I had recorded details of any pronoun intervention. This interview was audio recorded and provided the raw data for a qualitative thematic analysis.

The purpose of the qualitative part of the research project was to understand the client's experience when I intervened, asking them to use the FP pronoun ('I') following them using 2P or 3P pronouns ('you', 'there is', etc.) in situations where I felt they might be distancing themselves from the situation discussed and their feelings about it. The reason for recording all the sessions was so that I could refer in the qualitative interview specifically to those parts of sessions in which I had made an intervention on pronoun usage. I did not fully transcribe each session, or attempt to analyse them quantitatively (only the first and last sessions were so analysed). This approach echoes that used by van Staden (1999), the only other researcher to have attempted an analysis of change in pronoun usage between commencement and termination of therapy. The main difference between van Staden's approach and my own is that he analysed two sessions from the beginning and two sessions from the end of therapy. Van Staden's sessions were transcribed already, whereas mine were not. I analysed one session from the beginning and one at the end for pragmatic reasons concerning availability of time and resources.

My Notes

During the course of therapy I made notes subsequent to each session, as is my usual practice. One additional dimension when working with research participants was that I would also make a note of any pronoun usage interventions I made, my observations of the client's reactions and my own feelings, together with an estimate of the time during the session that this happened (to help me more quickly identify that part of the session in the audio recording).

The qualitative researcher's worldview shapes the entire project. From early curiosity about 'me' and 'I' all the way to writing the final report, the researcher's personal biography is the lens through which they inevitably see the world. Whatever I offered from this research would be experientially and culturally situated, influenced by my pre-understanding, and would perhaps later be assimilated into subsequent and similarly personal interpretations by other researchers. My own notes therefore became an important, reflexive, documentation of this.

Client Notebook

At the start of therapy I gave clients a notebook. I invited them to write in this whatever they wished about their therapy. Specifically, I asked them to record any thoughts, feelings or observations they had in response to moments in the session when I might ask them to restate something in a different way (obviously knowing that I would make interventions in which I asked them to rephrase statements using a different pronoun). I was conscious that many weeks or even months might elapse between the beginning and end of therapy and that some of the situations relevant to our post-therapy interview would have occurred early on in therapy. I therefore intended the notebook to be a means of clients capturing their responses to my interventions, whilst these reactions were fresh in their minds. I asked that they dated their entries. However, I also pointed out that the book was theirs to keep and emphasised that at no time would I require access to it. Nor would I ask them to divulge content to me–I merely asked that they make it available to use as an **aide-mémoire** in their post-therapy interview.

Each notebook contained a brief printed description of the purpose of the research (mentioning again their right to withdraw at any time), a reiteration of how I had invited them to use it, and a space in which they could write the dates and times of their appointments if they wished. I observed that in some cases I never saw the notebook in the session from the day I gave it to them to the post-therapy interview. In other cases, clients brought it with them to sessions, assiduously noting the time of their next appointment and sometimes even referring to it during the sessions. Some clients wrote very little, others rather a lot and one almost filled her notebook.

Partial Transcription for Qualitative Analysis

I fully transcribed the initial session following an assessment. This was for use in the quantitative part of the study. I also fully transcribed the final session of therapy for the same reason.

Sessions between the first and the last ones were not fully transcribed; I did on some occasions transcribe specific parts of sessions where I made a pronoun-based intervention. I was then able to refer to such examples during the post-therapy interview and gain some feedback, in a process reminiscent of that used in interpersonal process recall (IPR). Central to IPR is reviewing a recording in order to stimulate recall of one's thoughts, feelings and bodily sensations at the time of interview (Kagan, 1984); however, IPR itself did not form the basis of my inquiry process.

Post-therapy Interview

At the end of therapy, participants were invited to attend a follow-up interview in which they were able to review their experiences in therapy generally, with of course particular focus on my interventions around pronoun usage. Accepting that participants' experiences would not be completely transparent to them, they would nevertheless have at least partial access to them (Polkinghorne, 2005), and this awareness was enhanced by inviting them to draw upon the notes they had made.

Thematic Analysis

Raw qualitative data comprised audio recordings and transcripts of post-session interviews conducted following the conclusion of therapy. Data also included notes made by me immediately following each session, or between sessions, in which I reflected on my experience of working with the client. The client was also able to draw in the post-therapy interview upon their notes made after or between sessions in their notebook. The client's experience and the individual meaning for them of their experience were central to this part of the project. My aim was to understand and engage with those meanings, rather than measure their frequency, as this was addressed in the quantitative part of the project.

In order to do this in a systematic, transparent and structured way, I adopted a thematic approach to analysing and reporting participants' experiences of my pronoun-based interventions.

Thematic analysis is a term which can be used to describe several approaches to the analysis of qualitative research in psychological therapy. These approaches include content analysis, interpretive phenomenological analysis and grounded theory (Pistrang & Barker, 2010).

Thematic Approach

In thematic analyses, free-standing units of text are first separated from the raw data with their meaning intact, although they are often called by different names (segments, incidents, meaning units). Tesch describes a unit as "a segment of text that is comprehensible by itself and contains one idea, episode, or piece of information" (1990, p. 116). The units are then re-contextualised and assembled into themes based on an accumulation of evidence over the duration of the analysis (Braun & Clarke, 2006, 2014).

This analysis method seemed to me to be entirely appropriate here.

Unlike the quantitative part of the study, which takes no account of context or meaning, my thematic analysis, whilst systematic in approach, referenced the meaning behind the use of the language, in what is essentially a hermeneutic process (Joffe & Yardley, 2003) where the whole and its components are interdependent and neither approaches a full understanding without reference to the other (Dilthey, 1990).

The main question I asked myself during this process was "What is this expression an example of?" Other questions I kept in mind when coding include the following, inspired by Kathy Charmaz' (2008, p. 96) account of coding in grounded theory but relevant, I submit, in any qualitative coding process:

- What process is at issue here? How can I define it?
- Under which conditions does this process develop?
- How does the research participant think, feel and act while involved in this process?
- When, why and how does the process change?
- What are the consequences of the process?

The coding process was described as abduction (as distinct from induction or deduction) by Peirce (Douven, 2011), who described a process, relevant especially in the quest for concepts not explained by current knowledge, in which the researcher assembles a series of features of the data that are relevant to the inquiry. The researcher then abducts a provisional description, explanation or rule, which is incorporated into a code, checked against other occurrences of the same phenomenon within the data, and subsequently assembled into a category of similar codes and then later themes (McLeod, 2011, p. 34).

In addition to a code label, I also applied a longer and more user-friendly descriptive label, to remind my collaborators (see below) of what the code was trying to capture, and indeed myself. I gave the same code to instances of the same phenomenon or content and I generated new codes as required (cf. Cooper, 2005). Following editing revisions, at the end of this process I had a list of 79 codes. I then further grouped these according to themes.

Collaboration

Members of the Reflective Practice Group (RPG), a peer learning and development group for psychotherapists and counsellors, agreed to act as "critical friends", sometimes termed "critical colleagues" or "learning partners" (McNiff, 2002). Originally a concept from education reform, one definition of a critical friend is:

A trusted person who asks provocative questions, provides data to be examined through another lens, and offers critique of a person's work as a friend. A critical friend takes the time to fully understand the context of the work presented and the outcomes that the person or group is working toward. The friend is an advocate for the success of that work. (Costa & Kallick, 1993, p. 50)

Emerging Themes

Created awareness of (new) feelings
A common response I encountered in the interviews was participants describing how pronoun interventions enhanced or even created new awareness of their

feelings concerning what they were discussing. In some cases, these were feelings hitherto not experienced:

» It did make me realise how much I was keeping in if you like, how much I hadn't ... I wasn't really in touch with what I was feeling. (J626-10:09)

» I remember once when you invited me to say, you know, to actually say 'I am' whatever. And it was saying it out loud that made ... and I remember getting really upset — not getting upset because of what you'd asked me — getting upset with the realisation that I am actually struggling. And I am in need of a bit of help sometimes. (K666-32-11:15)

» I think those emotions that I was feeling were the same but it really hit home that it was happening to me. (K666-34-11:52)

Change in thinking or conceptualising

As well as creating new or deepened awareness of feelings, some participants reported that this was then accompanied by a change in the way they thought about or conceptualised their problem or situation.

This was particularly the case with C669, who really seemed to question himself about the way he had been thinking about things:

» I definitely thought it was helpful, as uncomfortable as it was. I think it made me think about it in a different way. What have I been doing to myself and how is that affecting either other people's view of me or how they react to me? (C669-30- 10:53)

» I feel like I am thinking about things a lot more rationally now. (K666-96-23:44).

» It just sort of challenges me a little bit to think ... even if I feel uncomfortable with something ... I mean erm, I suppose being aware that I feel uncomfortable about it makes you realise something about your thought processing and what you are feeling. (J626-21:53)

» I'm not used to saying 'I am'. So I suppose that at first ... I'd come not knowing who I was. (E631-13-6:30)

Created awareness outside of session

These changes in awareness of the connection between pronoun usage, thought and feelings sometimes extended beyond the sessions and clients reported such experiences during their post-therapy interviews:

» I think more in terms of perhaps me and [...] my thought processes ... I use pronouns more in my head if you like! (J626-14:11)

» I think now, in rephrasing things, I am making a conscious decision. (F632-188-58:28)

Writing was positive or helpful | Written about an intervention

Many clients commented positively on their experiences of writing and said they found it helpful. Frequently, this was because clients found it easier to write openly about their feelings than to speak about them:

» Writing things down — that's had a beneficial effect. It's definitely, definitely helped me that. And my mum's started doing it as well (laughs). I think that has a positive effect for me because in many ways I think I find it much easier to express myself in writing than I do verbally. (J626-42:31)

» For me personally, I have found it helpful and I'm glad I tried it. Whilst it might not suit everybody because they might not be able to get their feelings down, I do think everybody should try it. (K666-114-28:19)

» It has helped to write things down, I'll write frustrations if I feel like I can't vent or I'll write, you know, how truly sad I do feel. (K666-118-29:45)

Clients often wrote about my interventions and how they felt about them, so they could discuss them in the post-therapy interview. Many clients acknowledged that reflecting on their sessions or reviewing them in this way enhanced the benefits of therapy.

Quantitative Research Aims and Objectives

The aims of this part of the project were:
- To explore how, if at all, client pronoun usage changed between the first and last sessions of therapy;
- To investigate any correlations that might exist between client outcome as measured by the CORE-OM (Clinical Outcomes in Routine Evaluation Outcome Measure) and changes in client pronoun usage.

Clearly, this was an extremely small sample in quantitative terms and I regard this part of the project essentially as complementary to the qualitative work and as a means of introducing different perspectives and contexts for the qualitative project–a useful way to understand more about change, outcomes and pronoun usage.

CORE Monitoring

At the outset, and again in the final session, I invited clients to complete a CORE-OM questionnaire. This has been my usual practice since 2006, when I became convinced that services offering short-term and medium-term counselling needed to build an evidence base in order to demonstrate efficacy and value, and justify investment in services (◧ Fig. 12.1). Specific to this research, a reason for asking clients to complete CORE-OM was to enable me to explore any correlations between changes in levels of distress, measured by CORE, and changes in pronoun usage.

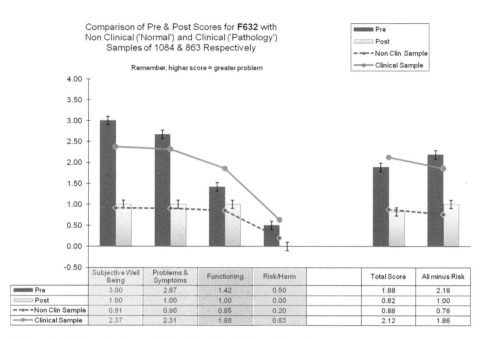

Comparison of Pre & Post Scores for **F632** with
Non Clinical ('Normal') and Clinical ('Pathology')
Samples of 1084 & 863 Respectively

Remember, higher score = greater problem

	Subjective Well Being	Problems & Symptoms	Functioning	Risk/Harm		Total Score	All minus Risk
Pre	3.00	2.67	1.42	0.50		1.88	2.18
Post	1.00	1.00	1.00	0.00		0.82	1.00
Non Clin Sample	0.91	0.90	0.85	0.20		0.88	0.76
Clinical Sample	2.37	2.31	1.86	0.63		2.12	1.86

□ Fig. 12.1 Example of a graph showing client's change in CORE scores pre- to post-therapy

Sample

The first session after assessment and also the final session before the post-therapy interview were, as mentioned, audio recorded and transcribed by me verbatim. These transcripts, stored in the form of Microsoft Word documents, provided the raw data for a linguistic content analysis of client, and indeed my own, use of language within the sessions. As mentioned previously, all sessions were recorded but only the first and last sessions were fully transcribed. These sessions were then used as the basis for a content analysis using *Linguistic Inquiry and Word Count* (LIWC) (Pennebaker, Chung, Ireland, Gonzales, & Booth, 2007). The case study illustrates this.

► Example

Linguistic Inquiry and Word Count — LIWC

The words we use in daily life reflect who we are and our social relationships (Tausczik & Pennebaker, 2010). In simple terms, LIWC (usually pronounced 'Luke') counts words. However, LIWC is more than a mere word counting program. After counting the words it analyses them and allocates them to one of 22 psychologically meaningful categories, for example articles (e.g. a, the), pronouns, emotion words (e.g. happy, angry), thinking styles (e.g. causal words, insight) and tentative language (e.g. maybe, perhaps, guess). LIWC's dictionary contains over 1.2 million words from over 2000 examples of speech from 850 speakers, collected during 10 studies on talking and conversation.

LIWC does not attempt to determine the context in which words are used. So, for example, the analysis does not consider if words are used ironically or sarcastically. In this sense it is described as a 'bottom-up' analysis, rather than ascribing word usage to predefined concepts and interpretations. This made LIWC ideal for this project. However, does this approach have validity and utility? Since its introduction, many studies have concluded that the way people use words remains stable over time and across different contexts (for a review see Pennebaker & King, 1999; Pennebaker, Mehl & Niederhoffer, 2003). Analysis of word use can predict real-life health behaviours and the use of words has been shown beyond any reasonable doubt to be related to psychological and physical health (for a review see Priest, 2013). ◄

The sample comprised eight clients, six of whom also participated in the qualitative study, plus a further two clients for whom, despite their not being interviewed, I was able to use transcripts of their opening and closing session or a later session in the quantitative study.

Content Analysis

In the quantitative part of my project I employed a structured coding scheme to label categories in the data (e.g. pronouns, emotion words) systematically recognising the occurrences of each content category to produce a quantitative output. In this part of the project I used LIWC to count the words used within sessions and to allocate them to one of a number of predefined categories, including of course pronouns. I then explored, amongst other things, how these counts changed over the course of therapy and investigated their relationship with other measures, as defined by CORE-OM.

Transcription for Quantitative Analysis

Each session took between four and seven hours to transcribe; much depended on the speech rate of the client, how much they had to say, and whether the session was punctuated by periods of silence or quiet reflection. For example, one client spoke at 175 words per minute; her opening session transcript was over 9000 words. The shortest session was 5150 words.

I undertook transcription myself, not only for reasons of maintaining accuracy and confidentiality (Patton, 2002) but also to familiarise myself with the client and their process. Transcribing sessions during the process of therapy provided me with new insights into the client and their way of being. I feel this benefited the way I worked therapeutically with clients participating in my research.

Given their use for content analysis, I emphasise that these transcripts did not represent meaning-based data, as would be the case in an interview analysed qualitatively. My analysis approach did not concern itself with the client's meaning (see my second case study). What was necessary was an accurate transcription of words and punctuation. I transcribed dysfluencies ('ah', 'erm', 'uhm', etc.) and pauses because I knew that these would also be counted by the analysis software I would be using.

LIWC analyses sentence length but as Lacan stated, "punctuation, once inserted, establishes the meaning; changing the punctuation renews or upsets it; and incorrect punctuation distorts it" (2006, p. 313–314, cited in Chapter 3 in Fink, 2007). I inevitably introduced a subjective judgement as soon as I inserted punctuation to create a sentence. Goffman noted that whilst well-formed sentences seem able to stand alone, they can have structural ambiguity. Consider "flying aeroplanes can be dangerous", for example (Goffman, 1981, p. 29).

It helped that I transcribed sessions myself as I was able to use punctuation in a way which preserved what I recalled being the intended meaning of the client. I am often struck by the way that clients quoted in textbooks speak in nice neat packages. Real clients never speak like this! Being in the session and having witnessed the context of the speech, I felt I was the best person to insert this punctuation. Finally, I time coded each turn of speaker and numbered each paragraph for later reference.

Data Processing and Analysis

I exported CORE-OM data from Microsoft Excel to IBM SPSS v19, where I conducted most of the analysis.

Rather than applying a data transformation technique to improve the normality of variables, I decided (because of the small sample size) to conduct analyses appropriate to both normally distributed and non-normally distributed data (Pearson's product-moment correlation and Spearman's rank-order correlation respectively, the latter being a non-parametric version of the former). I also calculated Kendall's rank correlation coefficient, commonly referred to as Kendall's tau (τ). I then compared the results of these and in fact found them to be very similar, as I am told is often the situation in cases such as this. Pearson's is generally considered to be a more powerful test than Spearman's (Roberts & Russo, 1999, p. 8). As a parametric test, Pearson's uses data which, if it is normally distributed and measured on a continuous interval scale, contains more information. By using ranks, the non-parametric Spearman's test does not consider differences in size of neighbouring data; it assumes that subsequent ranks indicate equidistant positions on the variable measured (George & Mallery, 2006). Spearman's is still a good statistical test of correlation, but it is weaker and less likely than Pearson's to detect a correlation. Pearson's test is robust and can be used even if data only approximate to parametric requirements (G. A. Morgan, Leech, Gloeckner, & Barrett, 2012).

Correlations between Pronouns

I found correlations between change in clients' pronoun usage.

- As 'we' increased, 'you' decreased.
- As 'I' increased, 'she/he' decreased.

- As 'you' increased, 'we' decreased.
- As 'we' increased so too did 'she/he'.
- There was no correlation in the relationship between 'you' and 'I'.

This is perhaps expected since a preponderance of any one of these in a discourse tends to exclude the others. For example, if I am focused on 'I', I might make little mention of 'his' or 'him'. Similarly, FP plural ('we') is negatively correlated with 'I' and 'you'. The only significant positive correlation between pronouns existed between 'we' and 3P ('she/he'). Again, this is perhaps understandable; if I am talking about any 'we', I may well also refer to 'he/she'. For example:

» We had to agree — because we couldn't agree — we had to agree contact. When he'd have [name of child]. (623-22-5:55)

Correlations between Pronoun Change and Change in CORE

In interpreting these data, the key thing to remember is that the figures analysed for correlation are:
- Increase in use of pronoun
- Increase in severity of symptom on CORE-OM.

Therefore, a positive correlation means that greater 'increase in the use of pronoun' is associated with smaller improvement in symptoms. A negative correlation means that greater 'increase in the use of pronoun' is associated with larger improvement.

There were six significant (p<0.01) positive correlations between aspects of change in CORE and the FP plural pronoun 'we'. A further two positive correlations approached significance. Spearman's revealed seven significant (p<0.01) positive correlations between change in CORE and 'we'. In addition, a further positive correlation approached significance. Spearman's rho for the correlation between 'we' and 'problems and symptoms' was 0.916 (p=0.001).

There were six significant (p<0.01) negative correlations between aspects of change in CORE and the 2P pronoun 'you'. In addition, a further negative correlation approached significance. Spearman's showed four significant (p<0.01) positive correlations between CORE and 'you'. Again, a further positive correlation approached significance.

Surprises

Remember that, perhaps counterintuitively, a positive correlation means that greater increase in the use of pronoun was associated with *smaller* improvement in symptoms, and a negative correlation means that greater increase in the use of pronoun is associated with *larger* improvement in symptoms.

I expected that there might be a slight increase in the frequency of FP singular usage between commencement and termination of therapy. This proved to be the case, echoing the work of van Staden (2003). One of my fears was that my chances of establishing anything significant in the quantitative study would be extremely low. Moreover, my chances of identifying anything significant within the different subscales of distress addressed by CORE would be lower still. The fact that I found such correlations in this sample therefore surprised me.

What also surprised me was that none of the significant correlations were between CORE and FP 'I'. Understandably, I attribute great importance to the use of the FP by clients. In the qualitative study, when clients accepted my invitation to restate phrases made originally in 2P or 3P, they reported several benefits, particularly in terms of awareness. Therefore, the fact that neither increases nor decreases in rates of usage of 'I' between beginning and end of therapy correlated with improvement on CORE was interesting and even a little disappointing. Given the strength of evidence from previous studies which suggest that increased rates of FP singular are associated with anxiety and depression (see, e.g., Tackman et al., 2019), I expected to find that increases in 'I' were correlated with lower reductions in symptoms on CORE. Given that all clients in the study achieved some measure of improvement on CORE and that all clients increased their usage of FP pronouns, this was obviously never going to be the case. This, to me, highlights one of the key benefits of a mixed methods approach. The findings of the qualitative and quantitative studies may support each other or, as in this case, they may not, but even here the researcher benefits from having two contexts in which to interpret the findings.

For example, one explanation may be that whilst clients in this study were using more FP pronouns start to end, they were doing so having perhaps been encouraged by my interventions to adopt a different attitude, that is, an attitude of ownership and self-responsibility. Again, with the benefit of the understanding gained from the qualitative research, I can provide an example wherein one participant (C669) benefited very significantly from my invitation to utilise the first person. He was a heavy user of cannabis, in danger of losing his partner "because what the smoking does to you" (by which he actually meant 'me'). When I invited him to own this by restating in the first person, he recognised *his* role in his relationship with cannabis and that it was a situation in which he had choices.

» I start thinking about it in terms of 'me' and 'I' and how do I change that, how do I change myself? Rather than it's just something that's happened. (C669 -32-11:18)

Ultimately, he made arguably healthier choices, and in so doing, improved his position in his relationship with his partner.

Moving to an analysis of correlations between other personal pronouns (such as 'she/he', 'you' and 'we') and CORE, I would not have been surprised if, against this background of highly individual and dynamic usage, no correlations were found to exist. However, this was not the case. In this sample at least, increases in FP plural ('we') and 3P ('she/he') were correlated with smaller improvements on CORE. Increases in 2P ('you') were associated with greater improvements on 8/11 symptom measures across CORE. What I also found interesting was that increase in 'we' was negatively correlated with increase in 'you'. In other words, as proportions of 'we' increased, rates of 'you' effectively decreased, across the sample, between beginning and end of therapy, and this decrease in 'you' was significantly correlated with degree of improvement as measured by CORE. This may suggest that thinking and talking less about a 'we self' leads to a reduction in distress, although a causal connection cannot of course be concluded.

I believe that mixing methods produced a more comprehensive picture and one which, although not necessarily simple to interpret overall, provided greater depth and perhaps therefore enabled me to know a little more about the highly complex nature of the linguistic interaction between client and therapist.

From an epistemological point of view, I have encountered nothing which I consider caused conflict with my perspectives. Some might perhaps argue that my use of a quantitative approach, based on positivistic principles, might form the basis for such a conflict. I disagree. I hope I have demonstrated here that using CORE and LIWC added an additional dimension to my analysis.

I believe that one of the main benefits of combining methods was that the qualitative findings produced valuable background and context, enabling me to suggest interpretations that quantitative data alone could not have provided, for example that lower increases in 'we' were correlated with greater improvements on CORE. Knowing the individual circumstances of clients and their issues enabled me to suggest that this was associated with greater individuality and independence in relationships that were characterised by difficulties. Had I merely asked clients to indicate their relationship status on a questionnaire at the start of therapy, this would not have been revealed. My knowledge of the initial session with F632 enabled me, for instance, to interpret a higher proportion of 'she/he' in my discourse as being related to my reflections on *her son's* behaviour, rather than my empathising with *her feelings* about his behaviour, as I would perhaps be more likely to do in other sessions.

Overall, I submit that in this study, with these clients, there is evidence that restating experiences in the first person was an enabling factor which facilitated their processing and their progress in therapy.

I further submit that this is interesting and important because these participants were essentially confirming from their own experience something which is a commonly accepted part of humanistic theory, that is, that language and in particular personal pronouns can be used as a way of avoiding responsibility and acknowledging feelings.

Stating, 'I did this' rather than 'this thing happened' or 'you felt scared' might be likened perhaps to 'owning up', even to confession. Indeed, it seems to me to echo Pennebaker et al.'s findings, which showed that writing about feelings—acknowledging them—allowed for their release, making it possible for experiences to be cognitively restructured and *integrated* into one's life story or narrative (Pennebaker & Chung, 2011).

Summary

Mixed methods research is an under-utilised approach which attracts debate. In this chapter, I have referred to my own mixed methods study into clients' use of pronouns. I have explored different reasons for choosing mixed methods and provide definitions of some terms. The chapter presents a study where each part illuminates the topic of inquiry, not only from different perspectives but also, to use a scientific metaphor, in different wavelengths of light. We see things in some types of light that we do not see in others; consider infrared versus normal vision or even x-rays, for example. Each part of the study also, I believe, challenges us as both researcher and practitioner to think deeply about different aspects of the same phenomenon. For example, in this study qualitative findings refocused me on the importance of the *relationship* between client and therapist, and on the need for a tentative and sensitive approach when making interventions that might be experienced by the client as useful yet also potentially powerful. The quantitative findings provided, in turn, evidence of a relationships between certain types of pronoun usage and outcome. That the correlation was so strong in so small a sample convinced me that, regardless of the highly individual nature of therapy, there are also some generalities; I do not believe that changing pronoun usage per se is driving therapeutic benefit, but I do believe that pronoun usage reflects the changes the clients made in their lives, as evidenced by improvements on CORE. In my opinion, a mixed methods approach worked well in this instance.

Adopting mixed methods methodology should ideally be because neither method *alone* can adequately illuminate the research problem. To illustrate this to my students, I use the metaphor of adding a side order when ordering a burger, rather than ordering an inclusive meal which would not be complete without each component. There is a difference, I assert, between combining methods independently as separate components and mixed methods, in which each component complements the other and is an essential part of the whole. I hope I have demonstrated in this case that the sum of the parts was greater than the whole and neither could be viewed as an extra portion of fries or onion rings!

References

Bond, T. (2004). Ethical guidelines for researching counselling and psychotherapy. *Counselling and Psychotheraphy Research, 4*(2), 10–19.

Braun, V., & Clarke, V. (2006). Using thematic analysis in psychology. *Qualitative Research in Psychology, 3*(2), 77–101.

Braun, V., & Clarke, V. (2014). What can "thematic analysis" offer health and wellbeing researchers? *International Journal of Qualitative Studies on Health and Well-Being, 9*. https://doi.org/10.3402/qhw.v9.26152.

Bryman, A. (1984). The debate about quantitative and qualitative research: A question of method or epistemology? *British Journal of Sociology, 35*(1), 75–92. Retrieved from http://dis.fatih.edu.tr/store/docs/533266hY7F4iOn.pdf.

Charmaz, K. (2008). In J. A. Smith (Ed.), *Grounded theory* (2nd ed., pp. 81–110). London: Sage Publications Limited.

Constas, M. A. (1992). Qualitative analysis as a public event: The documentation of category development procedures. *American Educational Research Journal, 29*(2), 253–266.

Cooper, M. (2005). Therapists' experiences of relational depth: A qualitative interview study. *Counselling and Psychotherapy Research, 5*(2), 87–95.

Costa, A. L., & Kallick, B. (1993). Through the lens of a critical friend. *Educational Leadership, 51*(2), 49.

Creswell, J. W. (2011). *Controversies in mixed methods research* In J. W. Creswell, N. Denzin, & Y. Lincoln, Eds. (4th ed., pp. 269–283). Thousand Oaks, CA: Sage Publications.

Creswell, J. W., Plano Clark, V. L., Gutmann, M. L., & Hanson, W. E. (2003). Advanced mixed methods research designs. In A. Tashakkori & C. B. Teddlie (Eds.), *Handbook of mixed methods in social and behavioral research* (pp. 209–240).

Dilthey, W. (1990). The rise of hermeneutics. In G. L. Ormiston, A. D. Schrif, & (Eds.), & F. Jameson (Trans (Eds.), *The hermeneutic tradition: From Ast to Ricoeur* (Vol. 3). New York, NY: State Univ of New York.

Douven, I. (2011). *Abduction* (Vol. 2012).

Evans, C., Connell, J., Barkham, M., Margison, F., McGrath, G., Mellor-Clark, J., & Audin, K. (2002). Towards a standardised brief outcome measure: Psychometric properties and utility of the CORE–OM. *The British Journal of Psychiatry, 180*(1), 51–60. Retrieved from http://bjp.rcpsych.org/cgi/content/abstract/180/1/51.

Fink, B. (2007). *Fundamentals of psychoanalytic technique: A Lacanian approach for practitioners (e-Book)*. New York & London: WW Norton & Co.

Gadamer, H. G. (2004). *Truth and method* (3rd ed.). London: Continuum Books.

George, D., & Mallery, P. (2006). *SPSS for Windows step by step: A simple guide and reference* (6th ed.). Harlow, Essex: Pearson Education (Allyn and Bacon).

Goffman, E. (1981). *Forms of talk*. University of Pennsylvania Press.

Goss, S. (2012). *From Multi-Methods to Pluralism. Expert Seminar. Institute for Work Based Learning, Middlesex University. London. 8th Nov, 2012*.

Greene, J. C., Caracelli, V. J., & Graham, W. F. (1989). Toward a conceptual framework for mixed-method evaluation designs. *Educational Evaluation and Policy Analysis, 11*(3), 255–274.

Guise, J., Widdicombe, S., & McKinlay, A. (2007). 'What is it like to have ME?': The discursive construction of ME in computer-mediated communication and face-to-face interaction. *Health, 11*(1), 87–108.

Hanson, W. E., Creswell, J. W., Clark, V. L. P., & Petska, K. S. (2005). Mixed methods research designs in counseling psychology. *Journal of Counseling Psychology, 52*(2), 224.

Ingarden, R. (1925). *Essential Questions* In E. Husserl, Ed.). (pp. 125–304).

Joffe, H., & Yardley, L. (2003). Content and thematic analysis. In L. Yardley & D. F. Marks (Eds.), *Research methods for clinical and health psychology* (pp. 56–68). London: Sage Publications Limited.

Johnston, O., Startup, H., Lavender, A., Godfrey, E., & Schmidt, U. (2010). Therapeutic writing as an intervention for symptoms of bulimia nervosa: Effects and mechanism of change. *International Journal of Eating Disorders, 43*(5), 405–419.

Kagan, N. (1984). *Interpersonal process recall: Basic methods and recent research (D. Larson, Ed.). In (pp. 229–244)*. Belmont, CA: Brooks/Cole Publishing: a division of Wadworth.

McLeod, J. (2001). *Qualitative research in counselling and psychotherapy*. Sage Publications Ltd.

McLeod, J. (2011). *Qualitative research in counselling and psychotherapy* (2nd ed.). London: Sage Publications Ltd.

McNiff, J. (2002). *Action research for professional development*. Dorset: September Books.

Morgan, D. L. (1998). Practical strategies for combining qualitative and quantitative methods: Applications to health research. *Qualitative Health Research, 8*(3), 362–376.

Morgan, D. L. (2007). Paradigms lost and pragmatism regained: Methodological implications of combining qualitative and quantitative methods. *Journal of Mixed Methods Research, 1*(1), 48–76.

Morgan, G. A., Leech, N., Gloeckner, G. W., & Barrett, K. C. (2012). *IBM SPSS for introductory statistics: Use and interpretation* (5th ed.). New York, NY: Routledge Academic.

Mueller, M., Kennerley, H., McManus, F., & Westbrook, D. (2010). *Oxford guide to surviving as a CBT therapist*. Oxford: Oxford University Press.

Onwuegbuzie, A. J., & Leech, N. L. (2004). Enhancing the interpretation of "significant" findings: The role of mixed methods research. *The Qualitative Report, 9*(4), 770–792.

Onwuegbuzie, A. J., & Leech, N. L. (2005). On becoming a pragmatic researcher: The importance of combining quantitative and qualitative research methodologies. *International Journal of Social Research Methodology, 8*(5), 375–387.

Patton, M. Q. (2002). *Qualitative evaluation methods* (3rd ed.). Thousand Oaks, CA: Sage publications.

Pennebaker, J. W., & Chung, C. (2011). In H. Friedman (Ed.), *Expressive writing and its links to mental and physical health* (pp. 343–359). New York, NY: Oxford University Press.

Pennebaker, J. W., Chung, C., Ireland, M., Gonzales, A., & Booth, R. J. (2007). *The development and psychometric properties of LIWC2007* (Vol. 2011).

Pennebaker, J. W., & King, L. A. (1999). Linguistic styles: Language use as an individual difference. *Journal of Personality and Social Psychology, 77*(6), 1296–1312.

Pennebaker, J. W., Mehl, M. R., & Niederhoffer, K. G. (2003). Psychological aspects of natural language use: Our words, our selves. *Annual Review of Psychology, 54*(1), 547–577. Retrieved from: http://search.ebscohost.com/login.aspx?direct=true&db=bth&AN=9688611&site=ehost-live.

Pistrang, N., & Barker, C. (2010). In M. Barkham, G. Hardy, & J. Mellor-Clark (Eds.), *Scientific, practical and personal decisions in selecting qualitative methods* (pp. 66–85). Chichester: Wiley-Blackwell.

Polkinghorne, D. E. (2005). Language and meaning: Data collection in qualitative research. *Journal of Counseling Psychology, 52*(2), 137–145.

Polster, E., & Polster, M. (1973). *Gestalt therapy integrated.* New York: Vintage.

Priest, A. (2013). *You and I Talking to Me: Towards an Understanding of Pronoun Usage in Psychotherapy. DPsych research project.* Middlesex University.

Roberts, M., & Russo, R. (1999). *Student's guide to analysis of variance.* London: Routledge.

Rogers, C. R. (1976). *Client Centred Therapy.* London: Constable.

Sandelowski, M. (2000). Combining qualitative and quantitative sampling, data collection, and analysis techniques in mixed-method studies. *Research in Nursing & Health, 23*(3), 246–255.

Silverman, D. (2010). *Doing qualitative research* (3rd ed.). Thousand Oaks, CA: Sage Publications.

Smith, J. K. (1983). Quantitative versus interpretive: The problem of conducting social inquiry. *New Directions for Program Evaluation, 1983*(19), 27–51.

Stewart, W. (2005). *An A-Z of counselling theory and practice* (4th ed.). Cheltenham: Nelson Thornes.

Tackman, A. M., Sbarra, D. A., Carey, A. L., Donnellan, M. B., Horn, A. B., Holtzman, N. S., et al. (2019). Depression, negative emotionality, and self-referential language: A multi-lab, multi-measure, and multi-language-task research synthesis. *Journal of Personality and Social Psychology, 116*(5), 817.

Tashakkori, A., & Teddlie, C. B. (2003). In A. Tashakkori & C. Teddlie (Eds.), *Major issues and controversies in the use of mixed methods in the social and behavioral sciences* (pp. 3–50). Thousand Oaks, CA: Sage Publications.

Tauszik, Y. R., & Pennebaker, J. W. (2010). The psychological meaning of words: LIWC and computerized text analysis methods. *Journal of Language and Social Psychology, 29*(1), 24–54.

Tesch, R. (1990). *Qualitative research: Analysis types and software tools.* London: Routledge.

van Staden, C. W. (1999). *Linguistic changes during recovery: A philosophical and empirical study of first person pronoun usage and the semantic positions of patients as expressed in psychotherapy and mental illness (Doctoral).* Warwick University.

van Staden, C. W. (2003). Linguistic markers of recovery: Theoretical underpinnings of first person pronoun usage and semantic positions of patients. *Philosophy, Psychiatry, & Psychology, 9*(2), 105–121.

Yates, S., & Hiles, D. (2010). 'You can't' but 'I do': Rules, ethics and the significance of shifts in pronominal forms for self-positioning in talk. *Discourse Studies, 12*(4), 535–551.

12

Understanding Randomized Control Trial Design in Counselling and Psychotherapy

Megan R. Stafford

Contents

© The Author(s) 2020
S. Bager-Charleson, A. McBeath (eds.),
Enjoying Research in Counselling and Psychotherapy,
https://doi.org/10.1007/978-3-030-55127-8_13

After reading this chapter you should be able to:

- Understand the fundamental elements of Randomized Control Trial (RCT) design;
- Appreciate the advantages and disadvantages of using RCTs in counselling and psychotherapy research;
- Understand some of the rewards and challenges of conducting an RCT and perhaps be inspired to conduct your own;
- Know how to begin critiquing published RCT studies.

Introduction

This book advocates an overarching pluralist framework for counselling and psychotherapy research, and Sofie and Alistair argue for an approach which is embedded in critical realism. Such an approach values each study design for what it can offer without a prior belief about design supremacy. As McLeod (2017) argues, we need to be willing to embrace the potential relevance of, and valuable insights gleaned from, all forms of research. My own view is that RCTs can sit alongside other designs, contributing to our overall understanding of what works in therapeutic research, as long as we understand their limitations.

Positioning Myself in the Chapter

I am aware that the use of RCTs in psychotherapeutic research can be contentious. When I have shared with peers and colleagues that I have been working on a randomized controlled trial (RCT), I have experienced a range of reactions which have included surprise, boredom, dubiousness and sometimes hostility. Research discussions could feel like particularly prickly spaces when I worked on mental health guidelines for the National Institute for Health and Care Excellence (NICE). This is an organization which promotes a specific evidence-based approach and regards RCTs as the 'gold standard' for gathering data on the effectiveness of health and social care interventions. How did I reconcile (I would be asked) the clash of values and principles underpinning a medical model approach and a psychotherapeutic approach? Was I aware of the constraints and drawbacks of attempting to apply such a paradigm to psychotherapeutic interventions? And even, *how could I work for 'the other side'*? I always felt these to be understandable questions, in part because they were questions I was so often posing to myself.

So, what is it about RCTs that we can find ourselves railing against as therapists? Well, to begin with, concepts such as 'hard science', 'manuals', 'diagnosis' and 'statistics' inherent to this methodology appear to be a world away from the relational, reflexive and idiosyncratic experience therapeutic work is usually concerned with, leaving many of us feeling a bit cold.

As therapists, we are constantly engaged in a process of exploration and making meaning through dialogue, relationship and the prizing of lived, social and subjective experiencing. Any kind of nomothetic research, with its emphasis on objectivity and quantification, feels to many of us like the anthesis of this pursuit. As a psychotherapist and researcher, I have often found myself caught in the knots and tangles of methodological debates about the most appropriate means to evaluate the effectiveness of counselling and psychotherapy.

Politics and Power Dynamics

Therapeutic practice and research have historically inhabited quite different worlds, leading to a 'research practitioner gap' (Moran 2011; McLeod 2017). This may also be because therapists often feel marginalized in research and political contexts that are dominated by RCTs, data points and *p* values. Moran (2011) argues that there is a lack of parity regarding which methodologies demonstrate quality and rigour in mental health. This is reflected on the one hand by NICE guidelines, for example, that 'downgrade' non-RCT research studies in meta-analyses concerned with assessing effectiveness of interventions; while on the other hand critics argue that NICE's hierarchy of evidence is too narrow (Jackson 2018).

I know that sometimes I have felt overshadowed, even crushed, in my attempts to offer an alternative perspective, highlight the value of a qualitative methodology or make room for the possibility of multiple truths and subjective realities.

However, the National Health Service (NHS) which is the largest employer of counsellors in the UK, institutions and policy makers all use results from RCTs to make decisions regarding therapeutic interventions for their patients and populations. Knowing the effect an intervention has on patients through clinical trials enables such stakeholders to make population-level decisions. With a population of almost 67 million people in the UK, such decisions are necessary and pragmatic. By ignoring RCTs, we could miss out on important and interesting research findings that support, improve or challenge our practice in significant ways.

My intention is to hold the tension between the advantages and limitations of an RCT and hope I do due justice to both, such that you are able to use and appropriately critique RCTs conducted in counselling and psychotherapy to inform your practice.

Gaining an Understanding

The best place to start is with a basic understanding of the design itself. Therefore, in this chapter my aim is to introduce you to the RCT design and some of the ways in which RCTs can contribute to our understanding of what works in psychotherapy. You may even be inspired to conduct one yourself!

Having been immersed in RCT design over many years, I hope to bring this methodology to life by drawing on my own experiences of conducting and evaluating RCTs in mental health, with particular reference to the *Effectiveness and cost-effectiveness Trial of Humanistic cOunselling in Schools* (ETHOS) study (Stafford et al., 2018) which I worked on with Professor Mick Cooper and our colleagues from 2016 to 2019 at the University of Roehampton.

The ETHOS study aimed to evaluate the effectiveness of reducing psychological distress in young people receiving humanistic counselling in a school setting, compared to schools' usual systems of pastoral care support. There have been many RCTs in the field of CBT, but humanistic therapy is often neglected in RCT contexts. This was the first trial of its kind powered to detect clinically meaningful differences, and has contributed significantly to the evidence base for mental health provision for adolescents. ETHOS also included a large qualitative component assessing helpful and unhelpful aspects of counselling from the perspectives of young people, school staff and parents. The focus of this chapter, however, is on the RCT design specifically. At the time of writing, the results of the ETHOS study had been submitted for publication, but were not yet available in the public domain. However, the protocol is available to view (Stafford et al., 2018).

Basic Methodology Part 1: Why Conduct an RCT?

Imagine that as part of an evaluation of your practice as a therapist you had been administering an outcome measure of psychological distress to your clients on a regular basis. Part of an evaluation of your practice as a therapist has been to administer an outcome measure of psychological distress on a regular basis. You have been plotting their individual scores on a graph over time and using this data to inform your overall understanding of their progress, and over the course of a year you have accumulated a significant body of data for a large number of clients. Aggregating their data, you find that on average, over time and across clients, there has been a large reduction in your clients' levels of psychological distress. 'Marvellous!' you think to yourself, 'I must be one of those super-shrinks!' This is certainly good news–using a validated measure of psychological distress, administered in the same way with each client over several time points, your data would seem to suggest that your therapeutic approach (or perhaps your particular brilliance and charisma as a therapist!) has resulted in positive changes to individuals who presented with pain and difficulties and were in need of help and healing. The picture looks good. However, there are a few issues with assuming that's the end of the story. Interpreting your data in this way assumes that without therapy, your clients would have either stayed the same or deteriorated. Therefore, consider:

- What if time is indeed a great healer and over the same time period, but without therapy, their scores would have improved anyway?
- What if (and this suggestion is a lot less palatable for most of us, but nevertheless very important to consider) without therapy, your clients would have had even bigger improvements in their scores (in other words, therapy made things worse)?

13

The 'C' in RCT

Using outcome measures alone makes it difficult to draw definitive conclusions about your therapeutic approach as the agent of change. If there was some way to compare your clients' scores with people presenting with the same issues but who did not receive any therapy, you would start to have a fuller picture of what is causing scores to decrease.

This is one of the first key elements to understand about an RCT–a 'control' group (the 'C' in RCT) provides a comparison to the group of people receiving the intervention of interest (in the example above, your therapeutic approach). The control group essentially tells you what happens in the absence of your intervention. This group might receive some sort of placebo, or no intervention at all, or something they are used to having already (usually referred to as 'treatment as usual').

The Need for a Control Group: Real-Life Example

Prior to the ETHOS study we were aware of a growing body of research in the UK that strongly indicated a beneficial effect of school counselling for young people presenting with a range of issues.

Any study begins by exploring earlier studies. Our literature review highlighted, for example, an evaluation of the Welsh School-based Counselling Strategy (2011) that used a naturalistic cohort design and assessed changes in young people attending counselling from pre-intervention to post-intervention using the Young Person's CORE form (YP-CORE) (Twigg et al. 2009) and the Self-Report Strengths and Difficulties Questionnaire (SDQ) (Goodman 2001). The research design adopted by the evaluation enabled the collection of a large body of outcome data derived from practices reflective of routine practice. Data from over 5000 cases indicated that school-based counselling was consistently associated with significant and large reductions in psychological distress. However, without a comparison group, researchers were unable to control for natural changes over time. A controlled trial was needed that could provide comprehensive data on the effectiveness of school-based counselling.

A control group therefore strengthens the overall design by increasing the confidence researchers have in the cause-and-effect relationship between intervention and outcome. This is, in part, why RCTs are useful in assessing the effectiveness of an intervention. Of course, a great deal of criticism has been levelled at the notion of cause-and-effect relationships existing in mental health, and this is something I come to later in this chapter. First, however, let's consider another critical feature of RCT design on the basis that a comprehensive understanding of any study design is necessary if we are to critique it appropriately.

Basic Methodology Part 2: The Importance of the 'R'

In an RCT study there are at least two groups of participants–one receiving the intervention of interest, the other acting as a comparison. These are known as the experimental group and the control group respectively. All participants entered into the study are assessed and compared at exactly the same points in time, to see how effective the intervention is, and differences in response between the two groups are assessed statistically.

A further pivotal and defining characteristic of RCTs is the way in which participants are assigned to these different groups. This is done through an entirely *randomized* procedure (this is the 'R' in RCT). The methodological aim of an RCT is to reduce certain sources of bias which affect the overall confidence researchers have in the effects of the intervention they observe. Randomization is one method by which one form of bias, known as *selection bias*, can be reduced. It's a bit like rolling a dice (◘ Fig. 13.1) to determine who goes where and who receives what. When researchers randomize all participants eligible for enrolment into their study, they are attempting to ensure that each person has an equal chance of receiving either the intervention or the comparison. Equally, they are aiming to generate groups that are comparable. That is, groups that contain people who are alike in important ways (such as known and unknown confounding or prognostic variables). Differences observed between groups at time points of interest to the researchers can then, in principle, be ascribed to the causal effect of the intervention.

One way of thinking about this is to imagine for a moment what might happen without randomization. Let's return to your evaluation of your own practice (See box below).

13

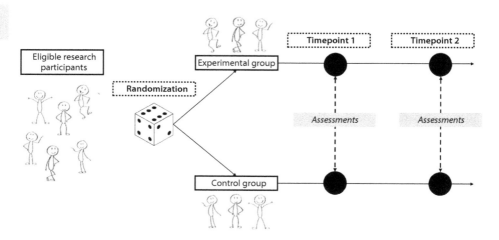

◘ **Fig. 13.1**   RCT design

> **Activity**
>
> Consider evaluating your own practice again. To increase your confidence in the outcomes you were observing you decided to include a comparison group. You then assigned all new referrals to one of two groups: the first group of people received therapy with you, the second group of people were put onto a waiting list where they weren't in receipt of any therapy. Wondering who to put in which group, you decided that all people referred by their GP would be put into the first group, while all self-referrals would be put into the second. While on the surface this may seem like an organized and systematic way to manage referrals, it is highly problematic. Using this method of group allocation, you have quite inadvertently introduced a source of selection bias. A *confounding factor* is some aspect or characteristic of a research participant that is associated both with the outcome of interest (e.g. psychological distress) and the intervention of interest (e.g. your therapeutic approach). Consider for instance:
>
> - What if, on average, GP referrals are more likely to be experiencing higher levels of psychological distress than self-referrals? In this example, as GP referrals are more likely to receive therapy, any observed relation between your intervention and the likelihood of change on your outcome measure would be confounded by type of referral.

Effective randomization and a comparable control group seek to reduce systematic errors, such as bias, in the overall design of the study. Such errors can impact the interpretation and generalizability of results. Some other key features of an RCT which also seek to reduce bias and increase a researcher's confidence in observed results, include an adequate sample size, employing appropriate eligibility criteria, sequence generation and allocation concealment, and 'intention-to-treat' (ITT) analysis. In the next section I unpack these methods using the ETHOS study as an example. Full details of the study can be found in Stafford et al. (2018).

Real-Life Example of Conducting an RCT in Counselling and Psychotherapy: The ETHOS Study

The Study in Context

The ETHOS study was timely. In both public interest and political arenas in the UK there had been a growing interest in the mental health of children and young people in preceding years. For example, the *Heads Together* initiative led by The Royal Foundation of The Duke and Duchess of Cambridge was set up in 2019, and highlighted the importance of working with children and young people and tackling stigma in mental health. In 2015, the Department of Health (DoH) published *Future in Mind* (DoH 2015), within which they expressed the aspiration that by 2020, "In every part of the country, children and young people [have] timely access to clinically effective mental health support when they need it" (ibid., page 16). Concurrently, the research world had seen an increasing evidence base for psychological and psychotherapeutic interventions which suggested that targeted school-based interventions led to improvements in wellbeing, mental health and educational attainment (Banerjee et al. 2014), and that school-based counselling in particular was perceived by children and pastoral care staff as highly accessible, non-stigmatizing, effective in reducing psychological distress (Cooper 2009) and associated with positive change (Cooper 2009; Cooper et al. 2013).

The Development of 'School-Based Humanistic Counselling' (SBHC)

In 2009, 'School-based Humanistic Counselling' (SBHC) was developed as a standardized form of school-based counselling (Cooper et al. 2010). SBHC is representative of the predominantly person-centred and humanistic style of British school-based counsellors and grounded in evidence-based competences for humanistic therapies (Roth et al. 2009). A series of four pilot RCT studies of between 32 and 64 participants compared SBHC to a control group–schools' pre-existing systems of supporting the wellbeing of students on roll ('Pastoral Care As Usual' or PCAU) (Cooper et al. 2010; McArthur et al., 2013; Pybis et al. 2014; and Pearce et al. 2017). A pooled analysis of data across these four pilot studies suggested that SBHC resulted in statistically significant, medium to large reductions in psychological distress as compared to PCAU, up to 12 weeks from assessment. However, sample sizes were small and therefore unable to detect 'clinically meaningful differences' required for more comprehensive interpretations of the data on the effectiveness of SBHC. A clinically meaningful difference refers to the smallest difference in an outcome measurement score that is considered to be worthwhile or clinically important.

Size Matters

In quantitative studies, size matters. Remember that in quantitative studies, broadly speaking, the aim is to summarize large amounts of data and facilitate comparisons across categories and for populations, rather than provide depth and detail on an individual level. Larger sample sizes allow researchers to better determine the average values of their data–the larger the sample, the more precise the mean (average).

Our ETHOS study intended to do just that. The sample size calculation conducted prior to participant recruitment indicated that we needed just over 300 young people to be able to detect clinically important differences between groups. We ended up surpassing this target over the course of five school terms, across 18 secondary schools in London. Clear eligibility criteria were used at the point of assessment to ensure that our sample was appropriate to the hypothesis being tested and results could be generalized and applied to the wider population. This is another key feature of a well-conducted RCT. For example, in ETHOS, young people needed to be between 13 and 16 years of age at the time of assessment, not to be considered at risk of harm, and experiencing moderate to severe levels of psychological distress as assessed by a score of ≥ 5 on the emotional symptoms subscale of the SDQ (Goodman 2001). This reflected the demographic and clinical profile of young people accessing school counselling described by Cooper (2009).

Study Procedures

All participants, once assessed, were allocated to receive either SBHC or PCAU. Allocation was randomized and, further, randomization was conducted via a computerized and remotely located application. This ensured that 'sequence generation' was concealed from the researcher conducting the assessment, the young person and the core researcher team. Concealment is often referred to as 'blinding' in RCT language. Essentially, this 'does what it says on the tin': the order in which participants are allocated to one group or another is masked, or hidden, from all key parties. All that is known to assessors, participants and researchers is that the order of allocations will be random. In other words, no one can choose which group a participant is assigned to. This is as important as the randomization itself. If we were able to decide who received what, it is highly likely that we would be biased in our selection, even if we were attempting to make our choices random. As a therapist and a researcher with a vested interest in the intervention, given any choice I would probably have found it difficult not to discriminate between participants at the assessment stage, and attempt to put as many young participants into the SBHC group as possible!

Once participants had been randomized, they completed a battery of measures. Our main clinical outcome was the YP-CORE (Twigg et al. 2009), a 10-item, self-report, 5-point Likert-type scale measuring psychological distress over the previous week. Individual item scores range from 0 ('not at all') to 4 ('most or all of the time') with a total score ranging from 0 to 40. The YP-CORE was chosen because it is a clinically relevant measure to assess changes in psychological distress in the age group of our participants and because it has demonstrated excellent psychometric properties (Twigg et al. 2009). Participants were then asked to attend research meetings at 6 (mid-point), 12 (endpoint) and 24 (follow-up) weeks following their assessment. The time points for assessment and list of all measures administered for the ETHOS study can be found in ◨ Fig. 13.2.

Experimental and Control Group Allocation

Participants in the SBHC group began 10 sessions of counselling with a qualified therapist who had completed SBHC clinical practice training and ETHOS proto-

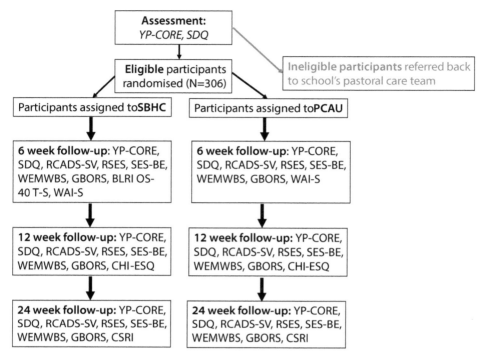

▫ Fig. 13.2 Study flow chart of referral, screening and allocation of participants to the ETHOS study from Stafford et al. (2017)

col training. Participants in the PCAU group were able to access their school's pastoral care services as they might usually and, for ethical reasons, were offered counselling 6 months later and once data collection was complete.

Allocation concealment is another important feature of an RCT. This is a procedure derived from drug trials and involves blinding (or masking) participants, practitioners and researchers, from the group to which participants have been assigned. It is easy to see how this would work in a drug trial where a placebo can be made to look like the drug under investigation, effectively concealing from research participants what they are taking. It is a process that is again designed to reduce the risk of bias, for example performance bias (where one group gets more attention from investigators than another group and/or participants change their responses on outcome measures as a result of knowing which group they have been allocated to) and attrition bias (an unequal loss of participants across groups).

The Issue of 'Blinding' Trial Participants

Of course, blinding of trial participants and practitioners is impossible in trials of counselling and psychotherapy. This is a good example of when attempting to apply the medical model approach to evaluation to psychotherapeutic interventions can feel like trying to force a square peg through a round hole. One way in which this issue has been addressed is to simply accept that blinding of participants and practitioners is unworkable, and instead focus on *blinding researchers.*

In our ETHOS study we employed a 'tester blind' design wherein testers (on-site researchers administering outcome measures) were blind to the participants' allocation from the outset and for the duration of the trial. To help ensure the success of the blind, we used a different tester at each time point and tested the success of the blind by asking testers to report whether the participant or any member of school staff had revealed what group the participant was allocated to. We also asked participants and school staff not to reveal the group to which participants had been assigned, as far as possible. Our principal statistician was also blind to group allocation.

Intention-to-Treat Analysis

A final key feature of a well-conducted RCT is the use of an intention-to-treat analysis (ITT). Analyses in RCTs are designed to estimate the size of the difference in predicted outcomes between experimental and control groups. Again, like other key features of an RCT, the aim of an ITT analysis is to reduce the risk of bias. One way in which researchers might arrive at an incorrect and biased assessment of results is by failing to evaluate patients according to the group to which they were originally assigned. You will recall that the goal of randomization is to ensure as far as possible that the experimental and control groups are comparable. The goal of an intention-to-treat analysis is to attempt to ensure this 'balance' is not disrupted in the analysis phase. ITT analysis is a method for analysing results where all participants who are randomized are included in the statistical analysis *and* analysed according to the group to which they were originally assigned, regardless of what happened following randomization (e.g. even if a participant accidentally received the wrong intervention, or wasn't able to attend a research meeting). The primary analysis used in the ETHOS study was based on this ITT principle. Last observation carried forward, a common technique for intention-to-treat analysis, was used. This is a method of data imputation, or 'filling in the blanks' for data that are missing using the last score the participant reported, and allows the data for all participants to be used.

The Complexity of Large-Scale Studies

The ETHOS study was enormous. It felt at times like a series of back-to-back marathons to try to complete successfully. As well as a large sample of young people, we were working with, and across, 18 separate school sites in the largest city in the UK. We employed a counsellor for every school and a team of supervisors to manage their clinical work, and commissioned a clinical SBHC manual to inform their training (Kirkbride 2018). Our on-site research team consisted of over 25 assessors and testers, all requiring training and day-to-day management to conduct, in total, 1500 research meetings with our participants. These all needed to be coordinated and scheduled to somehow fit both our research timelines and each school's individual termly, weekly and daily timetables. Karen Cromarty, who was the principal lead in this respect, must have used magic dust in order to make this all happen, because it was one of the greatest logistical challenges I've ever been faced with at work. The core ETHOS team itself consisted of 18 professionals from 9 different organizations, 5 of whom made up an Operational Group to manage the day-to-day running of the trial. In addition to this, we appointed a Trial Steering Committee and a Data Monitoring and Ethics Committee (DMEC). These are independent groups that monitor the scientific and ethical integrity of the trial, and assesses the trial quality and conduct, to ensure that the trial is being conducted in accordance with the principles of good clinical and research practice. I estimate that over the trial's total duration, well over 100 people were involved in its management and conduct. Naturally, this all came with challenges as well as rewards. I now turn to discussing some of these before focussing on the advantages and limitations of using RCTs in trials of psychotherapeutic interventions.

ETHOS: The Rewards and Challenges

The rewards and challenges that came with ETHOS were vast, too many in fact to list out in the space of the current chapter. Thus, my intention here is to focus on those that I believe future researchers could benefit most from understanding. These also happen to be those that are particularly memorable to me and I learnt the most from myself. My colleagues may offer you different insights.

Rewards

A high level of rigour is required to conduct an RCT well. By 'well', I mean with scientific integrity and ethical competence. It involves a methodical and systematic approach. While the operational side of the project was highly demanding and often unpredictable and the clinical management of over 300 young people was not, of course, without its challenges, an RCT design is a uniform procedure which on countless occasions felt to me like a lighthouse in a storm. There is a very precise way to do things, whether you like it or not. In many ways this is a world away from the work of a psychotherapist. As therapists we are taught, or perhaps at some level intuitively understand, the importance of being with and working with 'mess' and uncertainty. In my work as a therapist I seek to acknowledge complexity and all that comes with the co-createdness of human, interpersonal relating. For me, this is rich and valuable work. It is also often exhausting. The RCT lighthouse offered certainty, order and perhaps an occasional reprieve from my usual work. It may be these very things that make many quantitative methodologies so attractive to many researchers and practitioners. If I'm honest, the RCT design appealed to my inner obsessive-compulsive as well as a desire to lay my hands on some firm, objective ground.

The stringency of such a design is important in other respects too. We were working with a constant level of scrutiny regarding our hypotheses and adherence to our protocols. This encouraged discursive, active, sometimes challenging discourse within the team. Sometimes one of us would need to play 'devil's advocate' when we were collectively trying to think ahead to mitigate for possible problems and forecast into the future of the project. All of us needed to be able to articulate clearly and with research savvy why we expected to see the results that we did. We might not have always liked what we saw either. For those of us with a particular interest in humanistic therapy, we had to be prepared to engage with its potential imperfections in a non-defensive way, a way that could possibly enrich our understanding of what works in therapy. This was a big learning curve, and for me that is greatly fulfilling at both a personal and professional level. The learning was enhanced considerably by the professionalism, expertise and creativity of individual members of the team, as well as that all-important ingredient for any project—team spirit, which I felt we had in abundance.

Challenges

Managing Ethical Issues

An arguably universal ethical issue in all RCTs, present from the point of conception, relates to the necessity of withholding an intervention from people you believe could benefit from receiving it. This must be weighed up against the research context within which an RCT sits which has presumably indicated, but not proven, the effectiveness of the intervention of interest. In other words, the rationale for conducting your RCT needs to be crystal clear. You will recall that in the case of ETHOS, despite the prevalence of humanistic counselling in schools, only a limited body of research evidence existed supporting its effectiveness. ETHOS also sought to include a comprehensive cost-effectiveness analysis, and obtain long-term (6-month) follow-up data. The rationale and ethical grounds for conducting the study were clear. However, no ethical issue is even an issue if it doesn't cause you to question yourself and what you are about and result in at least a little discomfort.

During ETHOS, we had to work with two concerns that related to the above central issue with regard to: (1) young people who were deemed ineligible to take part in the trial and (2) providing information about other sources of support to the young people who we met at assessment.

Ineligible Young People

Approximately half of the young people we met with didn't meet trial eligibility. This constituted a significant number. Ineligibility was predominantly due to scoring <5 on the SDQ-ES (Goodman 2001), or being deemed at risk of serious harm. Of course, in neither instance did this mean that the young people in question weren't struggling with problems that could be helped through counselling, but rather that they didn't fall into the particular category of young people the trial was investigating (remember the importance of clear eligibility criteria). In fact the latter group—those at high risk—were excluded for clear ethical reasons: it would not be appropriate to enrol a young person at risk of harm into a trial where, should they be assigned to PCAU, they would not be able to access any immediate, specialist support outside of their school's usual provision of pastoral care. When a young person was assessed as ineligible, they were referred back to the school's pastoral care team. It was always made clear to the young person that this by no means reflected the view that their situation was not important, and that they were able to access the school's pastoral care for support if needed. Karen Cromarty and I were responsible for developing and leading the training of researchers conducting assessments and hence were principal assessors for the first cohort of participants. Despite the process we had in place for managing ineligible young people, we both reflected on the challenge of meeting young people who were in need of help, were recognizing and owning their need for help, and were also showing enthusiasm for the trial, only to find that they weren't eligible for the study. In this respect it was emotional work and we could both, oftentimes, feel a dissonance around what we knew was required methodologically and what we were experiencing clinically. RCT research is sometimes criticized for being more about numbers than people, statistics over humanity. My experience as a researcher is that this isn't the case. This is nicely epitomized by a sketch Karen drew one day of a hypothetical client, 'Bill' (◩ Fig. 13.3), who we used to think through the clinical and research pathway of our participants. We tried to think through the journey every young person would take when they expressed an interest in being part of the trial. We wanted to find a way of acknowledging these young people and the issues they were facing and be able to offer something more. Thus, together with other members of the operational group, we drew up a list of national and London-based support organizations offering help and support for this age group, and offered this out as an information sheet.

This seemed to help. We began to wonder if we could use the same information sheet with eligible young people assigned to PCAU.

Providing Information about Other Sources of Support

You may recall that the PCAU was the group with whom we were 'withholding' counselling. To offer information about additional sources of support, however, would have been to compromise the integrity of the control group. We wanted to compare SBHC to the typical and standard support young people are offered by school pastoral care services. By adding to that care in any way, such as providing information sheets to students, we would have tampered with the 'norm'. This, then, was an aspect of the design I had to learn to live with. It may be a particular and unique challenge to those of us who work both therapeutically and in research, as well as any professional involved in an RCT who believes resolutely in the intervention under investigation. I found I could hold this tension by focussing on the potential long-term gains of the work, above the short-term struggles.

Adverse Events: 'Above all, do no harm'

For drug-based therapeutic trials, adverse event (AE) monitoring is mandatory. AEs are negative events that occur for the research participants, and are not the goal of the research or intervention. Essentially this type of monitoring asks the question: 'Is it safe for participants in the trial to continue?' And 'Does the inter-

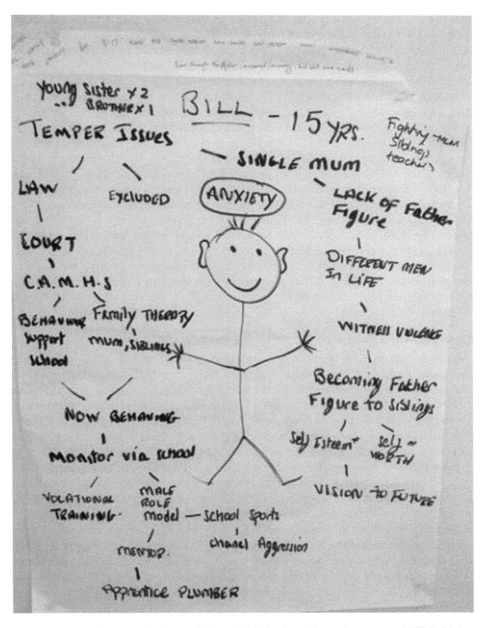

Fig. 13.3 'Bill' our hypothetical participant (With thanks to Karen Cromarty and Bill Suddes)

vention of interest cause any harm, as well as benefit?' These are important questions to ask as they inform both clinical assessment and decision making, as well as client preference. However, there is no mandatory reporting of AEs in trials of psychological and psychotherapy interventions and not all comply with these standards. The literature and general frameworks for understanding AEs are therefore rooted in pharmacological research, and a scant literature exists in counselling and psychotherapy. For example, the percentage of psychological intervention trials recording and reporting AEs has been estimated to be between 0% and 21% (Duggan et al., 2014; Jonsson et al., 2014). AE monitoring has thus, unsurprisingly, been described by Berk and Parker (2009) as "the elephant on the couch". Several reasons have been proposed as to why this aspect of RCT design is so neglected in our field. Jonsson et al. (2014) suggest that there may be no conceivable harm related to 'only talking' and point to the limited guidance in the psychological intervention RCT research. As a result, there is no consensus regarding the definition of some 'negative' effects of therapy. Therapists and researchers may also be subject to perception bias, which orientates us towards seeing the positive rather than negative effect of what we do (Linden and Schermuly-Haupt 2014). It may also be the case that our (researcher and practitioner) fear or pride may interfere with our willingness and capacity to engage with this material.

Developing a Protocol for Adverse Events

We developed an ETHOS protocol for the assessment and management of AEs using the literature that did exist, and by drawing on the clinical expertise within the core team. We defined an AE as any negative psychological, emotional or behavioural occurrence, or sustained deterioration in a research participant. Examples included running away from home, being excluded from school, a significant increase in emotional difficulties, a complaint made against the counsellor, self-harm and death, including suicide. We defined 'Serious AEs' (SAEs) as any event which was life-threatening or resulted in death, and developed a clear reporting and monitoring structure (including reasons for expediting reports) which was shared with school staff, counsellors and all on-site researchers. Members of the project team who had direct contact with the research participants were asked to report adverse events, and to indicate their seriousness (as defined above) as well as whether they believed the AE was related to the research or intervention. This latter assessment was known as an 'assessment of causality' and is a critical aspect of AE reporting as it speaks to the main reasons for monitoring AEs in the first instance. There were various issues that challenged us in developing and using our AE protocol, from trying to ascertain consensus on what constituted an 'adverse' or 'negative' event (Is a divorce a negative event? What about a house move?), to agreeing to where and to whom clinical responsibility should be delegated, to the thorny yet vital issue of how you define a benchmark for 'too much' adversity. However, assessments of causality probably presented us with one of the greatest challenges of the project.

Activity

Assessments of causality presented, as mentioned, one of the greatest challenges of our project. It is probably not difficult for you to understand why. In your own practice as a therapist, how do you make sense of the things that seem to go wrong for your clients? Who do you consider to be responsible? Do you ask 'why questions' about negative events and experiences? Do you ever consider that being in therapy is the reason for, or has contributed in some way to, what is happening for your client? The answer to all these questions is often that there exists a complex web of multiple possibilities, shared responsibilities and many influences. However, take some time and consider how you approach this in your practice: How does your modality inform you and how might you choose to research or more systematically evaluate this?

Assessing Causality

In ETHOS, we were aware that participants in psychological treatment research are often already vulnerable to experiencing AEs (e.g. suicide or self-harm), making attributions of causality when adverse events occur more difficult because there may be multiple causes. Nevertheless, as part of our assessment of causality we needed to try to understand why the AE had happened (paying careful attention to our ethical obligations regarding participants' rights to confidentiality). This included asking ourselves questions such as: Was the AE a feature of the presenting issue? Could we identify a specific aspect of research participation (or SBHC) that was harmful? Was the AE reflective and part of the process of change? Was the AE related to some element of the relationship between the participants and the study personnel (e.g. in the SBHC group, the school counsellor)?

Equally, we wanted to figure out what the consequences of the AE were and specifically whether these were transitory or sustained. This was important because we knew that transitory negative effects may be not only an acceptable component of therapy, but also an expected attribute of the psychotherapeutic process. For example, for someone unused to identifying and expressing their emotions, this process may feel uncomfortable, possibly extremely uncomfortable, initially resulting in reports of higher levels of anxiety, or problematic behaviour. We also needed to evaluate whether the professional role of the person reporting the AE might influence the judgement of causality. We were reliant on observation by ETHOS staff or school personnel involved in the study, or voluntary self-reporting by participants to these professionals. We wondered if participants in the SBHC group were more closely monitored in terms of AE reporting than those in the PCAU group because, in addition to meeting with ETHOS researchers, the SBHC group obviously met with their ETHOS Counsellor. Equally, we became aware that as therapists and researchers we were sensitive to certain events that we would describe as worthy of report but school pastoral care staff considered far more commonplace in the everyday life of a school and did not think to report (e.g. school exclusion, decrease in school attendance, poor behaviour).

For ETHOS, assessment of causality involved rating an AE as either 'related' or 'unrelated' to the study, meaning that either a causal link between the event and SBHC or PCAU *could not* be ruled out, or a causal link between the event and SBHC or PCAU *could* be ruled out. Given the complexities of assessment as outlined above, this may have set up a somewhat false dichotomy. The challenge of collecting and making sense of this data was arguably further compounded by our reliance on voluntary self-report and observation. If we had regularly screened all included participants for the occurrence of AEs, we may have had a more comprehensive data set that would have provided us with the opportunity to assess causality with the research participants themselves. Notwithstanding these challenges, our overall assessments were strengthened by drawing on epidemiological data as well as data derived from RCTs of other psychological interventions, where possible, to make sense of the incidence and prevalence of AEs in our sample. Our DMEC were also able to provide independent review of our data—including AE data—to determine the safe continuation of our trial. Overall, I am proud of our efforts (as taxing as it could feel) to monitor AEs in our trial and attempt to go where relatively few researchers had gone before.

The Advantages and Limitations of RCT Design in Counselling and Psychotherapy

Essentially, an RCT attempts to strip everything back to intervention and outcome through a series of methods and techniques designed to reduce bias. The design principles of an RCT mean that it is the most direct way to establish whether or not a cause-and-effect relationship exists between the intervention and outcome(s) of interest. In this way RCTs can establish whether or not an intervention makes a difference and, then, the average effect of that difference. They also offer an effective way to compare interventions. This makes them great designs for answering questions seeking to measure, quantify and compare interventions (*What is the difference between…? How much…?*). RCTs appeal to policy makers and commissioners because they can be used to determine the cost-effectiveness of interventions for population-level decision making. Trial results have implications for stakeholders such as policy makers and statutory advisory bodies—in the ETHOS study this included child welfare and parenting organizations, head teachers, therapists and, of course, young people themselves.

RCTs and Real-World Conditions

Increasingly, there is a call for data collected in routine practice and a practice-based evidence approach to research in counselling and psychotherapy, rather than the traditional approach of evidence-based practice. 'Pragmatic' RCTs (e.g. ETHOS) attempt to replicate usual clinical practice and so the important distinction between *efficacy* (the performance of an intervention under controlled conditions, e.g. a laboratory) and *effectiveness* (performance under 'real-world' conditions) must be understood. Despite this, the methodological ingredients that make an RCT what it is obfuscate its ability to truly mimic real life.

The process of counselling and psychotherapy is inherently complex and multi-faceted, involving an intricate dance between individual differences, interpersonal dynamics and external factors, as well as a range of possible outcomes. An RCT, put bluntly, does not speak to this or seek to understand it. This is not what it is designed to do. However, this means that vitally important aspects of the success (or failure) of our work and of client experiences and outcomes risk being either misunderstood or overlooked.

Many people who seek counselling and psychotherapy do so because of issues that transcend particular diagnostic categories, or specific symptoms, and present with various comorbidities. Hence, while the intention may be to reflect the larger population of interest and reduce selection bias in the trial, this is not usually possible because the larger population is not made up of simple, unambiguous presentations. The idea that we can measure presenting issues as discrete categories may therefore set up a false dichotomy. Equally, critics argue that the assumption that randomization of participant assignment controls for sampling bias, including the effects of moderators and process variables (e.g. participants' level of social support, self-reflectiveness, readiness for change), is valid only if study sample sizes are large enough to allow for adequate levels of power for valid statistical comparisons (Shean 2014). This is why appropriate and valid sample size calculations are so important.

Humans and our Contexts

The *Power Threat Meaning Framework* (Johnstone and Boyle, 2018) challenges the very attempt to measure cause-and-effect relationships in mental health. The authors argue that the idea of causality and the possibility of identifying specific factors and predictors of human distress is at best problematic–causal influences are always mediated and contingent upon other influences because humans are fundamentally inseparable from their context (Johnstone and Boyle, 2018). The idea that we can disentangle elements of counselling and psychotherapy, such as viewing the presenting issue like a classification, or an intervention as a set of techniques, may significantly underestimate these issues.

In reality, as in ETHOS, manuals can provide guidance, detail the values and principles underpinning an approach, and describe the therapeutic model being used (for an example see Kirkbride 2018). Intervention adherence can then be assessed using an appropriate measure such as the Person-Centred and Experiential Psychotherapy Scale (Freire et al. 2014) and recordings of counselling sessions, as we did in ETHOS. The process is not unlike that which many therapists go through at clinical VIVAs, wherein examiners have a set of criteria which guide them in ascertaining whether the candidate therapist is working in the way they purport to. However, we need to remain mindful of the limitations of such measurements and any tendency to overly emphasize what Rowan and Jacobs (2002) describe as the 'instrumental self', and be aware that the use of therapy manuals biases psychotherapy outcome research in favour of therapies that can be operationalized (Shean 2014).

Bias

You will now be familiar with the kind of attention that is paid to bias in an RCT study. Whereas in qualitative methodologies the focus is on recognizing, understanding and working with bias, in an RCT the intention is always to reduce it–not eliminate, but to constantly monitor in a different way. However, researchers are only human and embedded in context, just as their participants are. It is in fact not possible to eradicate bias, as research into researcher and therapist allegiance suggests. Findings have consistently indicated that interventions perform better in studies conducted by researchers who are committed to the approach under study than in studies conducted by others (Luborsky et al. 1999). This certainly assails the notion of the RCT researcher as a neutral, wholly objective observer.

Tips from a Trial Project Manager

For those Who Want to Conduct an RCT: What Do you Need to Consider?

A fully powered RCT is an extremely costly and timely venture. Funding is also challenging to obtain (ask Mick, who will tell you that he submitted four research proposals across 10 years before he was awarded the funds necessary to conduct ETHOS from the ESRC!). If these two things haven't put you off and you are continuing to read on, then you are probably made of some of the tenacious, hardy stuff required to withstand the RCT journey. A pilot study, however small, is a sensible and often necessary first stage in any research project. In preparation for an RCT it is an invaluable source of information regarding the feasibility of conducting your study and can also provide data in support of an application for a larger study. Here are my other tips for those of you interested in conducting your own RCT research:

1. *Think like a project manager, not only a researcher.* Good project management is about adherence to ethical principles and good practice in research *and* pragmatic, considered planning, implementation and decision making. Writing a detailed protocol can really help with this (and will also support you in writing your final report when the time comes). Becoming acquainted with relevant regulations, policies and guidance for this type of methodology is also important. For example, the International Committee of Medical Journal Editors state that RCTs must be prospectively registered in a World Health Organization-accredited trial registry such as ▶ clinicaltrials.gov.
2. *Forward planning means planning backwards.* Start at the end. By this I mean imagine where you want to get to–what data you want to have collected, the dates by which you want to have written your first report or paper, for example–and work backwards along your timeline, considering how many weeks, days or hours it will take to complete each of the tasks needed to get you to where you want to go. Have you worked your way back to today's date? If not, some aspect of your plan may need to be revised.

3. *Schedule review points.* Timetable regular reviews within your timelines to check scope, progress and the need to address any ethical issues. Different review points for different aspects of the study will likely be appropriate. These meetings will help you keep the project on track, probably help your focus and will also foster a sense of responsibility and ownership of your work. Monitoring the progress of your study will require you to work flexibly. If it's possible, I highly recommend building in contingency time–in RCT work if nothing is going wrong, something has almost certainly gone wrong! You'll need to give yourself time to manage this.

4. *Communicate, communicate, communicate.* Your team may be big or small depending on your study ambitions, but the most important and most helpful activity we engaged with during ETHOS was to simply talk to each other. This was supported by having regular meetings scheduled ahead of time. I would also encourage you to talk to people outside of the immediate team about what you're doing (within the boundaries of confidentiality). Getting multiple perspectives on a problem is a great gift–the key here is to work non-defensively!

For those Who Want to Know how to Read and Critique an RCT: What Are you Looking out for?

When you read a report of an RCT in an academic journal, your primary focus should be on the scientific integrity of the study and the design quality. This will indicate to you how much confidence you can have in the results that you see. Your secondary focus will likely be on the results themselves. Reading the results of a study is, for me, a bit like watching a news channel. However reputable the news channel might be, I am aware that the media is always selective about what it shares and will likely have a particular angle, or interpretation of what is happening in the world. This isn't a criticism (the particular interpretation may be of interest to you); rather it is something to be mindful of. The same is true of a research paper. Below I have provided a list of questions and criteria to help you start the process of assessing an RCT report, according to the focus on your critique. You may wish to refer to the published ETHOS protocol (Stafford et al. 2018) and assess the scientific integrity of our study using the list below.

Assessing Scientific Integrity and Design Quality

- Has the study been registered with ▶ clinicaltrials.gov or equivalent?
- Where was ethical approval obtained?
- Is there a clear rationale for the need to conduct this RCT?
- What have the researchers done to minimise bias?
  - Was the method used to generate the allocation sequence random?
  - What method was used to conceal the allocation sequence?
  - Are the procedures for outcome assessment for all participants across groups the same?

- Have the authors described all measures used to blind researchers from knowledge on which intervention a participant received?
- Have the authors described their sample size calculation and used an intention-to-treat analysis?
- Have the authors described the number of participants, with reasons, leaving the study in each group?

Assessing Results

- Are mean averages for each group at each time point clearly reported? (You don't have to be a whiz at statistics–results sections should contain simple and transparent reporting of results such that an independent researcher could analyse the data themselves.)
- Is the sample representative of the population of interest?
- Demographically and socio-economically, are there any under-represented groups?
- What contribution has this study made to the field according to the authors?
- What contribution has the study made to the field as far as you're concerned?

Summary

The RCT rests on a positivist approach, a medical model understanding of health, including a cause-and-effect view of human experience, function and distress. It is considered the 'gold standard' method for assessing effectiveness by many leading health organizations and governing bodies. Inequalities in perceptions of methodological value, as well as research funding, have led to an increasing concern that research is more about politics than scientific exploration. However, the supremacy of RCTs is increasingly being challenged in favour of a more pluralist framework for research in our field. Leading professional organizations in the UK, such as the British Association for Counselling and Psychotherapy (BACP) and the United Kingdom Association for Psychotherapy (UKCP), as well as leading researchers, stress the importance of this inclusive approach.

RCTs are not designed to investigate process issues, or the complex, nuanced experiences that happen in the therapy room. However, mixed methods approaches, such as the inclusion of qualitative components within a trial, are feasible (as demonstrated by ETHOS). Given the limitations of RCT design it would be a mistake to imagine they provide definitive answers to our important research questions. However, they do offer an opportunity to establish possible causal relationships between interventions and outcomes, establishing whether or not an intervention makes a difference. As part of a comprehensive variety of research studies, they can contribute to our overall understanding of effectiveness in counselling and psychotherapy.

References

Banerjee, R., Weare, K., & Farr, W. (2014). Working with 'Social and Emotional Aspects of Learning' (SEAL): associations with schools ethos, pupil social experiences, attendance, and attainment. *Br Educ Res J, 40*, 718–742.

Berk, M., & Parker, G. (2009). The Elephant on the Couch: Side-Effects of Psychotherapy. *Australian and New Zealand Journal of Psychiatry, 43*, 787–794.

Cooper, M. (2009). Counselling in UK secondary schools: a comprehensive review of audit and evaluation studies. *CPR, 9*, 137–150.

Cooper, M., Stewart, D., Sparks, J., & Bunting, L. (2013). School-based counselling using systematic feedback: a cohort study evaluating outcomes and predictors of change. *Psychother Res, 23*, 474–488.

Cooper, M., Rowland, N., McArthur, K., Pattison, S., Cromarty, K., & Richards, K. (2010). Randomised controlled trial of school-based humanistic counselling for emotional distress in young people: feasibility study and preliminary indications of efficacy. *Child Adolesc Psychiatry Ment Health., 4*(1), 12.

Department of Health. (2015). *Future in mind. Promoting, protecting and improving our children and young people's mental health and wellbeing.* NHS England.

Duggan, C., Parry, G., McMurran, M., et al. (2014) The recording of adverse events from psychological treatments in clinical trials: evidence from a review of NIHR-funded trials. *Trials, 15*, 335.

Freire, E., Elliott, R., & Westwell, G. (2014). Person Centred and Experiential Psychotherapy Scale (PCEPS): development and reliability of an adherence/competence measure for person-centred and experiential psychotherapies. *Counselling and Psychotherapy Research, 14*(3), 220–226.

Goodman, R. (2001). Psychometric properties of the strengths and difficulties questionnaire. *J Am Acad Child Adolesc Psychiatry, 40*, 1337–1345.

Jackson, C. (2018). It ain't what you do. *Therapy Today, 29*(4), 2–7.

Johnstone, L. & Boyle, M. with Cromby, J., Dillon, J., Harper, D., Kinderman, P., Longden, E., Pilgrim, D. & Read, J. (2018). The Power Threat Meaning Framework: Overview. Leicester: British Psychological Society.

Jonsson, U., Alaie, I., Parling,T., Arnberg, F. K. (2014). Reporting of harms in randomized controlled trials of psychological interventions for mental and behavioral disorders: A review of current practice. *Contemporary Clinical Trials 38*, 1–8.

Kirkbride, R. (2018). *Counselling young people. a practitioners manual.* London: SAGE.

Linden, M., & Schermuly-Haupt, M.-L. (2014). Definition, assessment and rate of psychotherapy side effects. *World Psychiatry, 13*(3), 306–309.

Luborsky, L., Diguer, D. A., Seligman, et al. (1999). The researcher's own therapy allegiances: a 'wild card' in comparisons of treatment efficacy. *Clinical Psychology: Science and Practice, 6*(1), 95–106.

McArthur, K., Cooper, M., & Berdondini, L. (2013) School-based humanistic counselling for psychological distress in young people: pilot randomized controlled trial. *Psychother Res., 23*, 355–365.

McLeod, J. (2017). Why read research? *Therapy Today, 28*(5), 3–5.

Moran, P. (2011). Bridging the gap between research and practice in counselling and psychotherapy training: Learning from trainees. *Counselling and Psychotherapy Research, 11*(3), 171–178.

Stafford, M. R., Cooper, C., Barkham, M., et al. (2017). Effectiveness and cost-effectiveness of humanistic counselling in schools for young people with emotional distress (ETHOS): study protocol for a randomised controlled trial. *Trials, 19*, 175–191.

Stafford, M. R., Cooper, M., Barkham,M., et al. (2018). Effectiveness and cost-effectiveness of humanistic counselling in schools for young people with emotional distress (ETHOS): study. *Trials, 19*:175.

Welsh Government Social Research. (2011). *Evaluation of the Welsh School-based Counselling Strategy: Stage One Report.* Social Research Division of the Welsh Government.

Twigg, E., Barkham, M., Bewick, B. M., Mulhern, B., Connell, J., & Cooper, M. (2009). The young person's CORE: development of a brief outcome measure for young people. *CPR, 9*, 160–168.

Roth, A., Hill, A., & Pilling, S. (2009). *(2009) The competences required to deliver effective Humanistic Psychological Therapies*. London: University College London.

Pybis, J., Cooper, M., Hill, A., Cromarty, K., Levesley, R., Murdoch, J., & Turner, N. (2014). Pilot randomised controlled trial of school-based humanistic counselling for psychological distress in young people: outcomes and methodological reflections. *CPR, 15*, 241–250.

Pearce, P., Sewell, R., Cooper, M., Osman, S., Fugard, A. J. B., & Pybis, J. (2017). Effectiveness of school-based humanistic counselling for psychological distress in young people: pilot randomized controlled trial with follow-up in an ethnically diverse sample. *Psychol Psychother T, 90*, 138–155.

Rowan, J., & Jacobs, M. (2002). *The therapist's use of self*. Maidenhead: Open University Press.

Shean, G. (2014). Limitations of Randomized Control Designs in Psychotherapy Research. *Advances in Psychiatry*, 1–5.

13

Navigating the Landscape of 'Evidence' in Research

Emma Broglia and Louise Knowles

Contents

© The Author(s) 2020
S. Bager-Charleson, A. McBeath (eds.),
Enjoying Research in Counselling and Psychotherapy,
https://doi.org/10.1007/978-3-030-55127-8_14

Learning Goals

After reading this chapter you should be able to:

- Explore a range of routes into research and identify which routes to pursue;
- Explain the difference between evidence-based practice and practice-based evidence;
- Understand the difference between efficacy and effectiveness and how to reach an equilibrium that suits your personal and professional style;
- Identify the impact research can have on practice and how research can be applied to daily practice;
- Practise refining and developing a shared language between researchers and practitioners in daily practice.

Introduction

Evidence-Based Practice (EBP) and Practice-Based Evidence (PBE)

Throughout this book, the issue of research-supported practice has been an under-lying theme. The authors have looked at ways in which we might navigate issues around research and practice by considering the different routes into research. In this final chapter, we will focus on building an evidence base born out of clinical practice. We offer a synopsis of evidence-based practice (EBP) and practice-based evidence (PBE) and consider the sliding scale of efficacy and effectiveness studies, whilst drawing attention to how we might reach an equilibrium to suit where we are in our own personal and professional development. We encourage you to consider the internal and external impact that research could have on your daily practice and the ways in which we might adopt a shared language that translates research and practice.

Reflections and activities have been provided throughout the chapter as well as brief case studies to help you apply the theory to your own practice. Reflecting on our practice and understanding how or why we might be interested in certain aspects of practice have been themes throughout all chapters in this book. This is a skill that is central to doing research. As Skovholt & Trotter-Mathison (2014) suggests: "As important as methods may be, the most practical thing we can achieve in any kind of work is insight into what is happening inside us as we do it. The more familiar we are with our inner terrain, the more sure footed our [work] – and living- becomes" (p.17).

In preparation for writing this chapter, we not only drew on our own personal experience of working together and with colleagues, but we also met with a number of trainees and practitioners to consult as much as we could along the way. Further to this, we have drawn on a range of literature that has been highlighted through-out this chapter and in the recommended reading at the end. Invaluable to or own understanding has been reading around the subject, and we would like to draw your attention to a number of key texts, including: 1) Barkham et al. (2010) who provide a guide for delivering practice-based evidence and 2) Bager-Charleson, du Plock & McBeath (2018) who explore practitioners' views on psychotherapy practice and research. We would highly recommend that you read these key texts in conjunction with this chapter.

Different Routes into Research

Navigating issues around research, bridging the gap between research and practice, and accessing or doing research are some of the many challenges you may face as a practitioner. We may have a natural preference to use research methods that are driven by practice or align with efficacy or effectiveness studies. You may already have connected with your preferences after reading this book. With each new research challenge is an opportunity to reflect, reassess and adapt for the benefit of our personal and professional development. These opportunities can arise at any stage during your professional career, and they may do so irrespective of whether you are embarking on research for the first time or are an experienced practitioner who has engaged with or led research in the past.

Sitting with our Clients

When you sit with your clients and seek to understand their frame of reference or presenting issues, consider how you are gaining more understanding and the skills you employ. Research starts in this sense quite simply in our daily practice. You listen to the words the client is using. You listen to the tone and pitch of their voice, looking at the client's body language and facial expressions, and you may use your sense of smell or your felt sense of the client. You may also enquire about what has brought them to your consulting room, what their history is and what their symptoms are. Through this process of enquiry, we collect a significant amount of data that we constantly sift and analyse.

14

'Analysing' our Daily Data

Supervision is also a formal structure within which we sift and analyse data. When we present at supervision, we may, for example, talk about our felt sense of the client, how we want to better understand why we may be losing our empathy for a particular client. We may even be reporting that we are experiencing a similar feeling with all our clients. Through a process of data analysis with my supervisor, I can gain better insight and understanding about my client work. I can begin to see and notice patterns and themes in the client work, and from this I can begin to formulate hypotheses about my clinical work. Whether we practise individually in independent practice or work within an organisation, when we are at the point of forming a hypothesis about

Personal	Intrapersonal	Contextual
• *"Feeling"* • Self-awareness • Self-exploration	• *"Thinking"* • Relationship with client • Relationship with supervisor • Analytical	• *"Applying"* • Practical & pragmatic • Adaptive • Overlaps with personal and inter-personal

Fig. 14.1　Reasons for research

a client, we may choose to give further discipline and structure to our experiences, hunches and hypothesis and engage in some structured practice-based research. Therefore, the research we undertake comes directly from our practice and the conclusions of the research will inform that same practice. We have broken this down into three main areas: personal, intrapersonal and contextual (see ● Fig. 14.1).

Personal

Your focus is on increasing your understanding about yourself and your internal world. This route is feeling orientated, where you are the researcher and place yourself in the frame with the aim of increasing your self-awareness and self-exploration. For example, we may be interested in our own counter-transference response to clients and how our own experience of personal therapy has shaped us as a practitioner.

Intrapersonal

This route into research is more about how you relate to others, and thus the focus is on the interactions between the researcher (you) and the other–our clients, our supervisees, our colleagues. Taking this route requires us to not only be aware of our own feelings and focus, but to also understand and harness what is happening between oneself and others. In essence, a focus on meta thinking and communications. For example, we may be interested in the transferential relationship or the parallel process in supervision.

Contextual

The third route into research is where the researcher is interested in shedding a light onto relationships between people and the context within which they sit. This best suits the researcher who wants to focus on how, for example, organisational culture impacts the client and client outcomes.

Activity

Think about your work with clients. Think about the sorts of clients you see and the challenges they bring to therapy. Do you notice a pattern? Does something interesting or unusual stand out? Take a few minutes and ask yourself:

- Why is my casework so easy/complicated compared to others?
- What is it about me that means I get [.....] sort of clients?
- Am I good at working with these types of clients and, if so, what is it that makes me 'good'?

We asked clinical students and newly qualified therapists to reflect on their work with clients and how they might access research; here is what one of them said:

» Most of what I do is independent learning – reading books and papers in my own time but it can sometimes take a lot of time getting to the main point of the paper. I find there's a part missing between reading a paper and then applying it to my practice and that's quite hard to do....It would be great to have more training in services and more hands-on experience, maybe even a research discussion group just to get us thinking about what's out there and how it might apply to what we're doing.

Navigating the Landscape of Evidence: Evidence-Based Practice or Practice-Based Evidence?

Is it possible to engage with quality psychotherapy research *and* maintain a full client caseload? Practitioners bring a wealth of knowledge from their therapeutic work and add endless value to the relevance of research. Engaging with research activities leads to both internal benefits for practitioners' development and external benefits for the service and wider field of psychotherapy (Bartholomew et al. 2017). Therapists who engage with data collection in their service or embed feedback into their daily practice feel more able to use evidence to inform the way they work and report positive client outcomes (Castonguay et al. 2010). Therapists who contribute to research activities increase the relevance of research by ensuring that the factors being explored are closely aligned with therapeutic practice (Youn et al. 2018). This, in turn, builds an evidence base on the effectiveness of therapy and provides recommendations for further service development. There are also service benefits from engaging with research and translating research findings into practice (see also Glasgow, Lichtenstein & Marcus 2003). For example, you may learn from the demographic information you collect that certain clients do not approach your service and you may redesign an element of your service to be more accessible and accommodate diverse demographics. This inquisitive and adaptive response to research findings not only ensures that you continue to develop your practice and offer a service that best fits your clients, but it also triggers a ripple effect for the wider sector.

The more practitioners engage with research, the closer we get to an evidence base that is grounded in clinical work and informed by therapists on the ground. The sector and policy decisions become more informed by the needs of clients and the profession gains the evidence to shape and protect the workforce. Perhaps the more relevant observation is that all therapists are engaging in research as part of their therapeutic offer and the theoretical base of our approach comes from years of active research (see also Rowland & Goss, 2013). We may vary on the different theories of counselling and psychotherapy, but we all employ research skills to confirm or discount theories. So perhaps the more fitting question is *how to* rather than *why* do research.

The Landscape of Evidence-Based Practice (EBP)

Evidence based-practice (EBP) informs standard health and psychological health care and is concerned with 'big questions', such as *Does psychotherapy work?* EBP often relies on treatment manuals and protocols with strict inclusion criteria to create homogenous client groups. By doing so, EBP favours certain types of evidence and drives the assertion that research is rigorous. EBP is overall concerned with highly controlled trials (i.e. Randomised Controlled Trials) that are often conducted across several sites with rigorous protocols and procedures to follow. Thus, EBP will attempt to control as many factors as possible in order to reduce the likelihood of a result being due to chance and provide confidence that the subsequent client improvement was the result of a therapeutic impact. These design characteristics overlap with *efficacy* studies, which explore outcomes under ideal or 'optimum' circumstances. EBP levies a hierarchy on trustworthiness with other types of evidence when higher methodological standards are not available, and as such, certain approaches to research can feel alien and threatening to practitioners.

Understanding EBP

However, it is important that we understand EBP and how it will continue to shape our profession. This way we can begin to engage and have a voice in some of the wider debates about our profession. There are also many benefits of EBP in the field of psychotherapy research as it can strengthen the reputation of the profession and foster relationships between researchers and practitioners (Allan, 2019). The bridge between research and practice is vast, with the high-end empirical evidence having little effect on what practitioners do on the ground, but we can apply the learnings from such research and adapt methods to be embedded into practice. Achieving this has potential to add credibility to your own professional reputation, the service or organisation you work in, and the overall field of psychological therapy.

The Landscape of Practice-Based Evidence (PBE)

As practitioners, we can feel more at ease and at home with PBE. PBE challenges the notion of a hierarchy and starts from a more level playing field. PBE adopts a 'bottom-up' approach that is firmly rooted in practice and shaped by the needs of the service. PBE is concerned with everyday practice, and its primary focus is generating research questions that are wholly grounded in practice and the routine context in which we practise. For example, we may be interested in using a new outcome measure with our clients and then discussing feedback with our client in sessions over time. We may already know the measure we want to use and have had training on how to use it, but we may not have the budget to use the form electronically and may not have administrative support to give clients the form. How do you find time for your client to complete the form without taking time away from the therapy session? What happens if a client arrives late or is too distressed to complete the form? Do you have the capacity to use the measure with every client? Rather than trying to tackle every challenge at once, you might decide to start using the form with a few clients until you find your new routine and feel ready to use the measure with all clients. You could ask your client to arrive 10 minutes early for their session and ask if they would be willing to complete the measure so that you can discuss it in your session. Over time you may observe that your clients naturally arrive early for their session as it becomes part of the way you work together. Alternatively, you may find that these changes do not work for you at first. You may decide to ask a colleague how they introduced a new measure into their practice, or you may raise it with your supervisor to find another solution.

The development of Practice Based Research Networks (PBRN) has enhanced the field of PBE even further by linking together groups of practitioners to collaborate, share good practice examples, conduct shared research projects and even pool service data (Zarin et al. 1997). The real strength of PBE is how encompassing it is in its application and use of a variety of different methods. Barkham and Mellor-Clark (2013) suggest that PBE is pluralistic when it comes to research methods, meaning that there is respect and value in the range of different approaches and methodologies. Its accessible application can, however, be its greatest weakness in that it can, in the eyes of some, lack rigour and solid empirical evidence. PBE can be revolutionary in two ways. First, PBE is building a sound evidence base that is born out of clinical practice and as such is driven by our clients and places clients at the very heart of research findings. Second, given its accessible nature and relevance to practice, more and more practitioners are engaging in, conducting and contributing to research evidence. The contrast between practice-based evidence and evidence-practice can at first seem quite stark, but it's perhaps more helpful to view the methods as being on a continuum, and depending on your experience and research intentions you may align more closely with one at a given time.

When we asked clinical students and newly qualified therapists to reflect on what gets in the way of doing research, here's what they said:

》 I'm relatively new in my counselling career and I'm working the max hours that I can for the safety of my clients, but still only making just enough money to support myself. I'm very aware that I have to be careful with what I do extra. I really hate that I'm at the point where I have to think about that. So, having some time protected within my role to do research would make a huge difference.

I think confidence. Would I be skilful enough to do research? Would my blind sidedness be too great for research that is valid and relevant? Am I going to drown before I get to the other side? I've started to realise that I don't have to go at it alone and that it might be a good idea to get involved with an ongoing project or maybe even help if the right study came along. I've found a couple of local events, workshop type things and a relevant conference so I hope to meet other people interested in research there. I've also asked my supervisor who's also an academic to see if they know of anything I could do.

These experiences were echoed among the counsellors we consulted, and they are not alone. Bartholomew et al. (2017) identified core factors that surround therapists' involvement in research, including 'making research feasible', 'the impediments to psychotherapy research' and 'benefits of doing research'. We've responded to these factors and applied both our own experience and the experience of colleagues and therapists we consulted to highlight the opportunity born from each challenge. ◘ Table 14.1 summarises the key themes with strategies to adapt the findings to your own personal and professional development.

The Sliding Scale of Efficacy-Effectiveness

Research methods can be used to evaluate interventions to determine whether they work and achieve the outcomes they set out to deliver. The methods we use to identify and reach these outcomes can be placed on a sliding scale from research that is

◘ **Table 14.1** Summary of challenges and opportunities surrounding therapists engaging with research

	Challenge	Opportunity
Making research feasible	Not all counselling services provide opportunities to do research	Talk to your service lead for support and time in your schedule to engage with research. If you're within an educational setting, link with staff doing research. Link with colleagues in other practices. Set-up a journal club to discuss research. When trainees do placements, think about incorporating research into their placement. Some organisations might be able to set-up a research clinic in their service and embed research into daily practice. Consider joining a practice-research network (PRN) in your area of interest
	Doing research can be time consuming	Collaborate with others doing research and shape (rather than lead) research. To meet others doing research, explore local workshops involving research. Attend a research conference in your field to help your professional development. Join a professional body engaged with research (e.g. BACP and SPR)

(continued)

■ **Table 14.1** (continued)

	Challenge	Opportunity
Impediments to research	Feeling guilty from taking time away from clinical time	Even when therapists do find time to do research, they can feel guilt from taking time away from clinical time. It's important to view the inquisitive and information sifting nature of your daily work directly translates to research and research supports your personal and professional development
	Clients' are more important than research	Often as clinicians, we are highly altruistic and can be tempted to place our clients' needs over our own needs. At times, we can neglect our own needs and feeling entitled to focusing on research is no exception to this. Research also makes us better practitioners and ensures that we are offering a service that stays up to date with our clients' needs
Benefits of doing research	Benefits to services. practitioners and client outcomes	Research allows practitioners to monitor their practice and client progression (e.g. using outcome measures). Research, like supervision, allows practitioners to reflect on what they're doing well and what they can improve on
	Keeping research momentum	It can be easy to be involved with research without fully engaging or benefiting from the process. Ensure that you apply your learnings to your work and share it with colleagues. Encourage colleagues to reflect on what they are doing in the room and how they know it's working (or not)

*Factors adapted from Bartholomew et al. (2017)

14

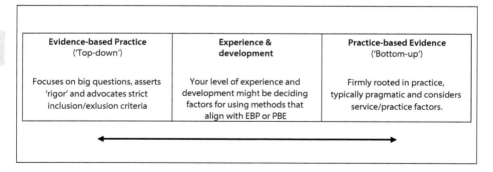

Evidence-based Practice ('Top-down')	Experience & development	Practice-based Evidence ('Bottom-up')
Focuses on big questions, asserts 'rigor' and advocates strict inclusion/exlusion criteria	Your level of experience and development might be deciding factors for using methods that align with EBP or PBE	Firmly rooted in practice, typically pragmatic and considers service/practice factors.

■ **Fig. 14.2** Navigating the landscape of evidence-based practice and practice-based evidence

conducted under optimum conditions and is often highly controlled–*efficacy* studies–moving to research that is applied, usually pragmatic and embedded in the 'real world'–*effectiveness* studies (■ Fig.14.2). Earlier in this chapter we explored the landscape of EBP and noted that this type of research aims to answer big questions that drive the future of health care and policy decisions, often relying on RCTs and using methods that attempt to control many components of the research (See also Kim, 2013). Systematic reviews are another example of research that applies methodical rules to combine study outcomes, often from RTCs, but also from broader research designs such as the systematic scoping review commissioned by the British Association for Counselling and Psychotherapy to compile evidence on counselling in children and young people (see Pattison and Harris 2006).

A key advantage of efficacy studies is that their controlled and manualised nature allows studies to be replicated, the findings of which can be pooled to provide a sound evidence base for the sector. For example, it was with these methods that Barth et al. (2016) were able to conclude that psychotherapeutic interventions for depression in adults are superior to receiving no treatment and that different psychotherapies have comparable benefits. A simple conclusion, but one derived from critically evaluating and extracting the findings from 198 RCTs including 15,118 adults receiving one of seven psychotherapies. However, such findings from efficacy studies, as essential as they are to evidence the profession, do not necessarily apply directly to practice, and the outcomes from efficacy studies are harder to achieve or may vary in practice (see Glasgow, Lichtenstein & Marcus 2003). Effectiveness studies are more liberal than efficacy studies and are typically less controlled with fewer methodological restraints. These characteristics go hand in hand with practice-based evidence and as such can seem more welcoming to practitioners. For example, whereas efficacy studies identify outcomes from an intervention in an ideal environment and then seek to replicate findings in a natural environment, effectiveness studies tend to start with the natural environment and will shape research methods around the intervention. Effectiveness studies still attempt to use rigorous research methods but will do so without dramatically changing the natural environment (i.e. a service). An example of this would be embedding a trial into a counselling service and rather than protecting counselling sessions so that clients in the trial have priority over other clients, all clients are scheduled to see a counsellor when they are available, as they would in routine practice (Broglia et al. 2017 and 2019). Such design components are not only more pragmatic and accessible, but they also address some of the limitations of efficacy studies that are often more difficult to replicate in routine practice. Some have also argued that effectiveness studies are more inclusive and representative than efficacy studies and as such are better able to respond to social justice issues (Allan, 2019). The strict inclusion criteria of efficacy studies and the need for large samples make it difficult to include clients that are less represented in therapeutic practice regarding characteristics that concern race, age, gender, religion, sexuality and disability. Aside from the limited client demographic, research inclusion criteria may also overrepresent clients of a certain clinical severity such as clients that meet a mild or moderate clinical threshold on a routine outcome measure. Similar sampling issues and the transient nature of certain client groups create further difficulty for researching more complex clients. These are common challenges of designing any research in the field of counselling and psychotherapy, and whilst it is not always possible to control for every extenuating factor, there is inevitably more variability (and therefore uncertainty) introduced when research is less controlled. It is for these reasons that perhaps it is helpful to view each research design decision as falling on a

Efficacy (ideal and controlled)	Context	Effectiveness (applied and real-world)
The extent to which an intervention does more harm than good, when provided under *ideal* circumstances (e.g. RCT)	The context and intentions of research are often the deciding factors for using methods that align more closely with efficacy or effectiveness studies	The extent to which an intervention does more harm than good, when provided under *usual* circumstances (e.g. embedded into a service)

◼ **Fig. 14.3**   The Efficacy—Effectiveness continuum

sliding scale that moves between efficacy and effectiveness studies, and some factors may be more feasible to control than others. ◼ Figure 14.3 presents this sliding scale and highlights that your research intentions will influence whether you adopt methods from efficacy or effectiveness studies.

Working with a Shared Language

We can take language for granted, and when we gain our own expertise we automatically make a set of assumptions regarding the level of knowledge of others. These potential language barriers aren't unique to the realms of research and practice–there are examples of different language use and assumptions being made between further and higher education institutions, psychologists and sociologists, and quantitative and qualitative researchers. Adapting the language we use takes practice and patience, and if either is lacking then it can add a further layer of confusion. It's helpful to bear this in mind when you're choosing your own language and to be mindful of the types of assumptions you might make before entering the conversation.

14

Internal and External Impact

Following the argument that the researching practitioner will inevitably place themselves within the research, it is important to consider the impact of any research on yourself as the researcher, your institution or organisation if relevant, and the participants–the clients. Whichever is your preferred route into research, as a practitioner you almost inevitably will be revealing a lot about you, your feelings, your clinical approach, your judgements and your views and values.

A precursor to undertaking this type of research is for you to consider whether you have the right level of support both professionally and personally to tolerate this level of exposure. Your findings may also challenge strongly held views within the profession, by your colleagues and your institution. As a practitioner you are very close to these groupings and have to be able to continue to work professionally after any findings are in the public domain. A critical way of sustaining yourself as a practitioner engaged in research is to establish a trusted and supportive relationship between yourself and the professional researcher where the research and research methods are built on co-design and co-authoring. Through this honest and authentic collaboration, your mutual skills and experience of practice and research will merge–then you will truly be involved in research in action.

Activity
Consider what research means to you:
1. What does research mean to you?
2. What do you associate with research?
3. What do you want to get out of doing research?

Summary
This chapter encourages you to address some of the challenges and opportunities practitioners experience when they engage with research. We hope to have encouraged you to build an evidence base born out of clinical practice. We need practitioners, such as yourself, to continue to engage with research and question your daily practice. In this chapter we presented some ways in which you might navigate issues around research and practice by considering the different routes into research. We referred to the broad remit of evidence-based practice and practice-based evidence and presented a sliding scale of efficacy and effectiveness, ideally with an equilibrium to suit where you are in your own personal and professional development. Our priorities for engaging with research will naturally vary over time. We explored examples of how to translate theory into practice and encouraged you to consider the impact that research could have on your daily practice. It is hoped that activities throughout the chapter provided an opportunity to reflect on your practice and understand how or why you might be interested in certain aspects of practice, and to recognise that such skills are central to doing research.

Throughout the book, the different authors have tried to convey the fundamentals of research and practice, woven into wider contextual aspects. We hope that this final chapter has contributed further to demystifying some of the thinking around evidence, whilst contributing to a basic map that will assist and support you further when navigating and pioneering your own research and practice. The most valuable asset to us in conducting any research has been relationships: our relationships with each other, with colleagues and with peers, as well as our relationship with ourselves. Our own personal insight has and continues to be invaluable to us as both researcher and practitioner–it is our common ground. From this common ground we can begin to explore our different contexts whilst remaining open to the empirical knowledge available to us. We hope that this chapter together with the others has triggered ideas and provided you with inspiration to enjoy many research projects, and that they have helped to build much needed knowledge in the fields of mental health and emotional wellbeing.

References

Allan, R. (2019). Teaching and learning evidence-based practices: Promoting dialogue for counsellors and psychotherapists. Counselling and Psychotherapy Research, *19(3)*, 206–213.

Bager-Charleson, S., du Plock, S., & McBeath, A. (2018). "Therapists have a lot to add to the field of research, but many don't make it there". A narrative thematic inquiry into counsellors' and psychotherapists' embodied engagement with research. *Journal for Language and Psychoanalysis*, (7), http://www.language-and-psychoanalysis.com/article/view/2603.

Barkham, M., Hardy, G. E., & Mellor-Clark, J. (Eds.). (2010). *Developing and delivering practice-based evidence: A guide for the psychological therapies* (pp. 329–353). John Wiley & Sons.

Barkham, M., & Mellor-Clark, J. (2013). Rigour and relevance. The role of practiced-based evidence in psychological therapies. In N. Rowland & S. Goss (Eds.), *Evidence based counselling and psychological therapies: Research and applications (pp 27–44)*. London and Philadelphia: Routledge.

Barth, J., Munder, T., Gerger, H., Nüesch, E., Trelle, S., Znoj, H., et al. (2016). Comparative efficacy of seven psychotherapeutic interventions for patients with depression: a network meta-analysis. *Focus, 14*(2), 229–243.

Bartholomew, T. T., Pérez-Rojas, A. E., Lockard, A. J., & Locke, B. D. (2017). "Research doesn't fit in a 50-minute hour": The phenomenology of therapists' involvement in research at a university counseling center. *Counselling Psychology Quarterly, 30*(3), 255–273.

Broglia, E., Millings, A., & Barkham, M. (2017). Comparing counselling alone versus counselling supplemented with guided use of a well-being app for university students experiencing anxiety or depression (CASELOAD): protocol for a feasibility trial. Pilot and feasibility studies, 3(1), 1–15.

Broglia, E., Millings, A., & Barkham, M. (2019). Counseling with guided use of a mobile well-being app for students experiencing anxiety or depression: clinical outcomes of a feasibility trial embedded in a student counseling service. JMIR mHealth and uHealth, 7(8), e14318.

Castonguay, L. G., Nelson, D. L., Boutselis, M. A., Chiswick, N. R., Damer, D. D., Hemmelstein, N. A., et al. (2010). Psychotherapists, researchers, or both? A qualitative analysis of psychotherapists' experiences in a practice research network. *Psychotherapy: Theory, Research, Practice, Training, 47*(3), 345.

Glasgow, R. E., Lichtenstein, E., & Marcus, A. C. (2003). Why don't we see more translation of health promotion research to practice? Rethinking the efficacy-to-effectiveness transition. *American Journal of Public Health, 93*(8), 1261–1267.

Pattison, S., & Harris, B. (2006). Counselling children and young people: A review of the evidence for its effectiveness. *Counselling and Psychotherapy Research, 6*(4), 233–237.

Rowland, N., & Goss, S. (2013). *Evidence based counselling and psychological therapies*. Routledge: Research and applications.

Skovholt, T. M., & Trotter-Mathison, M. (2014). *The resilient practitioner: Burnout prevention and self-care strategies for counselors, therapists, teachers, and health professionals.* London: Routledge.

Kim, S. Y. (2013). Efficacy versus effectiveness. *Korean Journal of Family Medicine, 34*(4), 227–227.

Youn, S. J., Xiao, H., McAleavey, A. A., Scofield, B. E., Pedersen, T. R., Castonguay, L. G., et al. (2018). Assessing and investigating clinicians' research interests: Lessons on expanding practices and data collection in a large practice research network. *Psychotherapy., 56*(1), 67–82.

Zarin, D. A., Pincus, H. A., West, J. C., & McIntyre, J. S. (1997). Practice-based research in psychiatry. *American Journal of Psychiatry, 154*(9), 1199–1208.

14

Supplementary Information

Index